Who Killed Jesus?

Who Killed Jesus?

THE AUTHORITY OF THE SANHEDRIN AT THE TRIAL OF JESUS

Norman D. Holcomb, Jr., PhD

Who Killed Jesus? The Authority of the Sanhedrin at the Trial of Jesus

Copyright © 2024 by Norman D. Holcomb, Jr., PhD

All rights reserved.

No part of this book may be reproduced or transmitted in any form or by any means without written permission from the author.

Published by Amazon Books

ISBN: 978-1-917281-98-0

Printed in the USA

In memory of my Dad, Norman D. Holcomb, Sr., who taught me how to rightly divide the Word of God; and my Mother, Georgia Ruth Webb Holcomb, who prayed for me without ceasing.

"Be diligent to present yourself approved to God, a worker who does not need to be ashamed, rightly dividing the word of truth" (2 Timothy 2:15, NKJV).

"Rejoice always, pray without ceasing, in everything give thanks; for this is the will of God in Christ Jesus concerning you" (1 Thessalonians 5:16-18, NKJV).

Table of Contents

Introduction 1

Chapter One 9

Chapter Two 69

Chapter Three 78

Chapter Four 91

Chapter Five 113

Chapter Six 139

Chapter Seven 179

Conclusion 185

Endnote... 283

Bibliography 220

Index 234

About the Author 243

Introduction

Who killed Jesus? This simple three-word question has implications that go far beyond the seeming simplicity of the question. The finger of guilt points to a cast of characters, each of which, in some way, is implicated in the death of Jesus. The New Testament scriptures make references to Herod Antipas, Caiaphas, Pontius Pilate, the priests, the elders and the Jews who comprise the population of Israel. And what of the role played by Judas Iscariot in the killing of Jesus? When all is considered, perhaps along with asking, "Who killed Jesus?" we should also ask, "Who helped to cause the death of Jesus?"

There are enough twists and turns in the consideration of these questions to make one's head spin. Where do we begin to isolate and identify a single motive for killing Jesus? The reasons for wishing his death are legion. The Jewish leaders wanted to defend their religious structures and the economic power advantages appropriated through their religious authority. Pilate did not want to lose political favor with his Roman bosses by losing control over the conduct of the common people, who might foment rebellion and disrupt the Roman-governed peace of Jerusalem and the surrounding areas.

Is there an easy and straightforward answer to the simple question of "Who killed Jesus?" I think the obvious answer is "No." However, my association with the general population of church-going Christians is that the question is seldom considered beyond the superficial acceptance of the standard belief that the Jews killed Jesus.

In my fifty years of service as a student pastor, parish pastor, and military chaplain, I have no recollection of anyone ever asking me to answer the question, "Who killed Jesus?" As I consider my childhood and adolescent Sunday School and worship experiences, I realize that I never once asked the question, "Who killed Jesus?"

I was born and raised in a rural coal town in southern West Virginia. The community was entirely defined by the rules and regulations established by the coal company that owned the coal mines from which the laborers earned their livings. Miners were paid in company currency called "scrip," and that currency could only be spent at the company-owned company store. The community doctor was on the company payroll. The company charged each employee one dollar a month and subsidized the balance of the cost for providing family medical care through the company doctor. Homes were heated with coal which was provided by the company at a minimal charge. The simply constructed houses were built and owned by the company, and families paid rent to the company with a fee for utilities being included in the rent.

The coal company had subsidized the building of five churches in the community. There was a Methodist, Baptist, Pentecostal Holiness, Roman Catholic and another Baptist church in the negro section of the coal camp. These churches represented the standard choices and preferences of most of the members of the community. Pastors serving these churches were known as lay pastors and did not have the benefit of a seminary education or any formal theological training. The Methodist pastor usually had some degree of training provided through the church hierarchy, but the Baptist, Pentecostal Holiness and negro pastors were simply selected for ordination by the local congregations based on everyone's claim to have been "called to preach." I assume that the Roman Catholic priest had some level of education as required by the Roman Catholic Church, but I do not know, nor would I have then known, the scope and extent of such a requirement.

The Roman Catholic Church served the families that had come from Italy, Hungary and other European countries to work in the coal mines. There was no cooperation between the Protestant Churches and the Catholic Church. As a matter of fact, the Protestant members of the community were highly suspicious of the Catholic Church and warned their children to stay away from the Catholic priest.

There were no Jews in our town. On more than one occasion, I recall hearing someone say in a bragging context that there were no Jews living among us. There was one Lebanese Jew who regularly visited our town. I don't know his name, and I doubt if anyone in town knew his real name. He was simply known as "Smiley," and he sold various items of clothing and household sundries. Everyone knew the days he was scheduled to travel to our town to deliver previously ordered goods and take orders for future delivery. I assume that Smiley did a very good business. On the days of his visits, many people gathered around his car to see what he was peddling for that week. When discussing business with Smiley, customers referred to the bargaining process as "Jewing him down" to arrive at the price they were willing to pay.

I suspect that many rural towns in America in the 1950s were much the same as my small hometown. Pastors were without formal education in theology and biblical studies and were ordained and appointed to perform ministry by neighbors who had the same or similar beliefs as their own. They had no Jewish element in their community, and the only Jew they personally knew was one who did not do manual labor for a living and was viewed as a shrewd person who might cheat and/or overcharge for the goods that he sold. Given such a narrow worldview of Jews and a literal reading of the New Testament, there was no reason for anyone to ask the question, "Who killed Jesus?" It was obvious and went without saying that, of course, the Jews killed Jesus.

Having said all of this, I am not yet willing to say that my townsmen were wrong in their unexamined and silently accepted claim that the Jews killed Jesus. In their insulated world and without the benefit of modern theological scholarship, it is likely that their powers of critical analysis were informed largely on the basis of local experience. They were limited by their own provincial knowledge and a very prejudiced view of Jewish individuals. While their lives lacked cosmopolitan sophistication and extended no further than the fences in their own backyards, it is possible that their answer was and is correct. Under those constricted circumstances of society and culture, it is not impossible to think that all of us would expect the entire world to be nothing more than an enlarged version of our own backyard. Knowing nothing else and not willing to learn anything else, it should not be unusual to assume that we might always try to see the entire world as only the world we already know.

The answer to the question, "Who killed Jesus?" more often than not, has been "The Jews killed Jesus." But there are other voices proposing other answers, and those voices need to be heard and examined. I propose to hear and examine some of those voices in what follows. I will examine the record as it is contained in the gospels of Matthew, Mark, Luke and John and in other New Testament scriptures as appropriate. Also, the *Lost Gospel According to Peter*, while not canonical, may be of some value.

Extra-biblical writings such as *The Works of Josephus* will be consulted for any information therein that might shed light on the issue. The *Nostra Aetate* document from the Second Vatican Council (1965) seeks to address an attempt of the Catholic Church to create a better rapport with Judaism. Father John Crossan's book, *Who Killed Jesus? Roots of Anti-Semitism in the Gospel Story of the Death of Jesus,* departs from the traditional exegetical findings of most scholars regarding the trial and death of Jesus.

Referencing various biblical commentaries and other scholarly works, I will look as deeply as I can into the question of "Who killed Jesus?" I will go where the evidence, as I find it and interpret it, will take me. While I approach this academic and somewhat intellectual adventure with tools, experience and resources that I and my neighbors of "coal town 1950s" lacked, I still do not rule out the possibility that their unexamined answer was and is correct. If I conclude that they were correct without the benefit of the ability to apply academic textual criticism, I will consider their answer justified by one of their own local phrases: "Even a blind hog finds an acorn every now and then."

Notwithstanding some differences and some disagreements among the four gospels, when viewed collectively, they represent a credible unified account of Jesus' ministry. Each of them reflects the importance of the earthly person and the work of Jesus. The central saving event highlighted in each gospel is the death and resurrection of Jesus. In proclaiming Jesus as the Christ, they ultimately proclaim that the emergence of the Christian church is the fulfillment of Old Testament prophecy. Through Jesus Christ, and the ministry of the church into perpetuity, the gospels point to and proclaim the final revelation of God's power, glory and ultimate victory.

For purposes of this book, I do not intend to rehash the issues of whether the names assigned to the gospels were written by those specific persons. Volumes of books and articles have been written addressing the issues of authorship, but interest in this question is maintained mostly in the world of academics. Christians who populate local churches are generally content to refer to the gospels by the names assigned to them, and that is the approach I take here. In this respect, while personally acknowledging the work of many scholars, I will make no attempt to introduce information that argues for or against authorship by either Matthew, Mark, Luke or John.

I am aware of the Marcan hypothesis suggesting that Mark is the earliest of the gospels and that the others drew from its content when writing their accounts. I subscribe to it as a valid tool in understanding the relationship of each to the other. It is a fact that has long been recognized that events recorded in Matthew, Mark and Luke (the Synoptics) are sometimes not the same and, at times, disagree with each other. Notwithstanding this, I do not intend to spend a lot of time sorting through the "hair-splitting" details that comprise the academic background of this observation, which I accept as being valid and proven by serious scholars of the New Testament.

Based on source criticism, form criticism and redaction criticism, it is entirely appropriate to point out that there are instances where Matthew and Luke have similar accounts of Jesus, and those accounts do not appear in Mark. It can be deduced from this that Matthew and Luke had knowledge and/or access to another source other than Mark. We may assume that even if written tradition was lacking, there was a strand of oral tradition that reflected the person and work of Jesus. William Barclay says, "The correspondence between the three gospels is so close that we are bound to come to the conclusion either that all three are drawing their material from a common source or that two of them must be based on a third."¹ Considering this, it is not my intention to play one gospel against another to try to prove or disprove the messages therein. I will boldly state at the outset that I accept the message of each gospel as reflecting the truth. Regardless of any differences or omissions, I see them as ultimately and collectively emerging in the form of a gestalt that comprises a unified whole.²

Chapter One

The Gospel According to Matthew

I am intentionally dealing with each gospel individually. I will conduct a verse-by-verse exegesis of Matthew 26:47-28:10 as being immediately pertinent to the trial, conviction and death of Jesus. However, before turning attention to these specific verses, I want to consider some general characteristics of *The Gospel According to Matthew*. As previously stated, I acknowledge the dating of Matthew near the end of the first century. For referential convenience, I will ascribe authorship as belonging to the traditional name of Matthew. Whether or not he personally wrote the Greek text as we now have it is not that important. What is of most importance is that a connection be made between the message of the gospel and the Jewish Matthew, who addressed a Jewish audience/community.

Matthew was a Jew writing for Jews. His goal was to convince Jews to believe and accept Jesus as the promised Messiah of Israel. Matthew portrays the birth and name of Jesus as the fulfillment of Jewish prophecy:

> She will bear a son, and you are to name him Jesus for he will save his people from their sins. All this took place to fulfill what had been spoken by the Lord through the prophet: 'Look, the virgin shall conceive and bear a son, and they shall name him Immanuel,'

which means, 'God is with us' (Matthew 1:21-23).

While the events leading to the trial and killing of Jesus involved the claim of the Jews that Jesus had violated the Law, Matthew clearly points out that Jesus did not come to violate or abolish the Law. To the contrary, he came to fulfill the Law: "Do not think that I have come to abolish the law or the prophets; I have come not to abolish but to fulfill" (Matthew 5:17).

When contrasted with the other disciples, we see that Matthew was not a fisherman. He was a tax collector: "As Jesus was walking along, he saw a man called Matthew sitting at the tax booth; and he said to him, 'Follow me.' And he got up and followed him" (Matthew 9:9). As such, he would be possessed of literary skills and accustomed to reading and writing and keeping records. This is a primary reason that I do not hesitate to simply refer to Matthew as the author of the gospel that bears his name. Regardless of how many hands contributed to the gospel as we now have it, it is more than likely that Matthew, the Jewish tax collector who became a disciple of the Lord Jesus Christ, had a significant impact on the accountings of the person and work of Jesus.

A further word might be relevant in acknowledging the possibility that the gospel of Matthew was written primarily for a Jewish audience. The text, as we now have it and as it was composed in the late first century, was written in Greek. The language of the Jews at that time was predominantly Greek. When Palestine came under the control of Antiochus III and the Seleucid dynasty, Judea was exposed to the processes of Hellenization. The use of the Greek language and the adoption of Greek customs became dominant forces in shaping the social and political life of the Jews. The governing authorities of the land dealt with the high priests at Jerusalem. Consequently, the high priests and the prominent and wealthy Jews were the first to come under the influence of the forces of Hellenization. As leaders and representatives of the customs and religion of the people, they were the prime forces in expediting the assimilation of Hellenistic tendencies into the everyday lives and activities of the Judean population.[1]

There is evidence that Matthew, as a tax collector, was familiar with the Hebrew and Aramaic languages. W. C. Allen claims that the gospel, or at least some of the sayings (logia), first appeared in Hebrew or Aramaic. He says, "The original language was either Hebrew or Aramaic."[2] Early writers connect Matthew to an earlier gospel or Matthean logia that existed in Hebrew or Aramaic. Origin says, "I have learned by tradition that the gospel According to Matthew, who was at one time a publican and afterward an Apostle of Jesus Christ, was written first; and that he composed it in the Hebrew tongue and published it for the converts from Judaism."[3] Eusebius quotes Papias as saying, "So then Matthew wrote the oracles in the Hebrew language, and everyone interpreted them as he was able."[4] In addition to the reports of Origin and Papias, Irenaeus says, "Matthew published his gospel among the Hebrews in their own language."[5]

Matthew does not identify any group specifically as "the Jews." His only specific reference to the Jews is found in four verses. The wise men from the East ask, "Where is the child who has been born king of the Jews?" (Ἰουδαίων, 2:2). Pilate asked Jesus, "Are you the king of the Jews?" (Ἰουδαίων, 27:11). The soldiers who mocked Jesus said, "Hail, king of the Jews" (Ἰουδαίων, 27:29). Regarding the bribing of the soldiers by the chief priests and elders Matthew says, "And this story is still told among the Jews (Ἰουδαίοις, 28:15) to this day." Writing as a Jew for a Jewish audience, Matthew did not have to repeat over and over the fact that he was dealing with the Jewish people in their relationship with Jesus. They innately and overtly knew that Matthew was calling the Jewish nation to an accounting of its confrontation with Jesus.

While Matthew does not need to speak in a general sense of the Jews, he chooses to identify their actions in terms of their various functions in the social, cultural, political and religious life of the Jewish nation. Throughout his gospel, he speaks of Pharisees, Sadducees, chief priests, scribes, elders, elders of the people and the crowds. I want to consider each of these groups and identify their functions in the life of Israel.

Matthew refers to the Pharisees (Φαρισαῖοι) twenty-seven times (3:7; 9:11, 14, 34; 12:2, 14, 24, 38; 15:1, 12; 16:1, 6, 11; 19:3; 21:45; 22:15, 34, 41; 23:2, 13, 15, 23, 25, 27, 29; 27:62). During New Testament times, the Pharisees may have been the most influential religious sect within the Jewish community. Referring to the Pharisees, Josephus wrote, "These are a certain sect of the Jews that appear more religious than others and seem to interpret the laws more accurately."[6] The word Pharisee probably has its source in a Hebrew verb meaning "to separate." If this is true, it would be appropriate to designate the Pharisees as "those separated or chosen by God for full obedience to the law."[7]

A significant characteristic of the Pharisees was their belief in the resurrection of the dead. Josephus says,

> They also believe that souls have an immortal vigor in them, and that under the earth there will be rewards or punishments, according as they have lived virtuously or viciously in this life; and the latter are to be destined in an everlasting prison, but that the former shall have power to revive and live again; on account of which doctrines they are able greatly to persuade the body of the people.[8]

Matthew clearly establishes the fact that the Pharisees are always in opposition to Jesus. Even when they appear to enjoin him in serious dialogue, it turns out that they are really trying to trap him or test him regarding some issue of the law (16:1; 19:3; 22:15). Josephus confirms this clever characteristic of the Pharisees and identifies them as "a cunning sect."⁹ The reputation of the Pharisees was that they were "supposed to excel others in the accurate knowledge of the laws of their country."¹⁰ Jesus did not deny that they were experts in the law. He knew that they were highly regarded in their role as teachers of the law, but he also knew that they were motivated by evil and cunning behavior. They reflected the policy of "Do as I say, not as I do." Jesus told the crowds and his disciples, "Do whatever they teach you and follow it" (23:2a). He did not condemn them because they had great knowledge of the law; rather, he condemned them because they were hypocrites." He told the crowds and his disciples, "Do not do as they do, for they do not practice what they preach" (23:2b).

Matthew's message of Jesus to the Pharisees is emphasized in a series of "Woe to you" exhortations (23:13, 16, 23, 25, 27, 29). Notwithstanding their ability as teachers and as experts in the law, Jesus defines and describes the Pharisees in very harsh terms. Repeating the Baptist's description of the Pharisees (3:7), he calls them a "brood of vipers" (γεννήματα ἐχιδνῶν, 12:34) and tells them that they are condemned by their own words (12:37). They are not curious about baptism because they see any need for repentance. They have a smug confidence in the historic continuity of the tradition which they have inherited from their fathers. While they claim preferential status on the grounds of their ancestry, Jesus warns them that they cannot satisfy God by claiming the positions of status held by their fathers. Going beyond that, he tells them that their fathers had nothing to boast of before God. Their legacy was that of being murderers of the prophets (23:31).

Matthew repeats his charge against the Pharisees, saying: "snakes, you brood of vipers" (ὄφεις γεννήματα ἐχιδνῶν, 23:33). He doubles down in his description, calling them snakes (ὄφεις) and then calling them vipers (ἐχιδνῶν). A snake (ὄφις) is a dangerous and malevolent animal that a person is better off avoiding.[11] In ancient literature, a snake (ὄφις) represented a symbol of cleverness and was figuratively applied to the character and reputation of depraved men.[12] Jesus had previously told the disciples to avoid the teaching of the Pharisees (16:11-12). They are to avoid them as they would avoid a dangerous snake.

Not only are the Pharisees snakes, but they are also "the offspring of vipers." The word "brood" does not capture the full meaning of γεννήματα. It is as if Jesus is saying, "Not only are you snakes in your current existence; you are also the offspring of snakes and vipers." As a poisonous reptile, it is of the very nature of a viper to be evil and destructive. The use of "offspring" (γεννήματα) furthers the claim of Jesus that their fathers were evil and that it is in their blood to be evil just as it was in their fathers' blood to be evil.[13] Snakes and vipers that are by their very nature poisonous and destructive produce offspring that are the same. Likewise, those who murdered the prophets produce offspring of their own nature. Therefore, "as the sons of those who murdered the prophets" (23:31-32), the nature of the Pharisees is of the same poisonous and destructive character as their fathers. Their wickedness is revealed in their false claims and obvious contempt for Jesus.

The Pharisees are exposed as snakes and offspring of vipers. As such, their true nature is evil, and it becomes axiomatic that they are not capable of speaking good things. Their wickedness is revealed in their false claims and obvious contempt for Jesus. Instead of seeking the truth that he represented, they test him, try to trick him, plot to trap him and finally, they call for his arrest and death. This public condemnation of the Pharisees, however, is not enough cause for them to lose their credibility in the eyes of the people (the crowds). Josephus says, "These Pharisees have so great a power over the multitude, that when they say anything against the king or against the high priest they are presently believed."[14] Again, he says, "The Pharisees have the multitude on their side."[15] What impact will this power have in creating the cry of "Crucify him!" among the people? Perhaps there are those who speak too quickly in absolving the Jews of the killing of Jesus.

Matthew makes six references to the Sadducees (Σαδδουκαῖοι). Attempts to reconstruct the specific origin and progressive growth of the Sadducees is difficult. One biblical scholar says, "The Saducean party cannot be said to have come into being at any particular point."[16] It is possible that the name derives from Zadok, a ruling priest under David. The class of priests that he represented became known as Zadokites, and by New Testament times, the Hellenized name became Sadducees.[17] The record of the Zadokites throughout their Old Testament history is replete with religious and political intrigue. While acknowledging this historical background, this book is concerned only with the Sadducees during the time of Jesus— a time when they had come to be identified as the priestly aristocracy.

The Sadducees were fewer in number than the Pharisees, but they were mostly members of the governing class of people. They were wealthy and generally cooperated with the Romans. As Sadducees, their political and religious leverage was very influential. They were extremely concerned with their own survival and could be viewed as being collaborators with the Romans. They were more than willing to cooperate with the Roman government if that enhanced the probability that they would survive and maintain their own privileges and favored status.[18] Even during the most volatile of times in Jerusalem, the Sadducees enjoyed a position of comfort and relative security. They are not known to have participated in any disturbance or protest that would put them at odds with the Romans. They guarded against creating or being party to any threat that might lead to the forfeiture of their comfortable and lucrative positions under Roman rule.

The religious perspective of the Sadducees differed from that of the Pharisees. Josephus says, "But the doctrine of the Sadducees is this; that souls die with the bodies."[19] He also confirms that they rejected the Pharisees' development of the Oral Law and only recognized and abided by the written Mosaic Law. He says, "Nor do they regard the observation of anything besides what the law enjoins them; for they think it an instance of virtue to dispute with those teachers of philosophy whom they frequent."[20]

Compared to the Pharisees, the Sadducees were a somewhat more conservative group. They were primarily concerned with functioning as the custodians of the cultic ceremony. Despite their obvious differences, the Pharisees and Sadducees can still be viewed as religious brotherhoods during the time of Jesus. The Pharisees focused on the authoritative interpretation of the Law, and the Sadducees focused on temple worship. While the Sadducees rejected the doctrine of resurrection, it did not follow that they disputed God's existence. They were, however, much more conservative in how they viewed life and God's involvement in the lives and affairs of people. They did not subscribe to a belief in the intervention of God in the miraculous stories recorded in the prophetic books. In fact, they contended that God does not interfere with the progress of history in general and that he does not recognize nor care for what happens to individuals. The accidents of prosperity, adversity, and the forces of good and evil all have their origin singularly in the free will of man.[21]

Except for questioning Jesus about the resurrection, Matthew shows no concern for the complicated relationship between the two groups. He makes six references to the Sadducees (3:7; 16:1, 6, 11; 22:23, 24). In five of those references, he lists them together in the phrase "Pharisees and Sadducees." Only in 22:23 does he mention the Sadducees without grouping them with the Pharisees. On this occasion, the Sadducees confront Jesus and plainly state that there is no such thing as resurrection from the dead. They pose a question about a woman whose first husband died. In accordance with Mosaic Law, she married the husband's brother, and at the death of each succeeding brother, she married another brother until she had been the wife of all seven brothers. They asked, "If there is a resurrection, which of the seven brothers will she be the wife of when they are all resurrected?" Obviously, they wanted to discredit Jesus by showing that he opposed the Law. Jesus tells them that they are wrong in their thinking. They are falsely defining the reality of heavenly life in terms of earthly understanding. Using their own Pentateuch, he shows them how the living God is the God of living men. He accuses them of being ignorant of the Scriptures. Having foiled their attempt to put him at odds with the Mosaic Law, Jesus silenced them and amazed those who heard the truth and power of his teaching. Other than in the above instance, Matthew shares the same familiarity with Sadduceeism as he does with Pharisaism. He warns the disciples to be equally aware and suspicious of the teaching of both groups (16:5-12).

The fact that one group believes in the resurrection and the other does not elicits no favor for either group. Matthew depicts both as "snakes and the offspring of vipers" (12:34; 23:33). He completely ignores the distinctive differences between both groups. From his perspective, Pharisees and Sadducees fall under the condemnation of both John the Baptizer and Jesus. For all their genealogical heritage and impressive political and religious connections, they are "trees that do not bear good fruit," and God has begun the process of cutting them down and throwing them in the fire" (3:7-10).

When all the factors are considered, it seems to me that the role of the Sadducees in the trial and death of Jesus cannot be easily denied. Although fewer in number than the Pharisees, it cannot be overlooked that the Sadducees wielded more political influence because they controlled the priesthood.[22] They supported the Herodian dynasty, and since it was the Roman rule that put the Herodians in power, it followed that they supported the Roman government.

Sherman Johnson says, "Most of the first century high priests and their friends were Sadducees, and it is this group which, more than any other Jewish group, instigated the crucifixion of Jesus."[23] The Sadducees observed that political disturbances and civil unrest were accruing to the person and work of Jesus. They knew that the Romans would not tolerate mob activity and riots and that they would react swiftly and viciously. This would be especially true if the peace of Jerusalem were threatened. Since many of these wealthy Sadducees lived in Jerusalem, the possibility of Roman retribution frightened them. It could not be guaranteed that their favor with the Romans would exempt them from the pain and punishment of Roman reprisals.

For the Sadducees, Jesus represented a clear and present danger. They stood to lose their prestige, power, wealth and titles if Jesus continued to be the source of public hostilities. For the Sadducees, in an existential way of thinking, it just made sense that one person's life was not worth the risk of losing all that they had and all that they were. They used their influence and their political power to ensure that Jesus would be killed. Surely that influence and power played an important part in fueling the cries of many in the crowd who shouted, "Crucify him!" Again, perhaps there are those who speak too quickly in absolving the Jews of the killing of Jesus.

Matthew refers to "scribes" (γραμματεὺς) twenty times (2:4; 5:20; 8:19; 9:3; 13:52; 15:1; 16:21; 20:18; 21:14; 23:2, 13, 15, 23, 25, 27, 29,

34; 26:57; 27:41). Of those twenty times, the scribes are linked with the Pharisees eight times, the priests and elders of the people five times and the crowd(s) one time. That which has been said about the Pharisees can also be attributed to the scribes. More specifically, however, the scribes were the Jewish theologians of Jesus' time. They were the experts in scripture and in the law. Joachim Jeremias says that "γραμματεὺς is a translation from Hebrew to Greek which means 'a man learned in the Torah.'"[24]

As a professional group, the scribes probably originated when Nehemiah and Ezra returned to Jerusalem from Persian captivity with the mission of rebuilding the city (ca. 464-404 BC). They became helpers in reestablishing the national life and identity of the Jews following their many years of captivity. While in exile, Ezra was appointed to serve as a member of the Persian civil service. The Septuagint (LXX) identifies Ezra as "a scribe (γραμματεῖ) of the Lord God of heaven" (Nehemiah 7:12). This identity represented the official title of the secretary who gave oversight to Jewish matters within the Persian government. When Ezra departed Babylon for Jerusalem, he was said to be "a scribe (γραμματεὺς) skilled in the law of Moses which the Lord God of Israel gave" (Ezra 7:6).

In Nehemiah 8:1, we read of an event that amounts to a national dedication of the people to the keeping of the Law:

> And the seventh month arrived and the children of Israel were settled in their cities; and all the people were gathered as one man to the broad place before the Watergate, and they told Esdras the scribe (γραμματεῖ) to bring the book of the Law of Moses, which the Lord commanded Israel.

This national assembly in Jerusalem was a historical event, the significance of which cannot be overestimated. At this assembly, the law was read and explained to all the people of Israel. It was essential that their memories be renewed and refreshed because they had forgotten much of the laws and ordinances during their long period of captivity.

The rebuilding of the post-exilic Jewish community in Jerusalem needed a unifying element to succeed. While the Temple would ultimately be restored, it remained that the cult of the covenant and the monarchy would not be restored. Out of necessity, the law became the dominant element in the survival and further development of Judaism.[25] The national assembly, described in Nehemiah 8:1, became the official force that moved Judaism toward a religion of written scriptures. With the advent of the written law, it followed that the power of any prophetic claim for authority was subordinate to the Law of Moses. In its pre-exilic life, the guidance and revelations of God to the Israelites were of a flexible nature. It was geared to the variables of place, time and condition which confronted them.[26]

In pre-exilic Israel, the commandments reflected the helping hand of God as the people moved through history toward their national destiny. Under these circumstances, the commandments served the people as they faced difficulties, dangers and the threats of heathen forms of worship. Absent the flexibility to adapt to history and circumstances, the law became "an absolute entity, unconditionally valid irrespective of time or historical situation."[27] Rather than the law and the commandments serving the people, the people now had to serve the law and the commandments.

The stage has now been set for the ascendancy of what might be called scribal religion. With the law reigning as the supreme authority, it became necessary to apply the law to all the details of daily life and to establish rules governing the details. As Ringgren points out, "In cases which the existing law did not contain any concrete regulations, it now appeared imperative to supplement the law with concrete rules."[28] Such issues as how far a person could travel on the Sabbath, what was allowed in the care of animals, what could be done to save a human life, what were the restrictions on carrying loads and many other details associated with the Sabbath needed to be explained. It has been accurately noted that these "rather vague biblical prohibitions cry out for clarification."[29]

The reorganization of the Jerusalem community based on the Law of Moses had the effect of elevating the scribes to a position of absolute authority.[30] One result of this was that the charismatic and prophetic influences were no longer constitutive factors in Israelite religion. This marked the beginning of scribal religion in Israel.[31] As a new religious class, it is not surprising that the scribes zealously defended their status in the government of Israel. They saw themselves to be the preeminent spokesmen for warning and exhorting the people.[32]

By the time of Jesus, the scribes had become theologians, teachers, and lawyers all at the same time. When the Baptist and Jesus named the Pharisees, Sadducees, scribes, and priests as the murderers of the prophets, it immediately created an adversarial relationship. It was a direct assault on their absolute authority. Furthermore, it validated the message of the prophets who often called Israel to repentance and a renewed commitment to the prophetic challenge as spoken by the Baptist: "Bear fruit worthy of repentance. Do not presume to say to yourselves, 'We have Abraham as our ancestor'" (Matthew 3:8-9).

Israel's religion, as defined by the scribes, had become little more than a litany of rules built on a system of very narrow legalism. Under scribal religion, God had become a far-away God who was enthroned in heaven. In opposition to this, Jesus declared that God interacts with each person in his or her everyday life. He proclaimed that mere participation in the written law, as interpreted by the scribes, does not provide the righteousness which God demands. True righteousness comes to each person in their own private daily living through their concrete encounters with their neighbors.[33]

In Matthew we hear Jesus voice a great protest, not against the law, but against Jewish legalism. He does not advocate abandoning the law; rather, he vigorously challenges the motives under which the scribes interpret the law and compel the people to conform to their legalistic interpretations. They taught that the singular purpose and desire of every person must be that of satisfying the demands of the law.[34] As pointed out before, this meant that the law no longer served the people, but the people served the law.

Jesus sets the motive of the love of God and neighbor against the motive of legalism as seen in scribal religion. Matthew tells his Jewish audience that it is not enough to fulfill the motive of the law and thereby claim a status of righteousness. Jesus says that they must go beyond the Law of God to the love of God. The smugness of simply fulfilling all the rules required by the written law is insufficient. Righteousness is intrinsically connected to concrete encounters with other people. Does God want each person to observe and respect the laws and commandments? The answer is "Yes," but it is not an unequivocal "Yes." Bultmann says, "What counts before God is not simply the substantial, verifiable deed that is done, but how a man is disposed, what his intent is."[35] Beyond the narrow legalism of scribal religion, Jesus teaches that the guiding principle of every human encounter should be based on the desire and intent to respond according to the motive of love. This is the conduct, behavior and action that God counts as righteousness.

There can be no question that the scribes vigorously opposed the person and work of Jesus. His litany of "Woe to you, scribes and Pharisees, hypocrites!" certainly provoked them to seek his trial, conviction and death. Jeremias says, "As members of the Sanhedrin, on which the leading rabbis sat as leaders of the Pharisaic communities and thus constituted one of the three parties of which this supreme assembly of the Jews consisted, they took part in the prosecution and condemnation of Jesus."[36] It is most likely that the people shared the same opinions of Jesus as did the scribes. This possibility cannot be minimized when we consider the respect and admiration that the people had for the scribes. Many of them did not originate from within the ruling classes and did not inherit their power and prestige because of any degree of family nobility. In fact, many of them were born into obscurity, lived in poverty and worked in what we would today call "blue-collar jobs." They became scribes only after studying for several years. It was the knowledge they gained which afforded them the respect of the people.

As working-class people, scribes became known among all the people. Bruce Metzger says, "Their services were needed not only in Jerusalem but in the villages throughout Judea and Galilee."[37] They became the incarnation of the entire population's commitment to recognizing the authority of the law above all other authorities. The understanding of the people was that if they hoped to attain the good life, they would have to be properly instructed on what was required of them. They expected that the scribes would provide this instruction. Given this important role in the life of the community, it should come as no surprise that respect and admiration for the scribe was overwhelming. Among the people, the scribe became "a kind of superman who could work miracles and compel God by his prayers and was honored even after death by memorial offerings."[38]

It is not too difficult to believe that many people would have based their conclusions about Jesus on the position taken by the scribes. Referring to the masses of the Jewish people, Josephus says of his nation, "They give credit for wisdom only to those who have an exact knowledge of the law and are capable of interpreting the meaning of the Scriptures."[39]

Their great learning and knowledge guaranteed their standing and credibility in the eyes of the people. As ordained teachers who transmitted and interpreted the tradition derived from the law, the scribes were respected by the people.[40] As they traveled throughout the length and breadth of Judea, they became well-known throughout the land. Indeed, they were "venerated, like the prophets of old, with unbounded respect and reverential awe, as bearers and teachers of sacred esoteric knowledge their word had sovereign authority."[41]

Having no noble background and no claim to position and authority by family or heredity, the scribes came to occupy a high position in the estimate of the common people and were given extraordinary respect by the populace at large.[42] The evidence strongly suggests, if not confirms, that they were highly esteemed and venerated throughout Judea. The voice of the scribe represented the voice of the people. "Their decision had the power to 'bind' or 'loose' for all time the Jews of the entire world." [43] Once again, perhaps there are those who speak too quickly in absolving the Jews of the killing of Jesus.

References to priests and the priesthood are common in both the Old and New Testaments. We would not be wrong in saying that none of the sacral offices in Israel has a longer history than that of the priesthood. Having noted this, one would think that it would be easy for a reader to understand the roles played and the functions performed by the priests; however, this is not the case. Gerhard von Rad says, "Unfortunately our knowledge of the history of the priesthood in Israel is very slight."[44] This book is concerned primarily with the authority and activity of the priesthood during the time of Jesus.

A cursory consideration of the history of the priesthood in Israel begins with Aaron and an unbroken line of priests by way of Zadok, the high priest in the time of Solomon.[45] However, the claim of unbroken succession by way of Zadok is not true. In 175 BC, Onias II was serving as a legitimate Zadokite priest. He was succeeded by his brother Jason who was arbitrarily appointed by Antiochus IV (Epiphanes). He then replaced Jason with Menelaus, who was a Hellenizing Jew. Menelaus did not belong to a priest's family, but he paid tribute to Antiochus IV, and, through bribery, he was appointed to the office of high priest.[46] His appointment broke the line of the Zadokites.

From the exile of the Babylonian captivity to the time of Jesus, there was a great deal of political and religious maneuvering to maintain the appointments and successions within the priesthood. This was especially true during the Herodian-Roman period (37 BC-AD 70). During this period, the historically hereditary nature of the office was abandoned by the political rulers, and arbitrary appointments were made. Traditional hereditary rights of the Zadokites were ignored, and members of other priestly families were recognized and appointed. In fact, during the time of Jesus, the dominant priestly families were no longer constituted of pure Zadokite blood. Schrenk says, "In the 106 years between 37 BC and AD 70, 28 high-priests discharged the office, and 25 of these were of non-legitimate priestly families."[47] By the time of Jesus, the years of confusion had weakened the influence of the office of the high priest. However, even with this reduced influence, "the high priest was still the supreme religious representative of the Jewish people."[48]

In Matthew, we find references to "the priest" (ἱερεύς), the "chief priests" (ἀρχιερεῖς, plural), and the "high priest" (ἀρχιερεύς, singular). There is only one use of the word priest (ἱερεύς), and that is in Matthew 8:4, where Jesus tells the cleansed leper to "go, show yourself to the priest." In comparison to "chief priests" and "high priest," the "priest" plays a very minor role in the sayings of Jesus. However, his recognition of the priest in this healing event confirms that Jesus accepts the requirement of the

Mosaic Law regarding matters concerning ritual purity and public health. Upon being declared clean by the priest, the man could then move freely among the population. Jeremias refers to these priests as "ordinary priests" and numbers them at approximately 7,200 during the time of Jesus."[49] Unlike the chief priests, most of them probably lived in the towns and villages outside of Jerusalem.

Matthew refers to the chief priests (ἀρχιερεῖς/plural) eighteen times (2:4; 16:21; 20:18; 21:15, 23, 45; 26:3, 14, 47, 59; 27:1, 3, 6, 12, 20, 41, 62; 28:11). The chief priests are listed alone on only three of those occurrences. Of the remaining fifteen occurrences, they are listed in various combinations with scribes, elders of the people and Pharisees. They agree with these power brokers on every occasion. They were selected from wealthy families who could claim a connection to Zadok, the high priest when Solomon was king. As pointed out above, the Zadokite bloodline had been broken, and the dominant priestly families in the time of Jesus probably represented an illegitimate aristocracy.

The chief priests consisted of a group of priests, many of whom were probably former high priests who came from prominent families. More than just a loosely formed group, they appear to have been an established college with specific duties and responsibilities. Schrenk defines them as "having oversight of the cultus, control of the temple, administration of the temple treasury, and supervision of priestly discipline"[50] Along with these duties, they also had seats in the Sanhedrin. Within the college and subordinate to the high priest, there was an order of precedence according to duties performed. With the high priest taking precedence in rank, Jeremias lists the order of the chief priests as follows:

1. The High Priest
2. The Captain of the Temple
3. The director of the weekly course

4. The director of the daily course

5. The Temple overseer

6. The treasurer[51]

With control of the most important offices of the Temple and the taxes and money, the chief priests wielded absolute power over the people. If need be, they had the capability to exercise this power physically and ruthlessly. They had considerable membership in the Sanhedrin and political leadership of the entire nation.[52] Along with this absolute power, the chief priests enjoyed the prestige of their historic positions and "were highly esteemed and given a leading role in their sectarian fellowship."[53] Notwithstanding the power and prestige of the chief priests, Jesus' words and actions irritated them. He challenged their power and authority, and for this reason, they began seeking to destroy him the very day he arrived in Jerusalem. Matthew says, "But when the chief priests and the scribes saw the amazing things that he did, and heard the children crying out in the temple, 'Hosanna to the Son of David,' they became angry" (21:15). They did not fear that the voices of the children would have any significant influence on the ultimate majority opinion regarding Jesus. Their anger was stimulated by the fact that this rebel-rousing false messiah should get any attention at all. Having both coercive and popular influence, there was little reason for them to doubt that the people would support them in whatever they wanted to do. It can be reasonably assumed that the voices of the chief priests and the voices of the people are one and the same.

Aaron was the first to fill the position of high priest. The power, prestige and influence of the office in Israel is seen in the fact that in the post-exilic period, when there was no monarchy, the high priest took over the function of the king.[54] Because of this, the high priest was afforded a great deal of the dignity that had previously belonged to the king. There could only be one high priest at a time in Israel, and he was the most important member of the total membership of the priesthood. The most important feature of the office of the high priest was that he was the only person with the right to enter the Holy of Holies. He was permitted to do this on only one day of the year, and that was on the Day of Atonement. On this annual day, he entered the Holy of Holies and sprinkled the Mercy Seat with the blood of the sin offering for himself and for the people (Leviticus 16:1-25).

As president of the Sanhedrin, the high priest was the chief representative of the people. The cultic character of his office raised him high above the total body of the priesthood and made him guardian of the sacred duties which all priests exercised on behalf of the nation. The influence of his office and the priesthood subsumed under that office created a permanent connection with the people, both sociologically and religiously. Eichrodt says, "His influence is not confined to the religious sphere but covers every department of life, with the result that the priest exerts a decisive influence on the practice of law, on politics, on art and on secular knowledge as well."[55]

Matthew makes six references to the "high priest" (ἀρχιερεὺς). All these references are to Caiaphas (Καϊάφα), who was the high priest at the time of Jesus' trial (26:3, 57, 58, 62, 63, 65). The high priest is not called by name in 26:59, but the reference to the "chief priests and the Sanhedrin" surely includes the presence of the high priest since he was the president of the Sanhedrin. Caiaphas attempted to remain under control as he interrogated Jesus. As the interrogation continued, Jesus' answers and his silence confused the high priest and sent him into a rage. Having been provoked into an outburst of angry frustration, the high priest accused Jesus of blasphemy and proclaimed that he had heard all that he needed to hear from this false messiah. Responding to and conforming to the decision of the high priest, the scribes, chief priests, elders of the people and others present unanimously declared that Jesus was deserving of death. In this instance, the leaders of Israel, speaking for themselves and for the people of Israel, used their influence to ensure that Jesus would be killed. After taking further counsel with each other, they proceeded to hand Jesus over to Pontius Pilate.

Apart from the New Testament references, there is very little reliable information about Caiaphas. Josephus mentions his appointment as high priest by Valerius Gratus.[56] His other reference to Caiaphas says only that he was removed from his office about AD 18 by the Procurator Vitellius during AD 36 or 37.[57] Josephus' references suggest that Caiaphas was probably appointed about AD 18 and that he served as high priest for about eighteen years.

Pontius Pilate, a contemporary of Caiaphas, was the Roman Procurator of Judea from AD 26-36. Caiaphas had been in the office of high priest for eight years when Pilate became a procurator. He served as high priest during the whole of Pilate's prefecture. From the Jewish point of view, Pilate was the worst procurator to have ruled over Judea.[58] He ordered a vicious attack on a group of Samaritans who were doing nothing more than watching a prophet perform a miracle. He looted the temple treasury and brought military insignia depicting the emperor's image into Jerusalem. He was blatantly insensitive to Jewish religious sensitivities and had little concern for their laws and customs. Strange as it might seem, however, Caiaphas and Pilate complemented each other in the exercise of their power, influence and authority. They had mutual reasons to work together. It can be argued that they built a working relationship that encouraged the high priest to appease Rome at the expense of quelling the Jewish revolutionary spirit that often antagonized Rome.

Both Josephus and the Gospels highlight a close relationship between the high priest and the Roman procurator/governor. Caiaphas and Pilate were pragmatic leaders, and survival and personal success were of paramount importance to each of them. Caiaphas knew that Jesus had to be killed if temple worship as he knew it was to survive with the continued permission of the Romans. Pilate knew that he could not risk word getting back to Rome that he could not control the population under his governance. For both these leaders, Jesus was a serious liability and risk on at least two counts: 1) He threatened the very way business/worship was conducted in the temple, and 2) His actions incited riotous behavior, which the Romans would not tolerate. This was especially true of Pilate because he didn't want word to get back to Rome that he was unable to preserve the peace and stability of Jerusalem.

Clearly, it was in the best interests of both men, whether spoken or unspoken, to acknowledge an arrangement or agreement that allowed them to coexist peacefully under the existing circumstances. Raymond Brown takes this position and says, "Perhaps the two of them had worked out a modus vivendi that would allow some Jewish actions to be overlooked so long as they would not endanger Roman governance or be publicly embarrassing to Pilate."[59]

Philo tells us something about Pilate's character when the people threatened to complain to the emperor Tiberius regarding the nature and style of his governing authority. The people and Pilate both knew that Tiberius did not want any of the Jews' laws and customs violated or destroyed. Knowing this about Pilate, Philo says,

> The people might go on an embassy to the emperor, and might impeach him with respect to other particulars of his government, in respect of his corruption and his acts of insolence, and his rapine, and his habit of insulting people, and his cruelty, and his continual murders of people untried and uncondemned, and his never-ending, and gratuitous, and most grievous inhumanity.[60]

Philo clearly shows that Pilate was a totally immoral man who would not hesitate to do whatever was necessary to protect his own position and ensure his success and safety. If Philo is to be believed, it appears that murdering untried and uncondemned persons was a commonplace occurrence under Pilate's governance.

Caiaphas most assuredly knew and understood the temperament of Pilate. He knew exactly what he was doing when he structured and orchestrated his "kangaroo court" to send Jesus to Pilate. Caiaphas worked with the precision of an engineer to manipulate the forces of power that would guarantee the death of Jesus. He set the stage for, and perfectly executed, a plan to blackmail Pilate. It seems obvious to me that Pilate was blackmailed into giving the Jews their way with Jesus. Caiaphas made an offer that Pilate couldn't refuse. He had to choose between the risk of losing his favor with Rome or giving the Jews their means to kill Jesus. Pilate opted for his own security and in defense of his own ambition by permitting the Jews to murder Jesus. Without speaking a word, both Caiaphas and Pilate knew that the most expeditious way to preserve the political status quo and the lucrative business of the Temple was to destroy Jesus. The message emanating from their mutual preservation pact was, "Kill this troublemaker, and we both will have an easier life!"

Before looking at the role of the elders (πρεσβύτεροι) in Matthew's Gospel, we need to consider the place of the elders in Israel's history. In the Old Testament, the elders were persons who maintained and upheld the Jewish community. They were grown men who were powerful by their strong and reliable personalities and because of their influence as members of respected and powerful families. The elders located their authority and origin in Moses' appointment of the seventy elders in the wilderness: "And the Lord said to Moses, 'Gather for me seventy men of the elders of Israel, whom you know to be the elders of the people and officers over them; and bring them to the tent of meeting, and let them take their stand there with you'" (Numbers 11:16). The men selected to be elders were "ripe in years as well as qualified by their wisdom to share the burdens of leadership."[61]

Jeremias refers to the elders as "the lay nobility."[62] Raymond Brown defines the elders as "a nonpriestly aristocracy, a nobility by heredity and wealth, who were consulted on important matters affecting people."[63] During the time of the monarchy, the role of the elders was strengthened significantly. The judgment of the elders was considered side by side with the decisions of the king. Walther Eichrodt says, "When it is a question of decreeing important laws of state, the elders have a share in the decision."[64] When the people returned from the exile of the Babylonian captivity, the elders played an invaluable role in reestablishing the Jewish community. They negotiated with the Persian authorities and represented the affairs of the people. They had a strong voice in directing the reconstruction of the Temple. Josephus calls them "men of worth and gravity."[65]

These elders, this lay nobility, secured a position in the Sanhedrin. In Matthew's Gospel, they are only mentioned as members of the Sanhedrin. Matthew refers to them eleven times. On seven occasions, they are grouped with the chief priests (21:23; 26:3, 47; 27:1, 3, 20; 28:12; twice with the chief priests and scribes (16:21; 27:41); once with the scribes and Caiaphas (26:57); and once with the chief priests and Pilate (27:12). In ten of these eleven references the elders and the chief priests are seen to be together. They are, in fact, conspicuously linked with the chief priests as mutual conspirators against Jesus. This triad of chief priests, elders and scribes comprised the highest court and council of the nation. While the conflict with Jesus was occurring in Jerusalem, we must not overlook the fact that the authority of the Sanhedrin was not limited to the city of Jerusalem. All Jews everywhere yielded to the authority of the Sanhedrin. F. W. Beare says, "Though it possessed no forces (apart from the temple police), its edicts were willingly obeyed."⁶⁶

The question I want to raise is, "As representatives of the people, to what extent is it likely that the voice of the elders and the voice of the people were essentially one and the same?" On four occasions, Matthew refers to "the elders of the people" (οἱ πρεσβύτεροι τοῦ λαοῦ) (21:23; 26:3; 27:1), and (πρεσβυτέρων τοῦ λαοῦ) (26:47). In the Septuagint ὁ λαὸς (people) is "a specific term for a specific people, namely Israel, and it serves to emphasize the special and privileged religious position of this people as the people of God."⁶⁷ In answer to the above question, the voice of the elders is synonymous with the voice of the people. Gunther Bornkamm says that the phrase "elders of the people" always indicates that the elders are representatives of the people, and the phrase presupposes the unity of the elders and the people.⁶⁸

It becomes clear that in the history of Israel, the elders are always the representatives of the whole people of the nation. Furthermore, the history of Israel was a history of the people accepting and obeying the Law of Moses and the regulations resulting from the application of that law. In this respect, the law was, for Israel, a very personal concept. Gerhard von Rad says, "It was God's will for order, which in the end could never become really stabilized and objective. This, however, means that understanding it became rather the concern of authority.⁶⁹" The people placed that concern of authority into the keeping of the elders, and when they spoke, so spoke all of Israel.

Throughout the history of Israel, the legitimacy and necessity of this office of the elders were never disputed. Gerhard von Rad identifies this office of the elders as "an organ of the will of Yahweh."⁷⁰ Since the elders had their origin by command of the Lord, it is unthinkable that the people would not comply with the opinions and authority of the elders (Numbers 11:16). Not only were they selected by command of the Lord, but they were also given some of the same spirit that was upon Moses so that they would be able to "bear the burden of the people" (Numbers 11:17). From the beginning the elders were elevated to a highly respected position among the people. Having been instituted at the direction of the Lord God and anointed with the spirit, Martin Noth says, "This led, among the chosen elders, to a remarkable combination of institution and charisma of office and vocation."[71]

As the lay nobility, the elders were distinct from the representatives of the priestly families. Nevertheless, as members of the Sanhedrin and representatives of the privileged patrician families in Jerusalem, we may assume that they identified with and followed the lead of the Sadducees.[72] Being distinct from the priestly families and members of the laity does not mean that they were denied the power and prestige of the title and office itself. They were often referred to as "the great men of Jerusalem" and "the nobles of Jerusalem."[73] As members of the Sanhedrin and having a voice that represented the normative authority of all of Israel, the voice of the elders of the people was synonymous with the voice of the people of Israel.

Referring to the office of "elders of the people" in the time of Jesus, Rudolf Bultmann says, "An elder was an office wherein respect for personal authority is united with the authority of office."[74] They identified with and followed the lead of the Sadducees, who had already called for the death of Jesus. Therefore, they joined the passionate clamor for the death of Jesus. Their authority in the eyes of the people enhanced their ability to persuade the masses. They persuaded the crowds to ask for Barabbas and to have Jesus killed (27:20). The elders of the people (οἱ πρεσβύτεροι τοῦ λαοῦ), which always refers to the Jewish population, are among those who wanted Jesus killed.[75] Matthew writes, "All of them said, 'Let him be crucified!'" "All of them" (πάντες) includes the people as well as the officers of the Sanhedrin. Perhaps we should not be too quick to absolve the Jews of the death of Jesus.

Reference to "the crowd" and "the crowds" appears fifty times in Matthew's Gospel. He freely switches back and forth between the singular and the plural forms of the noun. The singular, ὄχλος, appears nineteen times, and the plural, ὄχλοι appears thirty-one times. Since the plural is used more frequently than the singular, I will refer to "the crowds" unless there is some compelling reason to differentiate between the two forms. The role and composition of the crowds in Matthew's account are not easy to define. When he speaks of Pharisees, Sadducees, chief priests, high priest, scribes and elders of the people, we become more acutely aware of the roles they play. As specific entities, we can put a name, a face or certain personality traits to these characters. However, this is not the case where the crowds are involved. The crowds represent nameless, faceless non-specific characters about whom we know nothing as individuals. Because of this faceless anonymity, I believe that it is quite possible for a reader to pay little attention to, or at least minimize, the role of the crowds.

Notable scholars have advanced several opinions as to the composition of the crowds. Jack Kingsbury says that they form the "applauding backdrop for Jesus' teaching throughout the land."[76] S. van Tilborg argues that they represent those who have accepted Jesus.[77] Ulrich Luz says that the crowds represent "potential disciples of Jesus."[78] Paul Minear goes so far as to suggest that the crowds are comprised of the laity of Matthew's church, who are being tended to by the disciples. He says, "They were characterized from the beginning by their acceptance of Jesus' message and his authority as prophet of God."[79] Beare sees the crowds as appearing throughout the Gospel to provide an audience for observing the actions of Jesus and hearing his teaching.[80]

These and many other analyses of the role and composition of the crowds have been advanced by credible scholars. Their many diverse conclusions leave us somewhat perplexed in attempting to arrive at a conclusion as to the composition and role of the crowds. Andries van Aarde sums up the situation very accurately when he says, "The function of the crowd in the Gospel of Matthew is related to one of the most difficult exegetical questions in the Gospel of Matthew."[81] Considering this, we can say with certainty that no consensus exists regarding whether the crowds were sympathetic to the ministry of Jesus or whether they were simply curious in the interim and ultimately hostile to him when he was charged with being an enemy of Israel.

What can be said about the nature and general definition of "the crowds" as a participating entity in the New Testament? In non-biblical usage, οἱ ὄχλοι is often described as "the leaderless and rudderless mob, the politically and culturally insignificant mass where the people is said to have no power of judgment."[82] In Matthew as well as the other gospels, "the crowds" provide the anonymous background to Jesus' activity among the people. Rudolf Meyer offers the following descriptions of what a crowd might look like:

1. A gathering of men milling around or closely pressed together.
2. The public as distinct from the private person or the small closed circle.
3. A throng or tumult.
4. The anonymous mass as distinct from men of rank or officials.
5. The leaderless and rudderless mob.
6. The politically and culturally insignificant mass.
7. The banding together of great masses.
8. The population of the land.[83]

These descriptive phrases are not particularly flattering, and most suggest a degree of chaos or a situation becoming out of control. With a note of certainty, Meyer says, "In the first instance ὄχλος denotes a crowd of men milling around or closely pressed together."[84] In Jesus' own lifetime, he had been called a magician, a seducer of Israel through false teachings and a blasphemous pretender to divinity. It is not difficult to imagine how these accusations could, at any time and in any place, incite a public gathering to engage in mob behavior.

When we read in the English version of Matthew that "the crowds "followed Jesus," we might easily assume that the "following" represents acceptance of discipleship. This ambiguity would serve to confirm an assumption that the crowds were composed mainly of people who were committed to the ministry of Jesus. The Greek verb denoting the action of "following" is ἀκολουθέω and it must be understood as reflecting action in two different contexts. Gerhard Kittel points out that ἀκολουθέω connotes an external following involving physical movement, but also following "as when one is called by Jesus."[85] When Matthew says that the crowd followed Jesus, he means that they physically moved with him or after him. However, when Jesus calls for someone to follow him and they respond, it means that they are following his leadership and accepting the terms of discipleship. When the crowds followed Jesus, they accompanied him on the physical journey. The following occurs in this context on fourteen occasions (4:25; 8:1, 10, 23; 9:19, 27; 12:15; 14:13; 19:2; 20:29, 34; 21:9; 26:58; 27:55). When Jesus calls Peter, Andrew, James, John and Matthew (4:18-22; 9:9), they follow him both externally and internally. There is an attachment, a relationship to Jesus that responds to and embraces the messianic demand of "Come, follow me."[86]

Having recognized the contextual possibilities of what it means to follow Jesus, we might still respond by noting that the crowds appear to react positively to Jesus on some occasions. Conversely, it is equally true that they often display a lack of understanding, mere curiosity or hostility on other occasions. To correctly evaluate the relationship of the crowd to Jesus, we need to assess whether the context of the following is that of physical movement or that of internal relational attachment. Has the following been prompted by a response to the messianic call of Jesus, or is it based on a curiosity that explores the novelty of a sensational new teacher gone public?

Following Jesus in terms of discipleship means that the disciple leaves everything to accompany Jesus. This context of following demands a self-commitment that breaks all other ties with anyone or anything. In primitive Christianity, there was only one kind of following that signaled discipleship, and that was the one that represented an internal (spiritual?) relationship with Jesus as Lord. It would be wrong to confuse the physical following of the crowds with those who followed Jesus as disciples. To follow as a disciple meant that one had been called to participate in the salvation offered by Jesus.

Any positive reactions by the crowds can now be measured against the standard requirement of a relational attachment to Jesus. Even though they were amazed at Jesus' teaching, they did not accept him as their leader, and they still maintained ties to their scribes and elders. They continued to identify with their leaders and did not identify with the salvation that Jesus offered. While they were sometimes amazed at his miracles, they did not understand the gospel he was teaching, and they failed to enter into a personal/internal following. They were amazed at his power to heal, but their amazement did not transition to understanding. They lacked compassion for some who appealed to Jesus and rebuked them for their intrusion and interruption of his ministry. Perhaps the crowd's activity of 12:46 reflects the most conclusive evidence that the crowds did not consist of people who were committed to the person and work of Jesus. Warren Carter believes their appearance here confirms their role as outsiders. He says, "They are differentiated from the family of disciples which does the will of Jesus' Father in heaven (12:50), and they are allied with the Pharisees (12:14, 24) as well as with Jesus' own family (12:46, 50) and country (13:54) in not understanding Jesus' identity and what is required of them."[87] The crowds, as representatives of the public, often speak and argue about the person and work of Jesus, but they do not show any real commitment to Jesus. Their failure to commit to the leadership of Jesus amounts to cooperation with the authorities whose goal is to destroy Jesus.

Matthew leaves little room for doubt that the crowds and the people represent the Jews and that they are hostile to Jesus. J. Cousland says that "the crowd functions *pars pro toto*."[88] In this respect, the crowds are "a part taken for the whole" and are representative of the entire population. Throughout the Gospel of Matthew, the activity of the crowds invariably suggests Jewish participation. The leaders and governing authorities to which they relate and with whom they identify are Jewish. When they identify themselves with Israel and the God of Israel, they show that they are the people of Israel and, therefore, they are Jews.

Matthew describes the people of Israel as "sheep without a shepherd" (9:36), and as such, they are the people with whom God long ago made a covenant. Regardless of their past and present conduct, they were and are the object of God's loving care. Concerning this historic relationship, Cousland says, "Nevertheless they are also the people who continuously ignore his ministrations, follow their corrupt leadership and go so far as to persecute his ministers, and to kill his prophets."[89] It can be said that the crowds are attracted to Jesus out of curiosity and with the expectation that he can meet their immediate needs. While it is always possible for them to accept the gospel message of Jesus, they invariably take sides with their leaders and reject the commitment that qualifies them as disciples and followers of the Lord.

Finally, we must not overlook Matthew's ultimate identification of "the crowds" with "all of the people" (πᾶς ὁ λαὸς) in 27:25. At this time, my intention is to establish the synonymity of the terms. Further implications of 27:25 will be dealt with in my exegetical comments on the Matthean Passion Narrative. The construction of πᾶς ὁ with the substantive λαός literally means "all" and, as such, refers to the entire content of the singular noun λαός.[90] Matthew intends to press home the point that "all" the people failed to understand Jesus.

Joseph Fitzmeyer says that Matthew does not use "the people" in a generic sense but that, in most instances, he uses it as "an ethnic connotation equaling the Jewish people."[91] Luz goes beyond Fitzmeyer's qualifying claim of it being a reference to Jewish people "in most instances." He says that Matthew never uses λαός without the thought of the Jewish nation as such.[92] Anthony Saldarini makes a definite connection between "the crowds" and "all the people" in 27.25. He says that οἱ ὄχλοι and πᾶς ὁ λαὸς affect a "social and political description of the main body of Israel."[93]

The role of the Jewish authorities and leaders in killing Jesus is easily established. It is also obvious that the people of Israel cannot be acquitted of blame in the killing of Jesus. The leaders and the people are clearly corporate characters who are equally responsible for killing Jesus. While the leaders and the people may be representing classes of corporate characters, it remains that both groups are identified as Jews, and they must assume collective responsibility for killing Jesus. The encouraging shouts and the infectious madness turn into murderous desires. The voice of the collective crowd builds to a crescendo and will not yield to reason. They will not cease until they have satisfied their frenzied hatred. Having considered the role and composition of the crowds, perhaps we should not be too quick to absolve the Jews of killing Jesus.

THE MATTHEAN PASSION NARRATIVE: 26:1 – 27:66

Passion Prophecy and the Plot (26:1-5)

Jesus announces to his disciples that his betrayal, arrest and death are imminent. The plot against him will come at Passover, which is just two days away (26:1-2). The passion drama has begun, and everything that occurs from this point forward will be acted out under the shadow of the cross.

The chief priests, elders of the people and the high priest, Caiaphas, meet in the palace of the high priest. Immediately, the necessary members required to compose a Sanhedrin are assembled. To say that they "took counsel" is to state the intent of the meeting too mildly. In fact, they literally plotted to kill Jesus. The fact that they wanted him dead was a foregone conclusion and never a point of discussion. The plotting involved how they might take him into custody secretly and by deception. They wanted to seize him out of the sight of the Passover crowds. Including the members of the city and the visiting pilgrims, Jeremias assesses the Passover crowd that year to have been approximately one hundred eighty thousand. He says, "There can be no doubt that the influx of pilgrims at Passover time from all over the world was immense and amounted to several times the population of Jerusalem."[94] Any public disturbance had the potential to become volatile and totally out of control with all these people crowded together and under the influence of a festival atmosphere. The word for the disturbance that they feared is θόρυβοσ, and it suggests more than a minor disturbance of little consequence. It is the same word Josephus uses to describe the many "tumults" that occurred at Passover during the first century when several bloody insurrections broke out among the city population and the Jews.⁹⁵

The Anointing (26:6-13)

The action occurs in the house of Simon the Leper. Simon has not been mentioned before, and he plays no further part in Matthew's story. An anonymous woman approaches Jesus and pours a flask of ointment on Jesus' head. Matthew does not tell us the monetary value of the ointment but tells us that it is "very expensive and very precious" (βαρυτίμου). Matthew does not tell us who she is, but because of what she has done, Jesus says that she will be remembered wherever the Gospel is preached. The identity of Simon and the woman is incidental to the essence of this story. The emphasis is really on an act of love and adoration that was a "beautiful thing." It was not just a "good thing," as some would say. As the word καλός indicates, it was more than a "good thing."⁹⁶ What she did was very beautiful, generous, excellent, praiseworthy and an illustrious example of love for the Lord Jesus Christ. The act itself was an example of the full meaning of "doing a beautiful thing." Out of the heart of this anonymous woman, we see an act of love that is beautiful and indescribably beyond beautiful. Jesus chastises the disciples for criticizing the woman. Through the eyes of pragmatism and common sense, they see nothing but a great waste. She saw an opportunity that would never come her way again, and she acted on it. The disciples missed the significance of this unique moment. While the disciples calculate the value of a "thing," the woman has no thought for profit and gain in the marketplace. Instead, she seizes on the moment to do a beautiful thing that will never again present itself to her. Her sacrifice proved her love, and it was memorialized in history. Perhaps Jesus is teaching the disciples and us that in Christ's service, certain things should be done without counting the cost when opportunities arise. The poet said it very well: "A thing of beauty is a joy forever; It will never pass into nothingness."⁹⁷

The Betrayal (26:14-16)

Judas Iscariot, one of the twelve trusted disciples, provided the solution to the chief priests' and elders' desire to set a trap and secretly arrest Jesus. He went to them and informed them that he would lead them to Jesus, and they agreed to pay him thirty pieces of silver for his service. We may speculate as to why Judas betrayed Jesus, but Matthew does not provide us with facts that satisfy our speculations. He may have been a Zealot who was disappointed that Jesus refused to physically overthrow the Roman government. He may have had great faith in Jesus who, if he were the Messiah, would reestablish the kingdom of Israel if he were forced to demonstrate a public display of martial power.

While he did accept thirty pieces of silver, it is unlikely that he was motivated by greed. If the silver coins were shekels, the total bribe would have amounted to about a month's wages.[98] It appears that Judas tried to make Jesus to be what he wanted him to be. Regardless of why Judas betrayed Jesus, the message for us seems to be that none of us can use Jesus for our own purposes. We must conform to his will for our lives instead of trying to make his teaching conform to our often very selfish purposes.

The Passover With the Disciples (26:17-30)

The disciples are not asking Jesus if he will eat the Passover meal; rather, they are inquiring as to the place where the meal will be served. We must remember that the city was crowded with pilgrims. Meeting places and houses of lodging would have been booked by those seeking to stay in the city during the festival. Jesus shows that he is in charge and that overcoming these logistical issues is but a small thing for him. He has already made provisions for the meal and tells them what they must do.

Matthew's account of the meal with the disciples is straightforward and does not require an intense investigation of every act that occurs during the meal. We have already discussed the betrayal by Judas and have seen that we cannot know for sure what his motive was. We can assume that the meal proceeded in much the same way that was customary for a Passover meal. There is nothing unusual about his taking the bread, breaking it and blessing it with the usual formula of "Blessed art thou, O Lord our God, king of the world, who brings forth bread from the earth." He would then distribute it as would any father or host presiding over the meal. However, there are some things that we need to look at closely because they represent acts and words that fall outside what would be a routine part of the meal. First, it is helpful to ask what Jesus meant when he said, "My time is at hand" (26:18). Second, what dynamics are at work in Jesus' statement, "One of you will betray me" (26: 21). Third, what did Jesus mean when he said, "This is my body" (26:28).

When Jesus says, "My time is at hand," he is not speaking of time as we measure it in days, months or years. He is not speaking of time in the way that we would say, "I am going to a party on January the first of next year." He uses the word καιρός which does not suggest a specific date and is not used in referencing a spatial point. In non-biblical literature καιρός usually signifies a decisive moment or a crucial place or point. In the Septuagint, we see that God is the one who oversees the time of divine appointments. God says, "At the set time (καιρόν) which I appoint I will judge with equity" (Psalms 74:2, LXX; 75:2 RSV). He says, "It is time (καιρός) for the Lord to act, for thy law has been broken" (Psalms 118:126, LXX; 119:126, RSV). Ecclesiastes 3:11 says, "All the things which he has made are beautiful in his time (καιρῷ)." In the same sense, when Jesus says, "My time (καιρός) is at hand," he is proclaiming that the time determined by God has arrived for him. This is a time that has nothing to do with spatial time as humans measure it; rather, it is a time which is given by God's will.[99] The time of Jesus' betrayal, persecution, death and resurrection is a decisive point which stands under the divine appointment of God. Jesus consciously and willingly accepts all that is to happen in this time appointed for him by God. He voluntarily and obediently yields to the cup of suffering and death which this καιρός has placed before him. As disciples of the Lord Jesus, we cannot calculate the times of God's calling in our lives. We can only be prepared when the time comes and respond with obedience to whatever circumstances accompany that God-ordained decisive moment.

While they were participating in the meal, Jesus said, "One of you will betray me" (vs. 21). He had already told them that he would be "delivered up to be crucified" (26:3), but he had not given any clue as to the identity of the betrayer. The revelation that the betrayer would be one of the twelve who were eating with him would be unbelievable in the immediate moment. Jesus prefaced his revelatory statement with the word "verily" (Ἀμὴν). In this context, and in the vernacular of today, we might say, "You are not going to believe this but take my word for it; it is true." In the face of their immediate difficulty in believing what he is telling them, Jesus emphasises that the betrayer is, indeed, eating with them. Schlier says, "The point of the Amen before Jesus' own sayings is rather to show that as such they are reliable and true."[100] Perhaps Jesus is equating the moment to the experience of the Psalmist when he wrote: "Even my bosom friend in whom I trusted, who ate of my bread, has lifted his heel against me" (Psalm 41:9).

It is easy to understand that the disciples would be very saddened at the thought of having a betrayer among them. The question presents, however, as to why each of them had to ask whether it was them who was to be the betrayer of the Lord. Did they begin to take inventory of their relationship with Jesus? Did that act bring to mind some word, faithless thought or time when they had doubted the authenticity of the person and work of the one they called the Master? Each one cautiously asks, "Is it I, Lord?" We must wonder if each one begins to wrestle with some personal fear or inner weakness. The question suggests that a negative answer is expected, but an affirmative answer is not ruled out completely.[101] Jesus does not identify the betrayer. He says, "He who has dipped his hand in the dish with me" (26:23), but that does not identify the specific betrayer. They all had dipped in the dish with Jesus. While Judas knew that he was the betrayer, it is quite certain that the others did not know about Judas. Had they known, it is unlikely that they would have let him complete his deal with the Devil.

Jesus' proclamation of "this is my body" (26:26) and "this is my blood of the covenant" (26:29) establishes the institution of the Eucharist, communion or the Lord's Supper as the church knows it today. I do not intend to address the various and voluminous studies arguing for transubstantiation, consubstantiation or any other specific claim regarding these issues. From a broader perspective, it is important only for the believer to realize and affirm the fact that the death of Jesus has meaning and benefit for those who claim him as their Lord and Savior. Through the threefold action of taking, eating and drinking, believers are reminded that they are participating in a new covenant instituted by God through his Son. As faithful participants, they have forgiveness of sins and access to the great, glorious power and comfort of grace. With this comes the assurance that there will be a time when believers will sit at the table with Jesus in the triumphant environment of God's eternal kingdom (26:29).

Prayer and Arrest in Gethsemane (26:31-56)

After singing a hymn, Jesus and the disciples went to the Mount of Olives. Jesus said to them, "You will all fall away because of me this night; for it is written, 'I will strike the shepherd, and the sheep of the flock will be scattered'" (26:31). He told them that each of them would be confronted with a crisis of faith, loyalty and commitment. The nature and result of this impending crisis are contained in the verb σκαηδαλίζω which is variously translated as "fall away," "take offense," "be scandalized," "to desert" and "to be tripped up." Any one of these translations serves to let us know that Jesus is warning his most intimate disciples that they will have doubts about who he is and that they will lose faith in him. Filson says, "He told them they would take offense, be caused to stumble, led into sin by their relation to him; their loyalty to him would bring them into a danger whose pressure would lead them to act wrongly."[102] All of this will be in fulfillment of the prophecy of Zechariah: "Awake, O sword, against my shepherd, against the man who stands next to me, says the Lord of hosts. Strike the shepherd that the sheep may be scattered" (Zechariah 13:7).

After issuing this horrific prediction, Jesus lets the disciples know that the "falling away" and the "scandalizing" will ultimately give way to the good news of victory. He says, "But after I am raised up, I will go before you to Galilee" (26:32). Notice that Jesus speaks of his resurrection in the passive voice, "after I am raised up." He does not resurrect himself and lets them know that God is still in charge. He is letting them know that there is nothing that can happen that will be so bad or self-defeating that God cannot prevail. God will raise him up, and the pain of their falling away will be forgiven and overcome by the power and victory of God through Jesus Christ. Jesus tells them that he knows that they will be disappointed and will scatter from Jerusalem and return to Galilee. He tells them that when they arrive, they will find that he has already been raised from the dead and is waiting on them in Galilee.

Peter's response is one of rash confidence. He separates himself from the others and declares that even if all of them fall away, he will never forsake the Lord. His declaration of courage is an example of how little we can know of ourselves when we are threatened by pain, embarrassment and loss of confidence. Like Peter, we often put too much stock in the power of our own ego, and in so doing, we find that our "I amness" is not enough to withstand the wiles of the Evil One. Jesus knew the pain and horror of the awful ordeal which was before them all. He was unrelenting in repeating that Peter would most certainly deny him, even though Peter refused to believe it. Jesus was speaking and acting from the perspective of one who knew the whole story. He was not offended at the offense they would all commit. He knew that the scandals of our weaknesses could be forgiven and turned to gain for the Father's Kingdom.

In the Gethsemane prayer scene, we are reminded of the humanity of Jesus. In the face of anxiety and fear, he feels the need to pray. He takes the eleven remaining disciples with him to the place of prayer. One could even go so far as to say that in the Gethsemane experience, we see how much Jesus is one of us and like us. In these few verses, we find that Jesus is "sorrowful and troubled" (26:37). He reveals to Peter, James and John that his "soul is very sorrowful, even to death" (26:38). Under the accumulating weight of these emotional and psychological forces, "he fell on his face and prayed" (26:39). Nowhere else in the Gospel narratives does Jesus seem as vulnerable to the same forces that often visit us in our own humanity. In his hour of great need, Jesus asked his disciples to keep awake and be vigilant with him as he prayed. Treachery, betrayal, hatred, cruelty and fear produce agony and loneliness in all who are subjected to those debilitating forces. Jesus was wrestling with the ordeal that was before him, and it was human that he wanted the support of friends.

Jesus, no doubt trembling and hesitant, prays, "If it be possible, let this cup pass from me" (26:39). Of course, it was possible in that "all things are possible with God." However, should the cup of suffering be taken away, it would no longer be possible that Jesus of Nazareth could be Jesus the Christ and fulfill the victory over sin, death and the grave. The anguish reflected in this prayerful request is not "fear of a dark fate, nor cringing before physical suffering and death, but the horror of One who lives by God, at being cast from Him, at the judgment which delivers up the Holy One to the power of sin."[103] Jesus had taught the disciples to pray, "Thy kingdom come, thy will be done, on earth as it is in heaven" (6:10). Now, in his time of great anguish and need, he employs the same petition saying, "Not as I will, but as thou wilt" (26:39), and "thy will be done" (26:42). He places his will alongside the will of the Father, and he yields to the necessity that righteousness must stand in the place where sin is standing. Above the physical signs and strains of agony and sorrow, there is an absolute obedience to the will of the Father. His entire posture is one of fervent prayer, and it is significant that he only prays and makes no attempt to bargain himself out of the situation. Karl Barth rightly says that Jesus prayed "with only a view to God's own will and not with any bias in his own direction or favor."[104]

Jesus disengages from prayer three times and returns to his disciples. On each occasion, he finds them sleeping (26:40, 43, 45). It was but a short time ago that Peter and all the disciples declared, "I will not deny you" (26:35). Before the night is over, they will all be seen fleeing Gethsemane. Perhaps we should not be overly critical of their falling away. We share with them the same characteristics of fleshly weakness. Did they sense a note of fear in their otherwise fearless Master? Did their strength, gained in their confidence in him, begin to fail them? Did their thoughts of pain or death weaken their resolve? Did they feel powerless to change the circumstances of what was happening? Any one or all of these, and a host of other possibilities common to the human situation, could have been at play in their decisions to flee that night. Clothed in flesh as we are, Jesus would have them and us be on guard and be aware that "the spirit is willing, but the flesh is weak" (26:41).

Jesus announces that "the hour is at hand, and the Son of Man is betrayed into the hands of sinners" (26:45). His prayer to the Father is complete, and the failure of the disciples has reached its climax. James Mays calls the action that occurs from this point forward "a narrative of handing over." He says, "Judas hands Jesus over to an armed mob. They hand him over to judgment by the court of the High Priest. The court hands him over to the court of the governor. Pilate, intimidated by the crowd, hands him over to the troops to be crucified."[105]

The narrative will now become an account of what other people and authorities will do to Jesus. He will be subjected to arrest, trials, condemnation, verdict and execution. Through it all, there will be no miraculous intervention from the Father. Jesus will have to "faith" his way through the entire ordeal. When he obediently accepted the cup of suffering according to the Father's will, he also accepted the agony of the absence of God (26:42).

Fulfilling his contract with the chief priests and the elders of the people, Judas led an armed mob (ὄχλος) to Gethsemane, committed the kiss of betrayal and watched them seize Jesus. One of those with Jesus drew a sword and tried to resist by cutting off the ear of a slave of the high priest. Jesus stopped the resistance and told them that using force against force was self-defeating. Furthermore, if God's will required the use of force, Jesus was confident that God would provide a large army of angels to defeat any power that a human army could muster. Jesus exposed the irrational mob mentality that fuels the crowds. He reminded them that day after day, he sat peacefully teaching in the temple. Their ridiculous show of force in Gethsemane, inspired by blind hatred, was entirely unnecessary.

Jesus Condemned and Denied (26:57-75)

Jesus' solitude in facing the coming ordeal is seen clearly as the disciples leave him and the crowds take him away. The "handing over" has begun as they deliver him to Caiaphas, the high priest. On the information provided by Judas, the stage had already been set for Jesus' appearance before the high priest, the scribes and the elders. The "whole council" (τὸ συνέδριον ὅλον) reveals that a Sanhedrin had been constituted and assembled. We can identify this as the first trial to which Jesus was subjected. However, this is not to say that Jesus was fairly accused and given due process under Jewish law. In fact, there was no attempt to seek prosecution under the pretense of any established code of legal jurisprudence. The sole intent of the council was to cobble together any kind of charges that carried the death penalty and would support an indictment against Jesus. They solicited false witnesses against Jesus, and many such witnesses responded. To their displeasure, no two of them offered testimony that would require a death sentence. Finally, two witnesses, as required by Jewish law, testified that they heard Jesus say, "I am able to destroy the temple of God, and to build it in three days" (26:61). Caiaphas used the witness of these two non-disciples to press forward with his interrogation of Jesus. He tried to goad Jesus into defending himself, but Jesus stood silent before the accusers. Becoming more frustrated, Caiaphas demanded that Jesus testify under oath and said, "Tell us if you are the Christ, the Son of God" (26:63). Allen calls Jesus' answer "an evasive affirmative or ambiguous affirmative."[106] It is the same answer he gave to Judas (26:25) and the same one he will give to Pilate (27:11): "You have said so." It is the same as saying, "Your words, not mine."

To this point, Jesus has not said anything that Caiaphas can turn to his advantage. But Jesus amplified his short answer, and the high priest seized upon it as the condemning evidence he needed. Jesus said, "But I tell you hereafter you will see the Son of Man seated at the right hand of power, and coming on the clouds of heaven" (26:64). This was messianic language, and although Jesus does not say, "You will see me," the identification is plain enough to his hearers.[107] The pretend messiah stands arraigned before the high court of the messianic people. The high priest now has what he wants and proclaims that no further witnesses are needed. He declares that Jesus has uttered blasphemy. The whole council concurred and judged that "he deserves to die." The charade of false witnesses is joined by the false claim of blasphemy. Surely the council members knew that nowhere in Jewish tradition could it be found that a messianic pretender was to be regarded as a blasphemer.[108]

The council/Sanhedrin acted as a gang of power mongers who quickly arrived at an expedient and violent solution to the threat represented in the person and work of Jesus. The trial is broken off when it has hardly begun, and the death sentence is summarily pronounced. Karl Barth says that it is at this point that the passion story properly begins. He says:

"It is this admission, together with the prediction of His impending exaltation and second coming, that seals His fate in the eyes of His enemies. The high priest rends his clothes. There is no need for further evidence against Him, for this is blasphemy. The death sentence is pronounced forthwith, and the mocking and scourging follow."[109]

The physical mistreatment results in the fulfillment of a prophecy that described what the servant of the Lord would have to endure: "I gave my back to the smiters, and my cheeks to those who pulled out the beard; I hid not my face from shame and spitting" (Isaiah 50:6).

While Jesus was being interrogated, Peter was sitting nearby in the courtyard. During this time, he denied Jesus on three occasions. His denials brought the fulfillment of Jesus' prophecy into agreement with the prediction made in 26:34: "Truly, I say to you, this very night, before the cock crows, you will deny me three times." Those privy to the denials begin with a single maid, then another maid in the presence of bystanders, and finally, in the presence of bystanders who confront him and accuse him with certainty. The pressure of the accusations prompts Peter to emphasize his denial by an extended period of cursing and swearing. Allen says that Peter tried to convince his accusers that he was answering truthfully by invoking a curse on himself if his statement was not true.[110] His protest amounts to what we mean when we crudely say, "If I'm lying, I'm dying!"

At the third denial, the cock crows, and Peter is immediately reminded of his sworn allegiance to Jesus and Jesus' prediction that he would fall away and deny him. Confronted with the realization of what he had done, he was overcome with agony and shame. He left the courtyard and wept bitterly.

I remember a sermon preached by a shrill-voiced, red-faced, foaming at the mouth, hellfire and damnation revival preacher whose custom was to tell us that we were all sinners and in need of repentance. He told us that Peter committed a great sin because he "warmed his hands by the devil's fire" while Jesus was being sentenced to death. He warned us that we would never be guilty of warming our hands by the devil's fire if our faith was strong. He demanded that we should all come forward, confess our sins, and promise God that we would never warm our hands by the devil's fire. We never saw or heard from this preacher again. We later learned that he had been caught "warming his hands" with another revival preacher's wife.

We should always be willing to remind ourselves that before condemning Peter or any fellow human being we should ask ourselves how we might react under similar circumstances. When temptation ambushes us, how do we respond? While Peter did deny the Lord, he yet demonstrated the courage to remain nearby while the interrogation and mistreatment were taking place. It took a measure of courage to remain that close to the evil forces that had the power to apprehend him. Of the twelve, he alone had the courage to follow Jesus to the courtyard of Caiaphas. In the crucible of fear, terror and uncertainty, Peter wanted to remain loyal to the Master who loved him. Barclay sums up the denial in a positive way. He says:

> It was love that gave Peter that courage; it was love that riveted him there in spite of the fact that he had been recognized three times; it was love that made him remember the words of Jesus; it was love that sent him out into the night to weep—and it is love which covers a multitude of sins. The lasting impression of this story is not Peter's cowardice, but of Peter's love.[111]

Judas' Betrayal and Pilate's Acquiescence (27:1-24)

Some have argued that chapter 27 introduces a second meeting of the Sanhedrin. Is this a continuation of the meeting during the night, or is it the convening of another meeting? It could be that the first meeting was the vehicle for establishing a case against Jesus, and the morning meeting represented the formal affirmation of guilt. All that really matters is that "all (πάντες) the chief priests and elders of the people" were present and agreed that Jesus was guilty and deserving of the death penalty. The "handing over" continues as they bind Jesus and deliver him to Pilate.

The account of the death of Judas (27:3-10) rather awkwardly interrupts the flow of the "handing over" of Jesus to Pilate. When the reality of what was happening to Jesus became apparent, Judas became acutely aware of what he had done. His appearance at this point reminds us that the one who has been found guilty is, in fact, innocent of all charges. Judas admits and confirms this when he says, "I have sinned in betraying innocent blood" (27:4). Judas' repentance must not be equated to a "religious and moral conversion" or a "break with the ungodly and sinful past."¹¹² His repentance is represented by the verb "μεταμέλομαι" which refers to human repentance with no content of faith. Judas returned the thirty pieces of silver because he was filled with remorse. The reference in 27:4 is to remorse, not repentance. Michel says, "The remorse of Judas does not have the power to overcome the destructive operation of sin."¹¹³

Confessing that he had "betrayed innocent blood" and hoping to assuage his remorseful guilt, he returned the "blood money" to the chief priests. They showed no concern for Judas' state of remorse and grief. In fact, they say, "What is that to us? See to it yourself" (27:4). Their position is, "We don't care what you think, and we certainly don't have any feelings of remorse or pains of conscience regarding Jesus of Nazareth." Judas' reward has quickly become a moral and psychological liability with which he could not live. The verb "ρίπτω" designates the act of "throwing" the coins. This word always suggests "throwing away to get rid of something."¹¹⁴ Judas' "throwing" was more than simply returning the money. It was an attempt to get rid of his remorse. The "throwing" and the "hanging" both represent the act of a desperate man."¹¹⁵ That the money was used by the chief priests to buy a cemetery to bury non-Jews is seen as a fulfillment of Old Testament prophecy.

Matthew's reference to Old Testament scripture is not unusual. He attributes the references to the "thirty pieces of silver" and the purchase of the "potter's field" to the prophet Jeremiah. He doesn't mention Zechariah, but the reference itself appears to be a conflation of prophecies spoken by both prophets. Zechariah 11:13 says, "Then the Lord said to me, 'Cast it into the treasury'—the lordly price at which I was paid off by them. So I took the thirty shekels of silver and cast them into the treasury in the house of the Lord." This conflation and citing of Jeremiah alone does not represent any falsification of textual proof. Matthew is not interested in the exegetical interpretation of any Old Testament scripture.

Brevard Childs says, "Rather, the specific text functions as a transparency into the larger prophetic dimension represented by the entire Old Testament."[116]

Appearing before Pilate, Jesus neither confirms nor denies that he is the King of the Jews. Responding in the form of the "evasive affirmative," which he has used before (26:25, 64), he simply says, "You have said so," implying that "These are your words, not mine." The chief priests and elders accuse him, but they make no indication as to the specificity of their charges, and Jesus remains silent before them. He will not speak again throughout the remainder of this farce masquerading as a trial. His silence is reminiscent of the conduct of the Suffering Servant: "He was oppressed, and he was afflicted, yet he opened not his mouth" (Isaiah 53:7). Pilate finds the silence baffling and incomprehensible. Most men, when accused, whether guilty or innocent, typically protest that they are not guilty. As the charges and accusations increased, Pilate tried to prompt Jesus to defend himself, but he remained silent. He knew that nothing he said would make a difference, so he silently submitted to the will of his Father that he drink the sacrificial cup of death for the sin of the world.

Some scholars note that the claim that it was customary to release a prisoner of the crowd's choosing at the annual feast is not well-attested. Albright and Mann say, "We know nothing from external sources of the custom described for us by Matthew, Mark and John, and this account of a (local?) custom has from time to time been used to discredit the whole narrative of the trial of Jesus."[117] However, Filson disagrees and says, "The custom was known elsewhere, and is credible here. To let the crowd choose the prisoner they wanted was intended to pacify the Jews at a time of national enthusiasm in crowded Jerusalem."[118] There is no reason to doubt the authenticity of Matthew's statement. What would be the point of Matthew, Mark and John spinning a lie regarding this event? Other than comparing the criminal notoriety of Barabbas (27:16) to the righteousness and innocence of Jesus (27:19, 23), the story has no further interest in Barabbas per se.

The amnesty issue is intended to emphasize the case against the Jews. Matthew wants us to know that the religious leaders and "all the people" are desirous of the murder of Jesus. Given a choice, the chief priests and elders convince the people to demand that a criminal be favored over an innocent man. Pilate put the question before them: "If I release the criminal, what do I do with the innocent man?" With one voice, they demanded that he should be crucified. While Pilate was a cruel and vicious man with no history of demonstrating compassion, he seemed to be keenly aware of the injustice that was unfolding before him. Barclay says, "Pilate was warned by his sense of justice, he was warned by his conscience, he was warned by the dream of his troubled wife; but Pilate could not stand against the mob; and Pilate made the futile gesture of washing his hands."[119]

Pilate recognized that he could do nothing to change the mind of the crowd. To be honest, he was, as we would say, "Caught between a rock and a hard place." It was a matter of record that Emperor Tiberius did not approve of governors who dealt unfairly with his provincial subjects. On the other hand, he had no mercy for anyone suspected of treason. Knowledge of this gave the Jewish authorities leverage to get their way when dealing with Pilate. His final act was an attempt to defend himself from repercussions by the emperor and alienation from the Jewish leadership, which he needed to successfully manage his responsibility as governor of the province. He declared himself "innocent of this man's blood" and transferred all guilt to the Jews: "See to it yourselves" (27:24). All the people willingly accepted the responsibility for the murder of Jesus. Furthermore, they accepted the responsibility without any feelings of guilt, as evidenced by the fact that they made no concession that Jesus might be innocent. If Pilate exonerated himself from any guilt of the shedding of Jesus' blood and it remained that someone had to be responsible for that blood, all the people said, "Let his blood be on us and on our children" (27:25).

The Blood Curse (27:25)

If one holds that the Jews killed Jesus, one must also ask if the consequences of their guilt apply to all Jews into perpetuity. Or, should the guilt for that killing be applied only to the specific people living in the specific time in which the killing occurred? The words of the Jews in Matthew 27:25, "And all the people answered, 'His blood be upon us and our children!'" cannot mean that the people have accepted a curse on all Jews for all time. R. T. France reminds us that Matthew and his fellow apostles were Jews, and therefore, "to read into these words a 'curse' on all Jews for ever is ludicrous."[120] The logic inherent in France's statement is inescapable; however, the fact remains that multiple generations of Jews have suffered the scandal of being known as Christ-killers. The assumption that the Jews have placed themselves under an eternal curse has had tragic consequences for Judaism. Matthew 27:25 became the primary theme that produced hostility toward the Jews. Fitzmeyer says, "Probably no other New Testament text has been so often quoted against the Jews since it was first written."[121]

How is this troubling verse to be explained if it is not accepted as an irrevocable self-pronounced curse on all the Jews for all time? Brown refers to it as being "one of those phrases which have been responsible for oceans of human blood and a ceaseless stream of misery and desolation."[122] One explanation involves the response of the Jews to Pilate's final declaration of "I am innocent of this man's blood; see to it yourselves" (Matthew 27:24). Even in a rigged "kangaroo court," someone must accept responsibility for a sentence that is passed. If Pilate will not accept the requisite responsibility, who will? The Jews, sensing that their efforts to kill Jesus are in jeopardy of being terminated, accept the responsibility in order to salvage their plan to kill Jesus. It was a "snap" decision made in the immediate necessity of the moment. Given the circumstances, we must remember the nature of the God of Israel in relationship to Israel. Any presumed curse must ultimately be seen in consideration of the Psalmist's certainty that the anger of God "Is but for a moment, and his favor is for a lifetime" (Psalm 30:5). The Psalmist is so sure of this that he reinforces it: "For the Lord is good; his steadfast love endures forever, and his faithfulness to all generations" (Psalm 100:5). I do not believe that an impulsive decision made in a moment of frenzied panic could possibly have the power to endure forever against the love and mercy of God. If Matthew 27:25 is held to be true for all time, how can Christianity claim to have Jesus as its Lord? The magnificent, magnanimous cry from the dying Messiah on the cross speaks the last word to all sin, all curses and all failures: "Father, forgive them; for they know not what they do" (Luke 23:34).

The Christian understanding of the love of God in Jesus Christ should be a deterrent for using this verse of scripture as a springboard for condemnation of all Jews for all time. Both Jeremiah and Ezekiel remind Israel that the threat of the generational curse has ended. Jeremiah says, "The father's teeth have eaten sour grapes, and the children's teeth are set on edge. But everyone shall die for his own sin; each man who eats sour grapes, his teeth shall be set on edge" (Jeremiah 31:29-30). Referring to the same sour grapes proverb, Ezekiel says, "As I live, says the Lord God, this proverb shall no more be used by you in Israel" (Ezekiel 18:1-4). The children are no longer to be held accountable for any sins committed by their parents. Each individual will be required to give an account of his or her actions before God. Walter Zimmerli says that the prophets are making fun of the ancient belief that God would pass the guilt of the fathers on to their children. They are mocking the "ancient liturgical prediction of Yahweh as the God who punishes sins until the third and fourth generations."[123]

Considering their own prophetic history, the Jews did not have the power to place a curse on themselves. Any such corporate curse involving multiple generations would be meaningless since the prophets had made it clear that "everyone shall die for his own sin" (Jeremiah 30:30). The Christian tendency to read Matthew 27:25 as though it were an eternal curse on the Jewish race is beyond defending. It is not an eternal condemnation of the Jews and their descendants. Fitzmeyer says, "It was not the Evangelist's aim to point his finger at all the Jews of his own period—much less at the Jews of all ages since—and brand them as deicides."[124] It is sad but historically true that the words "His blood be upon us and on our children" have been the source of Jewish vulnerability and used to incite anti-Jewish sentiments throughout the world. Beare says, "It is appalling for a Christian to think of how much suffering has been inflicted on the Jews throughout the ages."[125] Appalling indeed! Wrong ideas and generational fears have taken a horrendous toll on an entire race of people. In the name of the Savior of the world, Christians have been blind to the Gospel of that same Savior. And the centuries-old crime of Christianity is that the Jews have been judged and punished again and again on the strength of a self-imposed generational curse that had been pronounced null and void by the prophets centuries ago.

The Handing Over (27:26-31)

With the blame having been established, Pilate had no reason to continue his defense of Jesus. He had him scourged and delivered him to be crucified. The "handing over" continued as the soldiers took Jesus to their barracks area and mustered the rest of their detachment so that they all might participate in some sadistic humor at Jesus' expense. It is unlikely that they had any personal interest in the farce that masqueraded as a trial. All they knew was that this beaten and bleeding man was accused of being a king. They matched his fake claim by adorning him with fake kingly accouterments. They did not have access to the royal robe of a king, so they clothed him in the red cloak of a common Roman soldier. While the crown of a triumphant king would have been made of a wreath of leaves, they made Jesus wear a painful wreath of thorns. A king's scepter would be a finely crafted staff trimmed with gold, but Jesus' scepter was a common reed, a stalky plant of no value whatsoever.

Jesus endured their mockery and physical abuse without saying a word. When they were finished with their sadistic games, they stripped him of the red cloak and struck him with the fake scepter. Their actions seemed to say, "You are not even worthy to wear a fake robe and carry a fake scepter." They dressed him in his own clothes, which certainly bore no resemblance to the garments of a real king. The soldiers then led him away to fulfill the demand of all the people that he should be crucified. What was happening would have lasting and awful consequences for the Jews, but for Pilate and the Roman soldiers, it was just another crucifixion.

Crucifixion and Death (27:32-56)

Matthew's account of the crucifixion and death of Jesus is straightforward and needs little in the way of exegesis or interpretation. As they leave the city and proceed to Golgotha, the Place of the Skull and the place of execution, Jesus is unable to carry his cross. The hours without sleep and rest and the merciless torture he has endured have left him without the strength to carry the cross to Golgotha. When Jesus faltered from exhaustion, the soldiers compelled and pressed into service a man known as Simon of Cyrene. Simon carried the cross the final distance to the place of execution (27:32). Beyond this reference to Simon as the cross-bearer, Matthew doesn't tell us anything else about him.

Jesus was offered wine mingled with gall before they raised him up on the cross. The wine was of a mild alcoholic content, and the gall was a bitter-tasting narcotic. The mixture of the two created a medicated drink that could ease the pain. Upon tasting it, Jesus refused to drink it. Having accepted the will of the Father, he was committed to accepting the total pain and agony represented in the cup of suffering (27:34). After raising him on the cross, the soldiers gambled for his clothing (27:35). Matthew is emphasizing the fact that all these things happening to Jesus are "according to the scriptures" and each one fulfills a prophecy from the Old Testament.

As was customary per Roman law, the crime of the condemned person was attached to his cross. The charge against Jesus was listed as, "This is Jesus, the king of the Jews" (27:37). He was crucified between two robbers (27:38) and was "numbered with the transgressors" (Isaiah 53:12). Those passing by slandered, mocked and made fun of him (27:39). Who are the ones passing by? Filson says, "They are not ignorant outsiders; they know and repeat the charge against Jesus."[126] The chief priests, scribes and elders join in and challenge Jesus to use his divine power to save himself. They tempt him in much the same way as he was tempted in the wilderness. They affirm that they will believe that he is the Messiah if he will save himself (27:41-43). The robbers join in the mockery and slander Jesus even as they face their own deaths on the cross (27:44). All these taunts, slanders and charges are based on falsehoods. Those who jeer and deride Jesus do it because they claim that he said, "I am the Son of God" (27:43). At no time has Jesus made that claim. To the question, "Are you the Christ, the Son of God?" he answered, "You have said so."

As Jesus approaches death, the earth becomes clouded with darkness from noon until three o'clock. In keeping with the miraculous things that will happen during the hour of his death, we can believe that the darkness is also a supernatural cosmic event. At three o'clock (the ninth hour), Jesus cries out loudly, "My God, my God, why hast thou forsaken me?" (27:46). These are the first words of Psalm 22, which begins in despair but concludes with a proclamation of God's deliverance. I have no doubt that Jesus knew this Psalm by heart, and I believe the Gospel writers when they tell us that Jesus appealed to this Psalm in the hour of his death. However, I believe that there is more to this anguished cry than simply serving as proof of fulfillment of an Old Testament scripture. I believe that he was identifying with all of us when we are confronted with those great fearful moments that are common to our human existence. Life flings great fearful words into our faces—words like cancer, heart failure, bankruptcy, divorce, death of a spouse, death of a child, death of a parent, death of a dear friend, the evil reports of gossip and lies told about us, and betrayal by those in whom we have placed our trust. In those moments, we can feel utterly forsaken by God.

I believe that Jesus did not fully understand everything that was happening as he hung on that cross. If he fully understood it all, I must complain that he pulled rank on my humanity. Who wouldn't die for the sin of the world if they knew beyond a shadow of a doubt that in three days, they would be raised from the dead and forever after sit at the right hand of God in power and glory? God help me, I must confess that there have been times when I did not know why things were happening as they were, and I did not have a clue as to how they would turn out. Therefore, I believe that Jesus entered completely into the depths of all that is possible in the human experience. He did not save himself, and he did not ask to be saved. What, then, did he do? He "faithed" his way through all the pain, suffering and unknowing of what was happening. He "faithed" that God would have the last word about his terrible predicament. Because of his example, we can have the courage to "faith" our way through whatever comes our way. God, through Jesus Christ, promises us that "whether we live or whether we die, we are the Lord's" (Romans 14:8).

Some of the bystanders thought that Jesus was calling Elijah (27:47). This presumption would be based on the Jewish belief that Elijah was the rescuer of the pious in their time of need.[127] Upon hearing this, one of the bystanders immediately filled a sponge with vinegar, put it on a stick and offered it to Jesus (27:49). This could have been an act of kindness, or it could have been an attempt to make sure that Jesus remained alive long enough for the bystanders to see if Elijah would come and save him. Matthew doesn't tell us anything about the bystander's motives.

We know that Jesus did not accept the drink but "cried again with a loud voice and yielded up his spirit" (27:50). The word used for "yielded up" is ἀφῆκεν (third person, singular, first aorist, active, indicative of αφίημι). In this context, it means "to give up, let go, send away, dismiss or yield."[128] I find it interesting to consider that this word, in various forms and derivations, is closely associated with forgiveness and the cancellation of sins. This is particularly evident in the Septuagint. When the Israelites sinned by making and worshiping a golden calf, Moses pleaded with God to spare the people. He said, "And now if thou wilt forgive (ἀφεῖς) their sin, forgive it (ἀφες)" (Exodus 32:32, LXX). Again, when the Israelites rebelled against Moses and God, Moses interceded and said, "Forgive (ἀφες) this people their sin according to thy great mercy" (Numbers 14:19, LXX). As atonement for transgressions, God directed Moses to offer "a calf of the herd without blemish for a whole burnt offering of sweet savour to the Lord" (Numbers 15:24, LXX). Upon making this sacrifice for all sins, intentional and unintentional, God said, "It shall be forgiven (ἀφεθήσεται) as respects all the congregation of the children of Israel" (Numbers 15:26, LXX). When God restored Job and "blessed the latter end of Job more than the beginning," Job also prayed for his friends, "and he forgave (ἀφῆκεν) them" (Job 42:10, LXX).

Chapters four, five and six of Leviticus catalog a list of sacrifices that must be made as a sin offering for acts that have broken the people's relation to God and endangered the welfare of the community. When the sacrifice is properly completed, the offender(s) will be forgiven. On all nine occasions of "it shall be forgiven him," the word used for forgiveness is ἀφεθήσεται (4:26, 31, 35; 5:6, 10, 13, 16, 18; 6:6). These sacrifices and the resulting forgiveness apply only to sins that are unwittingly or inadvertently committed. Perhaps this is why Matthew omitted Luke's "Father forgive (ἀφες) them; for they know not what they do" (Luke 23:34) and John's "It is finished" (John 19:30). The substance of both these sayings is resident in Matthew's use of (ἀφῆκεν). Relative to this, more will be said when I deal with the Lucan and Johannine passion narratives.

Bultmann notes that the Greek usage of αφίημι is used in every nuance, both literally and figuratively, from 'to hurl,' 'to release,' 'to let go' or 'to let be.'"[129] He says that in the Septuagint, the word is used for a whole series of Hebrew words. The Septuagint Greek uses αφίημι to capture the original sense of the Hebrew word, which points to the cultic removal and expiation of sin.[130] New Testament usage of αφίημι can include all the possibilities reflected in both Greek and Septuagint usage. For Matthew, Jesus' last action on the cross encompassed both completion of God's plan and forgiveness; "It is finished" and "Father forgive them; for they know not what they do."

Jesus' "yielding up his spirit" has far greater implications than our man-made rules governing petty morality and memorizing and reciting doctrinal codes that define us as Baptists, Methodists, Catholics, etc. Referring to Jesus' "Crying out with a loud voice and yielding up his spirit," Bultmann says, "God's forgiveness is not deduced from an idea of

God or His grace, but is experienced as His act in the event of salvation, so that preaching does not consist in illuminating instruction regarding the idea of God but in the proclamation of the act of God."[131] The forgiveness secured in the act of Jesus yielding up his spirit extends beyond that one moment in time. It represents an eschatological forgiveness that reaches into the future and maintains until the day when Jesus will sit at the table with us in the Father's kingdom (26:29). The power of our discipleship is not released in the words we read and repeat about our particular denominational pedigree or polity. The power is in the action that takes place on a cross—Ecce Homo! Behold the man!

Jesus' death is immediately followed by supernatural events. These events appear to be so fantastic that we may not choose to take them literally. If so, that is okay because there are lessons to be learned in each of the events. The veil that covered the Holy of Holies gave access once a year to one man. At Jesus' death, it was torn in two, indicating that not just one man but all men now had access to God all the time. That the tombs were opened was a guarantee that Jesus had conquered the power of death and the grave. In his resurrection, we have the assurance of our own resurrection. The earthquake represents a convulsion of the earth that only affected the splitting of the veil of the temple and the tombs of the dead saints. In keeping with Matthew's style, each of these supernatural events can be linked to Old Testament scriptures.

The centurion and those with him were fearfully impressed with the inexplicable demonstration of the natural phenomena attending the death of Jesus. This, along with the way Jesus endured his suffering and death, compelled the centurion to proclaim, "Truly this was the Son of God!" (26:54). Although the male disciples had fled (26:56), we learn that many women remained with Jesus throughout the crucifixion (27:55). They had followed him from Galilee and ministered to him, and now they would remain in Jerusalem until they could visit his tomb (28:1). Matthew does not include Jesus' mother among those women who remained with him.

Burial and Tomb Guarding (27:57-66)

Matthew begins the burial account by having it conform to Old Testament prophecy: "And they made his grave with the wicked and with a rich man in his death" (Isaiah 53:9). Joseph of Arimathea was a rich man and a disciple of Jesus (27:57). Under Roman law, relatives could claim the body of a dead criminal. If the body was not claimed, it was either buried in a common grave or left at the place of execution for the dogs and vultures to feed on it. Jesus' relatives were Galileans and had no tomb or burial place in Jerusalem. Joseph of Arimathea risked the anger of Pilate so that he might claim the body of Jesus and prepare it for burial. His courage was rewarded, and Pilate ordered that the body be given to him (27:58). Joseph treated the body with great respect, wrapping it in a clean linen cloth and placing it in a tomb that had not yet been used (27:59). The door is the open space marking the entrance to the tomb. Because of their great weight, rolling stones were used for security at the open entrance to a tomb or sepulcher. Joseph blocked the entrance to the tomb with one of these large stones to ensure that Jesus' body would not be violated or removed (27:60).

Having prepared the body and blocked the tomb, Joseph departed, but "Mary Magdalene and the other Mary were there, sitting opposite the sepulcher" (27:61). The men had left, perhaps out of fear for their lives or disappointed that the One in whom they had invested their trust was now dead. However, the women who had loved him in life were continuing that love at his death. Matthew says that they were sitting opposite the sepulcher. That they were sitting says a great deal about their psychological attitude as they waited near the tomb. Their sitting (καθήμεναι) expresses their grief and is a gesture of religious mourning.[132]

The next day, the chief priests and the Pharisees met with Pilate. They expressed a concern that the disciples might steal Jesus' body from the tomb and claim that he had been raised from the dead. This may explain why the Pharisees appear for the first time in Matthew's passion narrative. They, unlike the Sadducees, would be the only party giving any credence to the possibility of resurrection. They claim to remember that Jesus, the impostor, said, "After three days I will arise again" (27:63). To thwart any attempt to steal the body and compound the fraud regarding his resurrection, they ask Pilate to take special steps to guard the tomb. He approved their request and directed them to go and take care of the matter themselves. He authorized them to take a guard of soldiers and "make it as sure as you can," or "make it secure if you can" (27:65). So, the chief priests and Pharisees went to the tomb and "made it secure by sealing the stone and setting a guard" (27:66). We are not told what kind of seal was used to prevent an unlawful opening. Given that a large stone already blocked the entrance, it is quite likely that the sealing was, in fact, the act of setting a guard of soldiers to keep watch.

Chapter Two

The Gospel According to Mark

As previously stated, the issues of authorship and date and place of composition will not be given in-depth and extensive consideration for each Gospel. As pertaining to the Gospel According to Mark, I simply note that the author of Mark does not reveal his identity at any place in the Gospel. For purposes of this book, I accept the claim that "the great majority of scholars regard the composition of Mark by John Mark as certain."[1] As to the date of composition, Mark is probably the earliest Gospel, and most scholars date it in the years AD 64-70.[2]

While Mark is considerably shorter than Matthew, the groups referenced in both Gospels are almost equal in number. The following table reflects the number of occurrences of each group in each Gospel:

GROUP	MATTHEW	MARK
Pharisees	27	11
Sadducees	6	1
Scribes	20	21

Chief Priests	18	14
High Priest	6	5
Elders	11	7
Crowd	50	37
Pilate	9	9
Sanhedrin	4	3
Jews	4	4

Table 1-Occurrences in Each Gospel

Each of these groups has been dealt with previously. The descriptions, definitions and historical backgrounds remain the same and apply to the Gospel According to Mark as they applied to the Gospel According to Matthew. Avoiding redundancy, I will deal only with those Marcan passages which clearly show the responsibility and culpability of the Jews in the killing of Jesus. As pertains to the Marcan passion narrative, I will deal only with those verses which are not included in the Matthean passion narrative and those which show some deviation or suggest some difference from that which Matthew reports.

Early in his Gospel, Mark makes it clear that it is the Jews who bear the primary responsibility for the death of Jesus. A paralytic was brought to Jesus for healing (2:1-12). Jesus told the man that his sins were forgiven. Some scribes heard what Jesus said, and they accused him of blasphemy. These experts in the law were members of the Sanhedrin. The Sanhedrin served as their supreme court and functioned as the guardian of Jewish orthodoxy. An essential aspect of the orthodox faith was that only God could forgive sins. The charge of blasphemy was punishable by death by stoning (Leviticus 24:16). These experts in the law, members of the Sanhedrin, further expressed their opposition to Jesus by claiming that he was in league with Beelzebul and that he got his power from the ruler of the demons (3:22).

The real intent of the Jewish authorities is revealed in Mark 3:1-6. Jesus went into a synagogue and healed a man who had a withered hand. He performed this healing on the Sabbath, and this earned him the condemnation of the Jewish authorities. Instead of accepting the value of doing good on the Sabbath, they responded with an attitude of "hardness of heart" (3:5). Mark says, "The Pharisees went out, and immediately held counsel with the Herodians against him, how to destroy him" (3:6). C. S. Mann Says, "From this point in the narrative the threat of death is never far away."[3]

Throughout Mark's Gospel, there is an explicit antagonism between Jesus and the Jews. Jesus warns his disciples about this antagonism and tries to prepare them for the ultimate devastating consequences of that antagonism. On three occasions, he tells them the things that are going to happen to him in Jerusalem. In Mark 8:31, he confirms that the elders, chief priests and scribes will see to it that he will be killed. Citing these three groups of officials, Jesus is essentially saying that the Jewish Sanhedrin will facilitate his impending murder. The disciples responded to this news with disbelief and incomprehension. That Jesus would be killed by their own national authorities was not consistent with their idea of a messiah who would restore the kingdom of Israel. The second warning comes in Mark 9:31, where Jesus says, "The Son of Man will be delivered into the hands of men, and they will kill him." Vincent Taylor says that while 9:31 is briefer than 8:31, "it is practically the equivalent of 8.31."[4]

The third preparatory warning to his disciples comes in Mark 10:33-

34: "Behold, we are going up to Jerusalem; and the Son of Man will be delivered to the chief priests and the scribes, and they will condemn him to death, and deliver him to the Gentiles; and they will mock him and spit upon him, and scourge him, and kill him; and after three days he will rise." Mark includes more details in this third warning than in the first two. It identifies Jerusalem as the final destination of Jesus' journey. They were but a few common men going up to the great city of the Jews. Eduard Lohse says, "Jerusalem is the dwelling place of the enemies who exert themselves to bring Jesus to the cross. They confront him with pitiless hostility."[5] The city of Jerusalem embodied the "heart and soul" of the Jewish people. When one thinks of the Jews, it is natural to think simultaneously of Jerusalem. Hugh Anderson says the city of Jerusalem "is for Mark the seat and center of bitterest hostility to Jesus."[6] What chance did Jesus and his disciples stand against the concentration of power in Jerusalem? The members of the Sanhedrin were against them, and the Romans had military power over the land. The residents of the city and the pilgrims attending the Passover feast were packed into the city. They represented the crowds that would ultimately replace the shout of "Hosanna!" with the demand of "Crucify him!" The odds were stacked against Jesus and his disciples, and they knew it.

A close look at Mark 10:33-34 provides confirmation that the Jews were responsible for the death of Jesus. It provides the motive, the method and the mission of the Jews in their determination to kill Jesus. The motive is in the resentment and anger of the authorities who saw Jesus' ministry as a threat to the orthodoxy of the law. He healed on the Sabbath, taught with authority and assumed authority to pronounce the forgiveness of sins. Of the many acts of Jewish opposition, D. E. Nineham says, "Clearly they are, in fact, representative Jewish reactions to the Christian claim that sin could be forgiven by God in the name of Jesus."[7] The method they will use is to have the Sanhedrin condemn Jesus to death.

Having condemned him, they did not want to kill him by stoning (which they could have done). Their mission was to leverage their influence with Pilate so that Jesus would suffer death by crucifixion. They wanted Jesus' death to represent the public humiliation and total rejection by God, as was recorded in Deuteronomy 21:23: "For a hanged man is accursed by God."

The "Parable of the Vineyard and the Tenants" (Mark 12:1-12) confirms that it was the Jews who killed Jesus. The parable tells of a man who rented his vineyard to tenants. After a time, he sent one of his servants to get some of the fruit from his vineyard. The tenants beat the servant and sent him away without any fruit. The owner sent another servant who was treated the same as the first. He continued to send many servants, and they were mistreated. Some were even killed. Finally, he sent his son, thinking that the tenants would not dare to hurt him. To the contrary, "They took him and killed him, and cast him out of the vineyard" (12:7). The parable asks and answers this question: "What will the owner of the vineyard do? He will come and destroy the tenants, and give the vineyard to others. Have you not read this scripture: 'The very stone which the builders rejected has become the head of the corner; this was the Lord's doing, and it is marvelous in our eyes'" (12:9-11).

There is no doubt that the Jewish authorities who heard this parable knew exactly what it meant and that it was directed at them. The owner is God, the vineyard is Israel, the servants are the Old Testament prophets and the son is Jesus. Taylor says that the tenants are the "Jewish leaders or possibly the people as a whole."[8] Barclay sees the tenants as representing both the Jewish leaders and the Jewish people. He says, "If a man refuses his privileges and responsibilities, they pass on to someone else. The parable has in it the whole germ of what was to come—the rejection of the Jews and the passing of their privileges and responsibilities to the

Gentiles."⁹ The Jewish officials knew that Jesus "had told the parable against them, so they left him and went away" (12:12).

THE MARCAN PASSION NARRATIVE: 14:32—15:42

The Marcan passion narrative differs very little from that of Matthew. Therefore, I will limit my attention to those areas that require comments beyond what is reflected in my account of the Matthean passion narrative.

Barabbas

Matthew refers to Barabbas as "a notorious prisoner" (Matthew 27:19). As a "notorious" (ἐπίσημον) prisoner, the reason for his imprisonment would have been well-known by the public. Mark identifies the prisoner status of Barabbas as "a rebel who had committed murder in the insurrection" (Mark 15:6). Anderson says, "that the well-known Barabbas played some part in a minor insurrection of the time is more than likely historical fact."¹⁰ As a rebel involved in some act of insurrection, it is likely that Barabbas was considered by many to be a patriot. Anyone actively involved in throwing off the burden of Roman political tyranny would be popular with the crowds.

Pilate had to decide the fate of Jesus. He resorted to a familiar custom in an attempt to encourage the crowd to release Jesus: "Now at the feast he used to release for them any one prisoner whom they asked" (15:6). The crowd demanded the release of Barabbas, the well-known patriot. Suddenly, the solution to the problem became very clear for Pilate. With the introduction of Barabbas into the situation, Pilate now had two men before him who were guilty of the same charge. According to Ezra Gould, Barabbas became the scapegoat that Pilate needed. Gould says,

> These words tell the story of Barabbas. He was just what the Jews accused Jesus of being, a man who had raised a revolt against the Roman power. He was a political prisoner, and it was only such

that the Jews would be interested to have released to them. Their interests and those of Rome were opposed, and a man who revolted against Rome was regarded as a patriot. The fact that they asked for Barabbas shows that they were insincere in bringing charges against Jesus.[11]

The reaction of the crowd represented a fortuitous turn of events for Pilate, and he exploited the situation with all the cunning of a master politician. If he released one condemned man, it did not follow that he had to execute another in his place. He could grant amnesty to Barabbas and, at the same time, acquit Jesus. However, he knew that the Jews were more interested in killing Jesus than they were in releasing someone else. The only thing that would satisfy them was a one-for-one exchange. Barclay says, "To the chief priests this was a heaven-sent opportunity. Circumstances had played into their hands. They fanned the popular clamor for Barabbas and found it easy, for it was the release of Barabbas that that crowd had come to claim."[12] Pilate also saw this development as advantageous for his own position. By making a one-for-one exchange, he absolved himself of having to pass a formal sentence against Jesus. Without adjudicating the innocence or guilt of Jesus, Pilate handed him over to the Jews, thus making them solely responsible for the death of Jesus. This account of the release of Barabbas is crucial in establishing the responsibility of the Jews for the killing of Jesus. Nineham says, "The episode of Barabbas is interposed in the story of the trial before Pilate to make us understand that the governor did not condemn Jesus, but that he merely allowed him to be put to death in accordance with the sentence of the Sanhedrin."[13]

The Crowd

The crowd approached Pilate and asked that he grant their request to release a prisoner as he had done in the past (15:8). At this point, the crowd represented an anonymous mass of Jews distinct from the Jewish officials.¹⁴ The chief priests became involved with the crowd when Pilate, by way of his question, suggested that he understood them to mean that they were requesting the release of Jesus. They "stirred up" the crowd and incited them to call for the release of Barabbas. As Pilate continued to uphold the innocence of Jesus, the crowd became more stirred up and aggressive. Barclay says, "When they saw the possibility that Jesus might be released and not Barabbas, they went mad."¹⁵ The crowd increased its pressure on Pilate, and he released Barabbas and handed Jesus over to the Jews to be crucified.

Elias Canetti comments on the role of the crowd in the killing of Jesus. He says that the chief priests and the officials baited the crowd of Jews that had assembled. Those who bait the crowd incite them into a determination to kill a specific person. The crowd is worked into a frenzy so that everyone wants to strike a blow. The victim is always defenseless, and the crowd is not at risk in any way. All have agreed to the killing, and none need to fear any form of punishment or sanction for their participation. Everyone has a share in the victim's death, and the community as a whole does the killing. The real executioner is the crowd that is screaming for the death of the accused. Canetti says, "The account of Christ's condemnation contains the root of the matter. The cry of 'Crucify him!' comes from the crowd; it is the crowd which is truly active here."¹⁶ In the case of Jesus, it seems both improbable and impossible that the power of Rome would yield to the power of the crowd. Regarding this Canetti says:

> The sentence of death, which sounds abstract and unreal when pronounced in the name of justice, becomes real when it is carried out in the presence of the crowd. It is actually for the sake of the crowd that justice is done, and it is the crowd we have in mind when we speak of the importance of justice being public."¹⁷

As Mark reports, there can be no doubt that Pilate had the crowd in mind: "So Pilate, wishing to satisfy the crowd, released for them Barabbas" (15:15).

The Jews, along with the chief priests, elders and scribes, were dedicated to the murder of Jesus. Pilate ultimately accepted this, and he knew that the Jewish officials would continue to incite the crowd if they did not get what they wanted. With the city alive with the excitement of the Passover feast and overflowing with pilgrims, Pilate knew that the crowd could become completely unmanageable and cause problems that would reach beyond his jurisdiction. He gave the Jews what they wanted, and the pressure began to subside immediately. Canetti says, "Once a baiting crowd has attained its victim it disintegrates rapidly. Rulers in danger are well aware of this fact and throw a victim to the crowd in order to impede its growth."[18]

Mark makes it clear that the chief priests, elders, scribes, the whole council and ordinary Jewish citizens played crucial roles in securing the death of Jesus. The hatred of the Jews was not confined to any one group of officials or citizens. While the Jewish leaders planned, orchestrated and initiated the execution of Jesus, they could not have carried the plan to its fruition without the voice and energy of the Jewish people. Furthermore, Pilate absolved himself by not passing sentence on Jesus. He cleverly turned Jesus over to the Jews to execute the sentence of death by crucifixion, which they so desperately desired. Nineham concludes that "It is the Jews who must take the responsibility for the death of Jesus."[19] Amid the howling of the crowd (the Jews), the silent Son of God is handed over to be crucified while a condemned criminal goes free. As stated in other places in this book, perhaps we should not be too quick to absolve the Jews of the death of Jesus.

Chapter Three

The Gospel According to Luke

Saint Paul refers to Luke as "the beloved physician" (Colossians 4:14). G. B. Caird says, "The unfounded belief of ancient writers is that the author was Luke, the doctor whom Paul mentions as his companion and colleague.[1]" While some have argued for a date prior to the fall of Jerusalem in AD 70, Kümmel says, "We may regard the period between AD 70 and 90 as probable for the composition of Luke."[2] As for the place of composition, the only thing that seems certain is that it was not written in Palestine. The Gospel According to Luke has frequently been recognized as the "universal gospel." Without any concern for ethnicity, gender, or status, Jesus is portrayed as beckoning everyone to enter the Kingdom of God. Hated Samaritans and gentiles are included. The poor, outcasts and sinners, women, criminals, prodigals, and tax collectors all have a place within the Kingdom of God. Luke's Gospel places no limits on the expanse of God's love.

Luke is the most comprehensive of the synoptic Gospels, and it is the longest book in the New Testament. Luke would have his readers know that the life of Jesus was a "one-of-a-kind event." Salvation was not only proclaimed by Jesus; it was completely accomplished in his person and work. God entered into the everyday life of humankind in a unique way.

The life of Jesus was not just one more interesting human drama among many. His life and death was the fulfillment of all the promises made to the Jewish patriarchs. In Luke, we see the Jews' resistance to the inclusion of Gentiles as recipients of God's grace through Jesus Christ. The following table shows that Luke does not refer to the Jews as a group as compared to four references, each of Matthew and Mark.

GROUP	MATTHEW	MARK	LUKE
Pharisees	27	11	27
Sadducees	6	1	1
Scribes	20	21	14
Chief Priests	18	14	13
High Priest	6	5	2
Elders	11	7	5
Crowd	50	37	36
Pilate	9	9	12
Sanhedrin	4	3	1
Jews	4	4	0

Table 2-Occurrences in Each Gospel

As stated previously, I will deal only with those Lucan passages which pertain to the responsibility and culpability of the Jews in the killing of Jesus. My main concern is with what Kümmel calls "The Fifth Principle Part (19:28-24:53) Jesus in Jerusalem."[3] Luke essentially follows the sequence of Mark but does show some divergence in his account of the Passion narrative.

Early in his Gospel, Luke identifies the Jewish animosity and rejection of Jesus that will ultimately result in their demand for his death. Luke says that Jesus' first act following his temptation in the wilderness was to teach in the synagogues of the Jews. In accordance with the message of the prophet Isaiah (Isaiah 61:1-2; 58:6), Jesus announces that he has come to preach good news to the poor, to set the captive free and to proclaim the year of the Lord's favor. For Luke, the arrival of Jesus marks the arrival of the Kingdom of God. Jesus' fellow Jews in the synagogue at Nazareth initially accepted him as the one bringing salvation to Israel (4:22). He is their champion, and they accept his authority as long as he represents the Jewish people to the exclusion of everyone else. His popularity is very short-lived among the Jews in the synagogues. When Jesus recounted the miracles performed by Elijah and Elisha, the Jews saw that Jesus' preaching and promise of salvation were being extended beyond Israel and to the Gentiles as well as the Jews.

The Jews of the Old Testament became unworthy of God's favor when they rejected and persecuted the prophets. Therefore, the prophets went among the Gentiles and proclaimed the salvation of God. The Jews deduced that they, too, would be counted as unworthy if they did not accept Jesus' message that the Kingdom of God was not limited to Jews only. John Lightfoot says, "That by these instances he plainly intimated the call of the Gentiles, than which nothing could be more grating in the ear of the Jews. Elijah was sent to a heathen woman, and a heathen man was sent to Elisha: and both of them were turned from heathenism to true religion."[4] Jesus was rejected not because he claimed authority to preach the good news but because he was offering salvation to the wrong people. Jewish arrogance and the presumed identity as the "chosen people" afforded them a religious entitlement which they were not about to extend to or share with non-Jews. Their response to his universal offering of salvation was to drive him out of their presence with the intent to kill him if they could. Luke says, "When they heard this, all in the synagogue were filled with wrath, and they rose up and put him out of the city, and led him to the brow of the hill on which their city was built, that they might throw him down headlong" (4:28-29). Regardless of the many miracles that Jesus will perform and the many crowds that will follow him for the benefits they will receive from his ministry, this rejection by the people of his own hometown signals that the Jewish people will ultimately side with their leaders in demanding the death of Jesus. Their immediate offense at Jesus' teachings is an early indication that, in the end, the Jews will kill Jesus.

Luke's *Parable of the Pounds* (19:11-27) speaks of the persistent Jewish rejection of Jesus. A nobleman went on a trip to secure a kingdom (19:12). His fellow citizens hated him and did not want to be subservient to him; however, he did return to be a king over them (19:14-15). Upon his return, he demanded that the servants give an account of the money with which they had been entrusted. Two of them gave a favorable accounting and were rewarded for being faithful servants. The third had failed to put the money to good use and could show no gain on that with which he had been entrusted. In the eyes of the king, he had behaved with inexcusable irresponsibility. His punishment was to have the money entrusted to him taken away from him. The most severe punishment, however, was for those who hated him and refused to serve him as their king (19:14). The king referred to them as "these enemies of mine who did not want me to reign over them" (19:27). He said, "Bring them here and slay them before me" (19:27). Fitzmyer says that this parable "fits in with the Lucan theme of the rejection of Jesus."[5]

The "citizens" (πολῖται) who hated and rejected the king represent the Jews, the citizens of Israel.[6] Those who used the money irresponsibly, while being guilty of negligence, are not seen in as harsh a light as those who said, "We do not want this man to reign over us" (19:14). Plummer says, "The punishment of rebellious subjects and active opponents is far more severe than that of neglectful servants."[7] Throughout the Gospel According to Luke, the "active opponents" are the Sanhedrin authorities and the people of Israel. Describing the outcome of their rejection, Jesus says, "For great distress shall be upon the earth and wrath upon this people" (21:23). Luke is certain that the people of Jerusalem were the principle subjects in the condemnation and death of Jesus.[8] The citizens opposed their king and continued to do so throughout his earthly reign, and in the end, the citizens (the Jews) killed Jesus.

THE LUCAN PASSION NARRATIVE: 22:39—23:25

Prior to departing for the Mount of Olives, Jesus announced some new conditions for the future ministry of the disciples. Up to this point, they have been sent out with "no purse or bag or sandals" (22:35). Times have changed, and Jesus tells them, "But now, let him who has a purse take it, and likewise a bag. And let him who has no sword sell his mantle and buy one. For I tell you that this scripture must be fulfilled in me. 'And he was reckoned with the transgressors'; for what is written about me has its fulfillment" (22:36-37). Jesus recognizes that the attitude of the Jewish people will become exceedingly antagonistic toward him. Consequently, increasing hostility toward the apostles will be grounded in the people's hostility toward Jesus himself. In the past, they could count on some of the people to provide food and shelter. Jesus is now telling them that without his physical presence, their very lives will be at stake. Caird says, "Jesus is about to be executed as a criminal, and they as the criminal's accomplices, will find every man's hand against them."[9]

Jesus explains the change of circumstances as a necessity for fulfilling Isaiah 53, which sets forth the role of the Suffering Servant in the life of the nation of Israel. He specifically refers to being "numbered with the transgressors" (53:12). Being "numbered with the transgressors" has a far greater meaning than the standard explanation that Jesus was crucified between two criminals. Klaus Baltzer says, "The suffering Servant became in typology a foreshadowing of Jesus Christ. In the language of this text the Christian community could communicate its own experience."[10] Given this understanding, the transgressors represent Israel as a whole, and the cause of the Servant's suffering is the "unbelief of his people."[11] The nation's opinion of Jesus was that "he was despised and we esteemed him not" (53:3). Claus Westermann says, "He had lost all positive significance for the community,"[12] and Baltzer says, "He is of no account—not worth anything."[13]

The Servant of Isaiah 53 looks back to the leadership of Moses and forward to the leadership of Jesus. The suffering of Moses was caused by his own people, the Israelites. With Jesus in the role of the Servant of his people, we can say that his suffering and death was caused by his fellow Jews. That he "made intercession for the transgressors" does not mean that he merely made prayers of intercession for them. Westermann says, "With his life, his suffering and his death, he took their place and underwent their punishment instead."[14] This clearly shows that Jesus' being "numbered with the transgressors" goes beyond being crucified between two criminals. He could not take their place, and he could not prevent them from experiencing the punishment that had already placed them on their crosses. Who, then, were the transgressors? The people of Israel admitted their guilt. Isaiah says, "All we like sheep have gone astray; we have turned everyone to his own way; and the Lord has laid on him the iniquity of us all" (53:6). This is an admission of guilt in remembrance of the servant. The transgressors are those who had rejected the word and will of God. By extension, it can hardly be denied that the transgressors represented the leaders and the people of Israel. By fulfilling the scripture of Isaiah 53, Jesus tells us that the killer(s) of the servant will be all the people of Israel.

Jesus introduces his comment about the "sword" in his announcement of the new conditions under which the disciples will preach and teach. Fitzmyer says, "The introduction of the 'sword' signals the difference in the periods; the Period of the Church will be marked with persecution."[15] The mention of buying a sword is rather perplexing for us and probably for the disciples as well. They had to abruptly come to terms with the heretofore non-violent message of Jesus and ownership of a weapon of violence. The disciples said, "Look, Lord, here are two swords," and Jesus said, "It is enough" (22:38). This verse and the charge of Jesus to cease with the use of the sword (22:51), has been the source of many different interpretations among scholars. Jesus' short response without amplification contains its own explanation of his intent. Could anyone really believe that two swords would be enough to resist the Temple police or the Roman army? Lightfoot offers the simplest and most viable explanation of Jesus' comment about the sword. The disciples had just engaged in an argument about which of them was the greatest among the disciples. Jesus wanted to impress upon them the foolishness of arguing among themselves and the need for solidarity in facing the future. Lightfoot says,

> He warns them of a danger that is very near; and in a common way of speech lets them know that they had more need of providing swords against the common enemy, than be any way quarreling amongst themselves. Not so much exhorting them to repel force with force, as to give them such an apprehension of the common rage of their enemies against them, that might suppress all private animosities amongst themselves.[16]

So, the two swords are "enough," but the question is, "Enough for what?" The implied understanding is that they are as sufficient as any greater number would be. The disciples must remember that they are called to humble service and not to any amount of military or violent activity.

While Jesus was speaking with his disciples on the Mount of Olives, he was confronted with a crowd which was led by Judas. When his disciples saw what was happening, they asked Jesus if they should use their swords to defend him. Without waiting for a reply, Luke says that "one of them struck the slave of the high priest and cut off his right ear" (22:50). Jesus quickly put an end to the confrontation by saying, "No more of this!" (22:51). His refusal to be defended by the sword confirms that his comment about buying a sword was heuristic in nature and carried no intent or encouragement for the disciples to engage in violence.

The meaning of Jesus' response, (ἐᾶτε ἕως τούτου/no more of this), is not easy to determine and has been interpreted differently by many scholars.[17] David Matson advises that these words do not reflect a rebuke of the disciples; rather, "Jesus is reminding them of the divine plan to which he must not only submit, but which he must actively carry out."[18] Instead of rebuking the disciples, Jesus commands them, (ἐᾶτε is plural, imperative), that they must not interfere with the plan and the will of God. In this light, the command of Jesus is best understood as "allow them to continue with the arrest."[19] Having put an end to the violence, Jesus healed the ear of the servant of the high priest and showed that he never intended that the swords should be used. Furthermore, this act of healing shows that even in the presence of the Jews who reject him, he is not powerless, and he is acting under the authority of God.

The action from this time forward points to the cross. Jesus knew that the mission of the Jews who had come to arrest him had but one objective, and that was to orchestrate his death. He tells them how ridiculous they are to confront him with swords and clubs since they have always had many opportunities to arrest him. Now, they have come to seize him under cover of darkness. Their actions are appropriate since the physical darkness of night corresponds with the symbolic darkness of the evil power under which they are operating. The hour of success for the Jews corresponds with the hour of the power of darkness. In this fateful hour, the Jews seized Jesus and took him to the house of the high priest. For the remainder of the night, they insulted him, mocked him and physically abused him. During this time, they tried to trick him into saying something that could be construed as blasphemy or some other crime that could be held against him. When day came, the elders of the people, the chief priests, and scribes led him away and convened a meeting of the Sanhedrin.

Luke's account of Jesus before the Sanhedrin omits the actions of the authorities that are found in the other Gospels. For example, there is no search for witnesses, no claim of breaking the Sabbath, no appearance of false witnesses, no charge that Jesus is desecrating the temple, and no specific claim of blasphemy. They do not confuse their intentions to influence Pilate by charging Jesus with any transgressions of Jewish Law. Luke focuses only on two questions asked by the Sanhedrin: 1) "Are you the Messiah?" and 2) "Are you the Son of God?" The Jews foresaw that Pilate would have no interest in violations of Jewish religious laws. Knowing this, Luke represents the leaders of the Sanhedrin as presenting the Christological issue to Pilate. In doing this, they could raise the issue of conflating the title of "messiah" with the title of "king." They cleverly suggest that their charges are political in nature. They knew that the accusation that Jesus claimed to be a king would at least get the attention of Pilate. They set the stage for confirming this accusation by claiming that Jesus is "perverting the nation," and he is "forbidding us to pay taxes to Caesar" (23:2). The "perversion" to which they refer has nothing to do with religious beliefs, laws or customs. The verb is "διαστρέφω," and it has the various meanings of "to twist, turn, bend, steer, dislocate and confuse." In the charge against Jesus, the Sanhedrin is telling Pilate that Jesus is "wooing the people away from the Roman government."[20] The charge that Jesus is "forbidding, hindering, or preventing" the Jews from paying taxes to Caesar is indisputably false. When the Jews had previously raised the issue of paying taxes to Caesar, Jesus told them, "Then render to Caesar the things that are Caesar's" (20:25).

The Jews hoped to get Pilate's attention by introducing these two obviously false charges of a political nature. They tell Pilate that Jesus is "saying that he himself is Christ (messiah) a king" (23:2). Through their lies and cleverly constructed threat of political blackmail, they hoped to secure the favor of Pilate and ensure the death of Jesus. After questioning Jesus, Pilate delivered his verdict to the chief priests and the crowds: "I find no crime in this man" (23:4). The "crowds" who are condemning Jesus represent the Jews of Israel. Luke freely exchanges "people" (λαός) with "crowds" (ὄχλος) to identify hostile Jews.[21] Again, according to Luke, the Sanhedrin and the nation as a whole are responsible for killing Jesus.

The first two accusations against Jesus were blatant lies. Furthermore, Jesus did not tell the Sanhedrin that he was the messiah. He said, "But from now on the Son of Man shall be seated at the right hand of God" (22:69). To their questioning, "Are you the Son of God, then?" he answered, "You say that I am" (22:70). They immediately equated "Son of Man" with "Son of God" and made it a synonym for "messiah/king." Their goal was to get Jesus to admit that he was the Messiah, thereby condemning himself "out of his own lips" (23:71). By ignoring the difference between the two terms and interpreting them as synonyms, the

Sanhedrin hoped to successfully convince Pilate that Jesus was truly claiming to be a king and a rival to Caesar. In fact, the terms are not synonymous and are not to be exchanged one for the other.[22]

When Pilate learned that Jesus was a Galilean, he sent him to Herod. A trial before Herod is not mentioned in any of the other Gospels. Herod was excited when Jesus appeared before him. He had heard that Jesus was a miracle worker and thought that Jesus might entertain him by conjuring up a miraculous sign. He questioned Jesus at length, but Jesus remained silent before him. Jesus refused to serve as a spectacle, a figure of amusement for Herod. The Son of Man was not willing to accommodate a superficial curiosity that lacked any degree of seriousness regarding the Kingdom of God. Caird says, "His curiosity thwarted by Jesus' silence, Herod determined to treat the whole episode as a joke."[23] Herod and his soldiers dressed Jesus in royal clothing and mocked him. When Herod had satisfied his curiosity and grown tired of making sport of Jesus, he sent him back to Pilate.

Pilate notified the chief priests, the rulers and the people (the Jews) that neither he nor Herod had found Jesus guilty of any crime that deserved the death penalty. They "all"— the authorities and the people— demanded that Jesus be crucified (23:21). They would not accept the offer of releasing Jesus and demanded that Barabbas be released instead. Luke says, "but Jesus he delivered up to their will" (23:25). It was not the will of Pilate nor the will of Herod that Jesus should be crucified. It was singularly the will of the Jews that caused the death of Jesus. Having secured their way and will with Pilate, Luke says, "they led him away" (23:26). Gilmour says, "Luke's narrative almost suggests that it was Jews who took Jesus away to be crucified."[24] Fitzmyer is certain that it was the Jews who took Jesus away to the place of crucifixion. He says, "The 'they' has to refer to those who 'asked for' the release of Barabbas and to whom

Pilate handed over Jesus according to 'their will' (vs. 25). This must include 'the chief priests, the leaders, and the people' of v. 13 (cf. vv. 4, 18, 23)."²⁵

Luke includes the account of the crucifixion of the two criminals and tells us that one of them acknowledged his own guilt and recognized the innocence of Jesus. He asked Jesus to remember him when he "comes into his kingdom," and Jesus granted him inclusion in the kingly realm of Paradise (23:39-43). Jesus' death was preceded by darkness covering the whole land, and the curtain of the temple was split down the middle. With a loud voice, Jesus committed his spirit to his Father, and Luke says that he then "breathed his last" (23:46). The centurion, observing the death of Jesus, proclaimed that the dead man was "really a righteous, innocent man" (23:47). There is much irony in the fact that the heathen gentiles recognized the innocence of Jesus while the Sanhedrin and the people rejected him and demanded his death. Pilate made three declarations of his innocence; Herod, a half-Jew at best, found no reason to convict him; a dying criminal saw and said that Jesus was innocent; and a hardened soldier publicly and unequivocally declared that the crucified Jesus was innocent. The Jews, on the other hand, rejected Jesus to the very end. The people watched the crucifixion, and the rulers "scoffed at him" (23:35). Fitzmyer says that the leaders sneered at Jesus, and the people (ὁ λαὸς) joined them in the scoffing/sneering.²⁶

Throughout his Gospel, Luke supports the position that the whole people (ὁ λαὸς) side with the Jewish leaders in their rejection and hostility toward Jesus. When presented with the ultimate decision of life or death, they support a known murderer and insurrectionist and condemn an innocent man. A. R. C. Leaney says, "Luke is well aware that the whole people were responsible for the killing of Jesus and makes this point with emphasis at Acts 3:13 ff."²⁷ In the Acts passage, Luke records that Peter told the people, "But you denied the Holy and Righteous One and asked for a murderer to be granted to you, and killed the Author of life, whom God raised from the dead" (Acts 3:14-15).

Jesus was bound by blood, history, and kinship to his own people, the Jews. His love and concern for their spiritual health and security was evidenced in every fiber of his person and work. Rejected by his own people, he was the target and victim of political corruption, religious bigotry, and a catalog of outdated traditions that no longer honored the forgiveness, mercy, and grace of God. Caird says that the rejection of Jesus by Israel was the "national sin" of the Jews.[28] Perhaps Luke would not agree that we should absolve the Jews of the crime of killing Jesus.

Chapter Four

The Gospel According to John

Scholars have raised many perplexing questions about the Gospel According to Saint John. The questions of authorship and the relationship of John to the synoptic Gospels have been the subject of a myriad of studies across the years. Dwight Moody Smith, my teacher, and an acknowledged Johannine scholar, refers to the complexities encountered when studying John as often having a "sense of at once swimming against the stream and being borne away by the flood."[1] While recognizing the many scholarly opinions surrounding John's Gospel, I believe that F. F. Bruce's assessment suffices for the purposes of this book. He says, "From Irenaeus onwards there is virtual unanimity in the church on the canonicity and authorship of the Fourth Gospel."[2] The testimony of the early church favors "John, the disciple of the Lord" as the author and supports Ephesus in the AD 90s as the place and date of writing. While acknowledging the arguments opposing this position, Elwell and Yarbrough say, "At any rate, there seems to be no necessary reason to reject the uniform testimony of the early church in favor of speculative theories on which there is no agreement, even among the critics themselves."[3]

John's Gospel is different from the synoptic Gospels in several obvious ways. John tells us nothing about the birth and baptism of Jesus. He has no account of the temptations in the wilderness nor of the Ascension of Jesus in the presence of the disciples. John does not show us a picture of Jesus agonizing in Gethsemane. The parable stories that are so numerous in the Synoptics are missing from John's Gospel.

John's Gospel originates at a time when the early church was becoming institutionalized. Theology and doctrine were emerging as indicators of orthodoxy in support of the faith and teachings of the church. At a time when the faith was vulnerable to misinterpretation and the infection of heresies, John's Gospel provided a powerful response to the destabilizing forces of active heresies. He clearly and forcefully opposed a Gnosticism that depicted Christ as a heavenly figure who merely came through earth on a journey coming from the Father and ultimately returning to him. John emphatically announces that the eternal Word became flesh (1:14) and that as a man of flesh and blood, he experienced thirst and hunger and sat down to eat and drink with his disciples.

Of primary concern for this book is John's exposure of the Jews who opposed faith in Jesus Christ throughout his ministry. The Jews create and populate a daily environment of hostility and unbelief. The Jewish people and their leaders have but one objective regarding Jesus of Nazareth. From the beginning, they reject him with the ultimate goal of killing him: "He came to his own home, and his own people received him not" (1:11). It is incomprehensible that he was treated as a stranger—a despised immigrant in his own country and village. It was as if they had slammed the door in the face of an unwelcome visitor. The Jewish leaders resented him and opposed him at every opportunity. They disregarded his ministry to the people and accused him of breaking the law when he healed the sick and associated with those they regarded as sinners.

The following table shows that John refers to the Jews sixty-seven times as compared to Matthew and Mark with four times each, and Luke with no references to the Jews. On the other hand, John refers to the crowd nineteen times, while Matthew makes fifty references, Mark makes thirty-seven, and Luke makes thirty-six. John avoids the anonymous designation of "crowds" in most cases and specifically refers to them as the "Jews."

GROUP	MATTHEW	MARK	LUKE	JOHN
Pharisees	27	11	27	20
Sadducees	6	1	1	0
Scribes	20	21	14	1
Chief Priests	18	14	13	10
High Priest	6	5	2	12
Elders	11	7	5	1
Crowd	50	37	36	19
Pilate	9	9	12	18
Sanhedrin	4	3	1	1
Jews	4	4	0	67

Table 3-Occurrences in Each Gospel

As with the other Gospels, I will deal only with those Johannine passages which are germane to the responsibility and culpability of the Jews in the killing of Jesus.

The Jews Confront Jesus

Witness to Jesus (5:38-43)

Jesus accused the Jews of not believing that God had sent him to them. They prided themselves in searching the scriptures, but for all their knowledge of the scriptures, they did not understand that Jesus was the true Word of God as contained in the scriptures. Their problem is not one of intellectual or scholarly ignorance. They are capable of reading and committing to memory the words of the scriptures. Jesus tells them that their problem is one of pride and personal power. He comes in the name of the Father, and they reject him. However, they readily receive anyone who comes in his own name and who displays and brags about his own credentials. They rely upon their own dignity and power and are full of self-love but do not have the love of God amongst them. While they claim that they want abundance of life, by denying Jesus, they deny themselves the life that God intended them to have.

Attitudes Toward Jesus (6:29-7:5)

The Jews thought of the work of God as that of doing good works and living a good life. Jesus told them that doing the work of God was much more than that. Doing the work of God involved believing in the One whom God had sent among them. This was, of course, Jesus himself. They questioned Jesus as to what sign he could perform that would authenticate him as the One sent by God. Jesus does not answer their request for a sign. He compares himself to the manna which God provided in the wilderness and says that, in a like manner, he has come down from heaven to do the will of God. The Jews quickly point out that he is the son of Joseph, the carpenter, and that Mary is his mother. They know the family very well, and there is no evidence that Jesus is anyone other than a fellow citizen who grew up among them. They are offended at the claim of this earth-bound human that he "came down from heaven" (6:42). They limit their knowledge to that of human understanding and refuse to acknowledge the revelatory action of God in the person and work of Jesus. Bultmann says, "Thus the Jews with their objection do not see that the divine cannot be contrasted with the human in the confident way in which they say, 'How can an ordinary man claim to be the Revealer!'"[4]

Jesus again incurs the resistance and opposition of the Jews when he says, "He who eats my flesh and drinks my blood has eternal life" (6:54). Many of his disciples found this "hard to accept" (6:60). John says that the disciples "murmured" at the saying. Associating the "murmuring" with the Jews, Bultmann says: "Γογγύζειν" (murmuring) 6:41, 43, 61; 7:32 (γογγυσμός 7:12) means at first an inarticulate murmuring, then the suppressed grumbling and mumbling which is a sign of anger or dissatisfaction. In the Septuagint, it often refers to ungrateful obstinacy and doubt in God's faithfulness."[5] While the original twelve may have been in the audience to which Jesus spoke these offensive words, it is unlikely that they murmured, grumbled, or complained about what he said. The "murmurers" were from the outer circle of disciples whose allegiance and love had not yet been put to the test. Bultmann identifies these "many disciples" as "Jews who faltered and grumbled."[6] Peter's affirmation, "Lord, to whom shall we go? You have the words of eternal life" (6: 68) infers that the twelve remained when all others turned back.

The attitude of Jesus' brothers was one of disbelief. It is likely that they recognized that he had done some mighty works and that his arguments and teachings were based on sound wisdom. While they demonstrated solidarity with him because of familial dedication, they were disappointed that he did not comply with their preconceived notions of how he should display public power. J. H. Bernard says, "The brethren of Jesus did not believe in him as Messiah."[7] His brothers did not believe in him as the Messiah until after the resurrection (Acts 1:14).

The Murderous Will of the Jews (7:19-8:59)

Jesus entered into a debate with the Jews. As to their pride in the Law of Moses, he said, "Yet none of you keeps the law" (7:19). In truth, the source of their pride is also the instrument of their own condemnation. Jesus skillfully turned their appeal to the authority of Moses against them. He pointed out that they carelessly and with impunity break the law and, at the same time, want to kill him for healing someone on the Sabbath. The Jews who are listening to this debate break into the exchange and exclaim that Jesus "has a demon." The accusation is that he is demented and suffering from madness. They want to know where he came up with the idea that they are trying to kill him. Jesus doesn't bother to answer their question because he knows that from the very beginning, the Jews have sought his death.

The Jews continue to misunderstand Jesus. He said to them, "I go away and you will seek me and die in your sin; where I am going you cannot come" (8:21). Jesus warns them that after he is gone, they will recognize the error of their disbelief and will look for him, but they won't find him because they cannot follow him. Consequently, they will "die in their sin." As usual, the Jews fail to comprehend what Jesus is telling them, and they assume that he is going to commit suicide. Thinking only in terms of life in this world, they say, "If we cannot follow you, it must be because you will be no longer alive."[8]

The Jews try to legitimize their opposition to Jesus by claiming Abraham as their father. Jesus agrees that they stand in a direct relationship with Abraham as his children. Given that fact, he finds it puzzling that they should want to kill him. Apparently, they don't understand their own history as children of Abraham. Jesus is acting on the Word he has received from his Father. The Jews have taken the faith and history of Abraham and made it into something that is frozen in the past. The history of Abraham was a dynamic history that directed them to a God-given future. Bultmann notes that the Jews who opposed Jesus had distorted their Abrahamic history and relegated it to "mere past so that it had become a power that robs them of the future, i.e., that robs them of life."[9] If they are truly Abraham's descendants, how is it possible that they want to kill the very God of Father Abraham? Jesus tells them that the very fact that they want to kill a man who has told them the truth is evidence that their real father is the devil. While they may claim to be Abraham's children in the natural sense, they have no moral or spiritual relationship with Abraham. Bultmann says, "The murderous will of the Jews is proof that they are not Abraham's children."[10] Who, then, is their Father? Jesus says,

> You are of your father the devil, and your will is to do your father's desire. He was a murderer from the beginning, and has nothing to do with the truth, because there is no truth in him. When he lies, he speaks according to his own nature, for he is a liar and the father of lies (8:44).

The Jews have consistently shown that they are unwilling to accept the truth that Jesus has brought from his Father. Completely under the control of a liar, they cannot begin to comprehend the truth of Jesus. Unyielding in their hatred, "They took up stones to throw at him" (8:59). This evil, murderous will of the Jews will obtain until they finally succeed in killing Jesus.

The Jews Are Spiritually Blind (9:13-40)

A man born blind from birth prompted the disciples to ask Jesus about the origin of the man's blindness. If the man was born blind, how could he have sinned before he was born? Perhaps there was some ancient idea of pre-natal sin, but Jesus gave no credence to this. It would have been possible for his affliction to be the result of his parents' sin, but Jesus would not endorse this assumption. Jesus told them that his blindness had nothing to do with sin. He offered no explanation other than that the man's blindness presented an opportunity for displaying God's grace, mercy, and glory. However, when the Pharisees and Jews heard of the blind man receiving his sight, they saw it as an opportunity to attack Jesus for healing on the Sabbath.

The Jews were determined to discredit Jesus and did not believe that the man was blind to begin with. This is indicative of their absolute refusal to believe anything involving the person and work of Jesus. The power and hatred of the Jews for Jesus is seen in the response of the blind man's parents. They refused to answer the Jews and deferred to their son's account of the healing because they did not want to stir up the anger of the Jews. They affirmed that the son was of age and could speak for himself. John says, "They feared the Jews, for the Jews had already agreed that if anyone should confess him to be Christ, he was to be put out of the synagogue" (9:22). Raymond Brown says that they feared "the solemn curse of excommunication imposed by Jewish authorities, permanently excluding one from Israel."[11]

Unwilling to accept the man's account of his healing, the authorities called him before them a second time. With no other intent than to discredit Jesus, they implored the man to call Jesus a sinner and to give all glory to God. Given all the facts of the encounter with Jesus, the man said, "If this man were not from God, he could do nothing" (9:33). The Jews summarily called the man a sinner, and, as such, he was not capable of explaining what he experienced. Consequently, "they cast him out" (9:34). Bruce says, "The context suggests that they not only pushed him out of the place where the interrogation was held but expelled him from synagogue membership as his parents had feared might be done to them."¹²

In the aftermath of the action of the Jews, Jesus went to the man he had healed and explained to him why the Jews had abused him and excommunicated him. The man became an example of those who see and those who fail to see. He said, "Lord, I believe, and he worshipped him" (9:38). The man born blind confessed his faith and received his sight. With his whole being, he bowed in reverence before the light that opened his blind eyes. It is supremely ironic that the Jews, who were born with perfect vision, became spiritually blind and remained in their sin because of their rejection of Jesus, who was "the light of the world."

He Has A Demon (10:20-39

After describing the relationship between the true shepherd and his sheep, the Jews once again raise a protest against the message of Jesus. The authorities recognize that he is portraying them as thieves, robbers, hirelings, killers, wolves, and false shepherds. However, portraying himself as the "good shepherd," Jesus says that he will lay down his life for the sheep, and because of this, the Father has given him the power to reclaim his life. The unbelieving Jews have found everything that Jesus has said to be incomprehensible. The works he has performed and their traditional preconceptions are clearly in conflict. It infuriates them to think that Jesus would claim that he could lay down his own life and retain the power to "take it up again" (10:18). Brown says,

> This is a failure to understand that in NT thought the resurrection is not a circumstance that follows the death of Jesus but the essential completion of the death of Jesus. In Johannine thought, the passion, death, resurrection and ascension constitute the one, indissoluble salvific action of return to the Father. If Jesus is to give life through the Spirit, he must rise again (vii:39; and so

resurrection is truly the purpose of his death.[13]

Unable to deny the good works and unwilling to believe in the legitimacy of Jesus' relationship with the Father, the Jews resolve their conflict by claiming that "He has a demon and he is mad; why listen to him?" (10:20). With the renewal of the old charge of "demon possession" (7:20; 8:48), the Jews again confirm their rejection of Jesus and become further motivated to kill him.

The conflict intensifies, and the anger of the Jews burns hotter when Jesus says, "I and the Father are one" (10:30). C. K. Barrett says, "This claim provokes another murderous attack, the Jews asserting (rightly) that Jesus is claiming to be divine."[14] The Jews "took up stones to stone him" (10:31) and "tried to arrest him" (10:39). The Jews are furious because Jesus has clearly refuted all their charges and complaints. The merciful deeds he has performed speak for themselves. When they have claimed the authority of their own law, Jesus has turned the tables on them and proved that they did not keep their own law or that they did not understand it. The truth and power of Jesus' message have served to challenge the security they have in themselves and in their traditional claim as the "sons of Abraham." They will find no rest or satisfaction until they have killed Jesus.

The Plot to Kill Jesus (11:46-57)

Some of the Jews reported the raising of Lazarus from the dead to the chief priests and the Pharisees. They convened a Sanhedrin and initiated the formal plot to kill Jesus. Their initial fear was that Jesus would become so popular that a rebellion would break out over the land, and the Romans would destroy the temple and the nation. Caiaphas and most of the chief priests belonged to the party of the Sadducees. They comprised the wealthy party among the members of the Sanhedrin, and they readily collaborated with the Roman occupiers. They would do anything required in order to maintain their positions of wealth, comfort, and authority. News of the raising of Lazarus had created great concern bordering on panic for them. In the assembled Sanhedrin, they did not know what they could do to preserve their status and their wealth. Caiaphas, the Sadducean high priest, was a clever politician. The solution was self-evident, and he criticized his fellow chief priests for not immediately recognizing the answer to their frantic questions. In clear and simple terms, he said, "You do not understand that it is expedient for you that one man should die for the people, and that the whole nation should not perish" (11:50). His solution required no further explanation. It was and is the way of the world when expedience is the easiest and less costly course of action. In the case of Jesus, the lesser evil was that the life of one innocent man was not worth the destruction of the beautiful temple and the punishment of an entire nation. In their presumption of superiority and their contemptuous arrogance regarding their own importance, Barclay says, "It never even occurred to them to ask whether Jesus was right or wrong. Their only question was: 'What effect will this have on our ease and comfort and authority?'"[15]

Although Caiaphas was not aware of it, his clever counsel to secure the safety of the nation also echoed an unconscious prophecy to "gather into one the children of God who are scattered abroad" (11:52). The irony is that the killing of Jesus resulted in his resurrection and the gift of eternal life for all who believed in him. Conversely, the attempt to preserve the status of political and religious power resulted in the destruction of the temple, the nation and the loss of Jewish freedom. Bultmann says, "It is precisely the cleverness and deliberation that find acceptance in this world and always knows a way out that here lead to destruction."[16]

The prevailing fact is that the Sanhedrin gathered for one purpose, and that was to devise a strategy to kill Jesus. John says, "So from that day on they took counsel how to put him to death" (11:53). They no longer masked or hid their murderous intentions but publicly "gave orders that if anyone knew where he was, he should let them know, so that they might arrest him" (11:57). This transparent plot of the Jews to kill Jesus makes it clear that they planned, initiated, and completed the murder of Jesus. The powers of imagination, and far less the power of rational thought, cannot be stretched far enough to produce a credible reason to absolve the Jews of the killing of Jesus. It has now become a foregone, indisputable conclusion that, one way or another, they will kill Jesus.

THE JOHANNINE PASSION NARRATIVE: 18:12-19:30

Jesus Before Annas (18:12-14, 19-24)

The force that arrested Jesus consisted of Roman soldiers and their supervising officer along with members of the temple police. John does not tell us the size of the force, but it was large enough to secure the arrest and deal with any resistance that might be raised. After binding the hands of Jesus, they took him to appear before Annas. John identifies Annas as the father-in-law of Caiaphas, who was the sitting high priest. He later refers to Annas as the "high priest" (18:19). Questions as to whether Annas was the official high priest are without warrant. He had held the office of High Priest, and four of his sons and his son-in-law had succeeded him by Roman appointment. There can be little doubt that Annas retained great influence regarding the political environment of the day. Bernard confirms that the title of ἀρχιερεῖς (high priest) included all ex-high priests, and they were "often called 'high priest' in a loose way."[17] But if Annas was not the official high priest, what might have been the purpose of taking Jesus before him for an initial examination? The most likely answer to that question is to be found in Annas' money-making business in the Court of the Gentiles, where temple sacrifices were sold.

The sellers' booths were called the Bazaars of Annas, and the sacrificial offerings were sold at extortionary prices. Barclay says,

> Now we can see why Annas arranged that Jesus should be brought first to him. Jesus was the man who had attacked Annas's vested interest; he had cleared the Temple of the sellers of victims and had hit Annas where it hurt—in his pocket. Annas wanted to be the first to gloat over the capture of this disturbing Galilean.[18]

Annas doesn't ask Jesus about blasphemy or messiahship. He merely asks Jesus about his disciples and his teachings. Since he has done nothing in secret and has "spoken openly to the world" (8:20), Jesus refers Annas to those who have heard him teach. If Annas is really looking for information about the subject of his teachings, he can get an accurate account from those who have heard him speak openly in the synagogues. His response is interpreted as disrespect and earns him a slap from one of the guards. Jesus continued to firmly refuse to cooperate with Annas and the Jews. As an ex-high priest, Annas knows that he doesn't have the authority to pass an official verdict on Jesus. This, however, is of no consequence since the decision to kill Jesus has already been agreed upon by the Jewish authorities. Having satisfied his need to humiliate Jesus, Annas sent him on to Caiaphas, the official High Priest who will advance the pre-orchestrated Jewish plot to kill Jesus.

Jesus Before Pilate (18:28-19:16)

John tells us that Jesus was taken from the presence of Annas and sent to appear before Caiaphas (8:28). We do not know what happened in the interim between the action of 8:24 and 8:28. Was the appearance before Annas a pre-trial interrogation or was it considered to be a Sanhedrin session and a regular trial? Information provided in the Synoptic Sanhedrin scenes include the following elements: 1) the calling of witnesses; 2) a report of Jesus speaking about the destruction of the temple; 3) questions about the messiah and Son of Man/Son of God; 4) blasphemy; and 5) condemning Jesus to death. While John does not enumerate any of these details in the appearance before Annas, he does introduce these issues in other places in his Gospel (1:51; 2:19; 9:47-53; 10:24-25, 33, 36). The themes of the Synoptic Sanhedrin sessions are known by John and are included throughout his Gospel.

Careful research indicates that there is no absolute reconciliation of attempts to harmonize the Synoptic Sanhedrin accounts with John's account of what happened and when it happened. Lynn Boughton says, "Scholars have long pondered the meaning and purpose of each canonical gospel's account of a συνέδριον and an imperial inquest."[19] Brown claims that there are no successful results for the many attempts to provide reasonable explanations for differences.[20] There does, however, appear to be sufficient reason to believe that the appearance before Annas was equivalent to a legitimate Sanhedrin hearing. Lightfoot advises that John gives the only answer we need regarding Jesus' appearance before Annas. That answer is, "because he was father-in-law to Caiaphas and he was the older man, of greater skill in the law."[21]

Is it possible to identify the "they" (8:28) who led Jesus from Caiaphas to Pilate? Brown thinks that "they" refers to some authorities of the Sanhedrin who were present in the interim period, of which John tells us nothing.[22] This could very well mean that a second Sanhedrin session was held during the hiatus between 8:24 and 8:28. Bultmann supports this possibility. While some refer to the session before Annas as an interrogation, Bultmann says, "In John, as in the Synoptics, the examination counts as a court session.[23]"the quote marks should be after the period instead of including the endnote number While John does not name either session as a Sanhedrin, Bultmann does not see this as a problem. He says, "In John it is not expressly stated that the trial takes place before the assembled Sanhedrin, nevertheless it may be allowed as self-evident."[24]

The many scholarly "ponderings" regarding the harmonization of the canonical Sanhedrin accounts are important only in the world of academic gymnastics. Brown's conclusion might be the most appropriate final word on the issue. He says, "The harmonization of John and the Synoptic accounts does not overly concern us."[25] What is important is that each of the Gospel writers, in their own way, reveals that there was never any possibility that Jesus would be treated justly. The Jews had determined that he should die the death of a criminal and be publicly humiliated. They clearly and systematically exercised each step of their plot to kill Jesus.

It is probable that Pilate had been briefed regarding the situation with Jesus before he asked the Jews to state their accusation against Jesus. Their evasive response indicated that they expected Pilate to immediately accept their charges and dispose of Jesus without further discussion of the matter. Bernard paraphrases the response of the Jews as, "That is our business; we would not have brought the prisoner for sentence, if we were not satisfied with his guilt."[26] Pilate was intolerant of their insolence and directed them to take Jesus and judge him by Jewish law. This prompted the Jews to reveal their true intent and total disregard for any process of justice. They had already decided on the death penalty and announced that "It is not lawful for us to put any man to death" (8:31). I will address the authenticity of this claim when I address the authority of the Sanhedrin in the next chapter. For now, I maintain that the issue for the Jews is not that they can't execute Jesus; rather, the issue concerns the manner of death they can impose upon the victim. To achieve their goal, they will use political pressure akin to blackmail to make Pilate the tool of their murderous plot to kill Jesus.

Pilate could have walked away and left the Jews with his answer and his tacit approval for them to do as they pleased with Jesus. However, he chose to continue to question Jesus and was drawn further into the orchestrated plot of the Jews. Pilate remained narrowly focused on the question of kingship, and Jesus participated in the exchange. He asked Pilate if he was personally curious about his status as a king or if he was just asking about what others had told him. Pilate's answer, "Am I a Jew?" (18:35), indicates that the matter is of no great importance to him. It is obvious that Pilate had no personal complaint against Jesus. He did not seek to bring him to trial and had no idea why the Jews had brought Jesus before him. He asks, "What did you do to earn this kind of hostility from your own nation and the chief priests?" (18:35). Jesus did not answer the question but replied that his mission is "to bear witness to the truth" (18:37). Pilate understood that any association of kingship with Jesus was not the kind of kingship that Rome recognized or saw as a threat to the state. Neither did he have any understanding of or interest in an otherworldly kingdom of truth. Interested only in worldly power and convinced that Jesus had no revolutionary intentions, Pilate cynically asked, "What is truth?" (18:38). His question is rhetorical, and he does not wait for an answer.

Pilate issued his verdict to the Jews and offered to release Jesus. As in the synoptic accounts, they reject his offer and ask for the release of Barabbas. Jesus is scourged and mocked, and Pilate once again declares him to be innocent. Despite this, Pilate already knows what the Jews want. Although he has declared the innocence of Jesus, the outcome is a matter of indifference to Pilate. He knows that the Jews want nothing less than the death of Jesus. He responded to their cries of "Crucify him!" by again declaring his innocence and telling the Jews to "take him yourselves and crucify him" (19:6). Notwithstanding the claim of the Jews that they couldn't put any man to death, it could be that Pilate was tacitly telling them that he would look the other way on this occasion if they wanted to kill Jesus. Again, however, they do not want to kill him by stoning, strangulation, beheading, or burning. These were the methods that their law allowed them to use in capital punishment cases. They wanted to humiliate Jesus and show him to be cursed by God through the death of "hanging on a tree." This could only happen through Roman crucifixion. Countering Pilate's third declaration of innocence, they say that their law demands death "because he has made himself the Son of God" (19:7).

Pilate tried to get more information from Jesus, but he remained silent during the extended examination. Irritated and frustrated by the refusal to answer, Pilate scolded Jesus and told him that he had the power to either spare him or crucify him. Jesus notified Pilate that he had no power except that given to him by a higher authority. As Pilate basked in the glory of his assumed power, Jesus told him that he was nothing more than an instrument through which the power of God was at work. Pilate is just the "middleman" in this criminal drama. While he has some culpability in the injustice that is taking place, the real sinners are the ones who brought Jesus to Pilate for punishment. Bultmann cautions that it is neither Judas nor Caiaphas who individually "has the greater sin." He says, "The initiative lies on the side of the Jews, who delivered Jesus to him in their hatred."[27]

Pilate's future attempts to release Jesus are futile. Abandoning any form of religious argument, the Jews play their trump card against Pilate and turn the entire affair into a political issue. They say, "If you release this man you are not Caesar's friend" (19:12). Pilate understood the threat implicit in this, and he abandoned his reluctance to release Jesus. His negotiations with the Jews are over, but he still will not deliver a judgment because he is convinced that Jesus is innocent. Confirming their recognition of the power of Rome, the Jews renounce any idea of the kingship of Jesus and declare, "We have no king but Caesar" (19:15). Upon hearing this, Pilate's political fears are relieved, and he hands Jesus "over to them to be crucified" (19:16). Smith says, "The trial ends abruptly, with no actual verdict from Pilate. He hands Jesus over to 'them' (αυτοῖς), which in the immediate context can only mean the Jews."[28]

The Cross and Crucifixion (19:17-27)

Crucifixion could not take place within the city, so the chief priests, the Jews and presumably some Roman soldiers led Jesus to Golgotha. John says that he "carried his own cross," and there is no mention of assistance by Simon of Cyrene. Pilate affixed a placard to the cross, which identified Jesus as "the King of the Jews" (19:19). The Jews blackmailed Pilate as they relentlessly sought to enlist his support to satisfy their desire to kill Jesus. It is likely that he placed this title on the cross to exact some revenge by irritating and annoying the Jews. The Jews, having proclaimed, "We have no king but Caesar," protested the sign which named Jesus "the King of the Jews." They wanted him to write, "This man said, 'I am King of the Jews,'" but Pilate refused to change what he had written (19:21-22). Written in Latin, Greek and Hebrew, the universal languages of the day, the sign proclaimed the judgment of the world against Judaism. It stood as a witness to the guilt of the Jews who had succeeded in killing their Messiah, the prophesied Savior of Israel.

The clothes of any executed man belonged to the executioner(s). Jesus' outer garment was a cloak and was sewn together from more than one piece of cloth. The four soldiers assigned to the death detail divided the cloak at the seams, and each took an equal part. The inner garment—the tunic—was one complete seamless piece of material and, as such, was more valuable than the sewn-together cloak. To maintain its value as a seamless garment, the soldiers gambled for the tunic, with one winner taking possession of the intact tunic. John passes this account on from the standpoint of tradition. The Church has typically seen it as a fulfillment of Psalm 22:18: "They divide my garments among them, and for my raiment they cast lots." We may concede that this account represents the soldiers' unwitting participation in the fulfillment of scripture. Nevertheless, Barrett reminds us that "This was an incident that might very well happen at any execution."[29] There is no connection between the action of the soldiers and the malice of the Jews. Referring to John, Bultmann says, "One could ask whether the episode has a particular meaning for him, but there is nothing to indicate such."[30]

Jesus was not alone as he faced his last moment of life. At least four women and one disciple were standing nearby. They were there because they loved the man who was suffering on the cross. Love requires no explanation beyond itself, and further speculation about why they were there is pointless. The many shabby, romantic, sympathetic attempts to symbolically explain the exchange between Jesus and these onlookers diminish the meaning of what was transpiring. The raw recognition of death and grief can only be overcome by the same transparently pure and honest acknowledgement of unqualified love. Suspended vertically between heaven and earth and horizontally spread-eagled on the cross, heaven spoke to earth, and earth spoke to heaven. In that fantastic, glorious exchange between humanity and divinity, we learn that nothing less than love can span the chasm that unites us to and with the God of the universe who created us in His own image.

The End and the Beginning (19:28-30)

Many pages have been written by competent scholars regarding Jesus' final words from the cross. John says that his final words were spoken "to fulfill the scripture" (19:28). Jesus' declaration of "I thirst," the nature of the drink offered to him, the use of hyssop as a sponge and the instrument used to lift the sponge to his lips all make for interesting consideration and speculation. Notwithstanding this, they have no connection to the intent of the Jews to kill Jesus. Brown suggests that these phrases might represent the fulfillment of scripture and might also represent some symbolism intended by John.[31] The massive body of research indicates that it is probable that both these possibilities credibly obtain when considering an exegetical study of these specific issues; however, they have no connection to this study.

John does not tell us of a final great cry as do the Synoptic Gospels. In one Greek word, "τετέλεσται," John tells us that at the very end, Jesus said, "It is finished" (19:30). Jesus is not saying that mercifully, the entire painful ordeal is over. His final word is spoken in the perfect tense. The action of God has come full circle, and the mission of the Son has been perfectly completed: "In the beginning was the Word; the Word became flesh; and the only Son who is in the bosom of the Father has made the Father known to the world" (1:1-18). Chronologically and theologically, through his person and his work, Jesus has demonstrated perfect obedience to the will of the Father. Bultmann says, "So now everything has happened that had to happen; the work of Jesus is completed; he has carried out that which his Father had commanded him."[32]

This is not a simple ending to a successful plot to kill Jesus. The Jews may think that they have once and for all brought an end to the work of this alleged blasphemer and enemy of the nation. They scrambled to take his body down from the cross and dispose of it as soon as possible. It is true that their law required that the dead body of a criminal should not remain on the cross after sunset (Deuteronomy 21:23). In this case, there was a more urgent matter to dispose of the body than that of complying with the law. They were infuriated, humiliated, and embarrassed by the spectacle of a crucified criminal being publicly displayed as the "King of the Jews." They wanted to be done with him and have him immediately removed from their presence and their memory.

When Jesus said, "It is finished," he was speaking of the drama that had been initiated at his birth into the world. His message from the cross was a testimony that he had done all that his Father had sent him to do. His every act was one of obedience. In effect, he was saying to the Father, "I have done all that you have commissioned me to do. If there is anything that remains beyond this, it is in your hands to see that it is done." How wrong the Jews were to think that their murderous victory had rid them of Jesus the Christ, the Son of the living God. What they thought was the end was, in fact, the beginning of a great triumph. The world had not witnessed an ending; rather, it witnessed the completion of God's plan to save the world. John has forever defined the victory that the unbelieving Jews could not thwart through political chicanery, subverted justice, and premeditated murder: "For God so loved the world that he gave his only Son, that whoever believes in him should not perish but have eternal life" (3:16). Karl Barth offers the following explanation of "It is finished":

> The crucified Jesus knew that all things were now accomplished. And his last word when he died was, 'It is finished.' Jesus knew what God knew in the taking place of his sacrifice. And Jesus said what God said: that what took place was not something provisional, but that which suffices to fulfill the divine will, that which is entire and perfect, that which cannot and need not be continued or repeated or added to or superseded, the new thing which was the end of the old but which will itself never become old, which can only be there and continue and shine out and have force and power as that which is new and eternal.[33]

The canonical Gospels bear witness that a combination of priests, Pharisees, Sadducees, elders, and hostile crowds affected the murder of Jesus. John makes no distinction in the title or individual identity of the membership of this combined entity. He refers to them as the "Jews." All of them were blind and hostile as to who Jesus really was. Perhaps it can be argued that the Pharisees opposed Jesus because of a genuine concern for maintaining and preserving the religious laws and peculiarities of their religious beliefs. No doubt, the wealthy Sadducees opposed Jesus because he threatened their wealth and positions of power and prestige. It might be argued that the "crowds," the citizenry at large, were caught on the horns of a dilemma. They were confronted with the choice of believing their leaders or thinking for themselves. Even so, that very conflict and ambiguity of choice amounted to a rejection of Jesus. They preferred their historic and essential Jewishness to the message of life offered by Jesus.

John identifies all those who populated this stronghold of rejection and resistance as the "Jews" (οἱ Ἰουδαῖοι). Gutbrod says that the Johannine use of οἱ Ἰουδαῖοι (the Jews) "is a name for those who reject the claim of Jesus to lordship, and remain Jews because they do."[34] A rational understanding of the Gospel According to John makes it very difficult, if not impossible, to absolve the Jews of the killing of Jesus.

Chapter Five

The Sanhedrin

Scholars and historians are not confident that it is possible to reconstruct the exact history of the Sanhedrin. It probably did consist of seventy-one members, as reflected in Moses' organization of seventy elders plus himself. He formed this group to function as a governing body over the large population of Israelites that he led out of Egypt (Numbers 11:10-24). The Babylonian/Persian period of captivity produced a hiatus in the functionality of the Sanhedrin as a governing institution in the life of Israel. However, when the exiles returned to Jerusalem, Ezra immediately reorganized the Sanhedrin as a regularly constituted authority. Throughout its remaining history, the Sanhedrin saw its authority and membership vary according to prevailing political factors. During the time of Jesus, the Sanhedrin was composed of Sadducees who represented the aristocratic priestly class, Pharisees and scribes who were experts in the law, and elders who were respected men among the people. There was only one sitting High Priest at any given time, and he was a Sadducee.

The Sanhedrin possessed administrative authority and had the power to arrest any suspected criminal. Apparently, it had access to its own independent police force (Matthew 26:47, Mark 14:43, Luke 22:52, and John 18:2). Obviously, the powers of the Sanhedrin were very broad during the Roman era of occupation. The Jews could decide matters germane to the life and affairs of the cultic community and could punish individuals for offenses against the Torah. The question that is at hand and has yet to be answered satisfactorily is this: "Did the Sanhedrin have the power to impose the death sentence and execute a condemned prisoner?"

There are no precedents from the time of Jesus to serve as historical guidance in answering this question. The only legal case of capital punishment associated with the competence of the Sanhedrin is the case of Jesus as presented in the canonical Gospels. A. M. Okorie says, "Hence, outside the trial of Jesus, no conclusive decision can be substantiated for or against the complete judicial competence of the Sanhedrin."[1] Fortunately, we do not have to go outside the trial of Jesus to arrive at a conclusive decision. We do know that the Jerusalem Sanhedrin was destroyed by Titus in AD 70. What is often overlooked is that little to nothing is known about the exact rules, methodologies, and legal protocols that were in force, much less strictly adhered to before AD 70. The Mishnaic code of legal procedure wasn't organized, codified, and meticulously applied until the reorganization following the destruction of Jerusalem and the dispersion of the Jews. Disregarding this known fact, we find that too often, the legal procedures codified in the second and third centuries are used to explain and interpret the actions of an early first-century Sanhedrin. Consequently, faulty premises produce erroneous conclusions upon which many studies are based. The truth is lost as arguments are based on theoretical deductions and personal preconceptions, which have no connection to the defining conditions that prevailed during the actual time of the event(s).

It is a mistake to assume that the Mishnaic rules compiled following the destruction of Jerusalem can be used as references for Sanhedrin procedures prior to AD 70. No one can confirm that the codified laws compiled at the end of the second century AD existed in Jesus' time. Furthermore, Kümmel points out that "if they did exist, we do not know that they were acknowledged as binding by the members of the Sanhedrin."[2] Absent the imposition of these post-AD 70 Mishnaic rules, we can proceed to look more clearly at the competence of the Sanhedrin during the trial of Jesus.

Arguments Concerning the Authority and Responsibility for the Death of Jesus

Many attempts have been made by lawyers to recreate the trial of Jesus before the Sanhedrin. Brandon says,

> Attempts have sometimes been made by eminent lawyers to explain the trial of Jesus. Their forensic knowledge and experience seem to befit them preeminently for such an undertaking. Unfortunately, such attempts have foundered on a primary misconception. It is supposed that the four Christian Gospels provide severally, four accounts of the trial of Jesus, which are basically authentic; allowance having to be made only for minor differences.[3]

Some of these attempts conclude by claiming that the rules of the Sanhedrin were strictly observed and that Jesus received the proper considerations and protections afforded by Jewish law. Finding him guilty as charged, but not having the power of capital punishment, the Jews passed him on to the Roman governor to carry out the sentence of death. Others have argued that the Sanhedrin was not convened according to Jewish law; therefore, the Jews could not be held accountable for the actions of a rogue tribunal. Numerous other assessments regarding the authority, competence, and jurisdiction of the Sanhedrin have been advanced. Many diverse views have been expressed by scholars, lawyers, and historians, resulting in countless divergent conclusions, some credible and some incredibly unbelievable.

My starting point in assessing the authority and competency of the Sanhedrin is to affirm that my study of the canonical Gospels credibly establishes the fact that the Jews killed Jesus. For my purposes, this is no longer an issue that requires further proof. Going forward, the issue is to discover the role of the Sanhedrin in killing Jesus. All the previous studies, conjectures, and hypotheses regarding this subject are too numerous to be included within the scope of this study. To narrow the results of my research, while simultaneously maintaining relevancy, I will specifically consider the following Jewish arguments relating to the authority and competency of the Sanhedrin in the time of Jesus: 1) Jewish arguments against the canonical Gospels; and 2) the argument of Haim Cohn in his book *The Trial and Death of Jesus*.

Jewish Arguments Contra the Canonical Gospels

Rabbi Michael J. Cook serves as Professor of Intertestamental and Early Christian Literature at Hebrew Union College, the Jewish Institute of Religion. Rabbi Cook has extensive expertise in Jewish Christian relations and is the only rabbi in North America with a full professional chair in the New Testament. His scholarship is representative of the many Jewish arguments rejecting the authenticity of the trial of Jesus as presented in the canonical Gospels. Cook immediately declares his distrust in the truth of the canonical Gospels. He states that "there is a propensity by Jewish scholars to misconstrue as actual history Gospel 'facts' that are purely fictional."[4] He rejects any attempt to treat Gospel data as being factual. He considers it a mistake to even speak of the Gospel accounts of the trial and death of Jesus as though they represented history. He claims that he particularly locates fabricated stories in the accounts of the Last Supper, the Sanhedrin trial, the charge of blasphemy, and the release of Barabbas.

For purposes of this book, my concern is only with his position regarding Jesus' Sanhedrin trial. Cook refers to it as a "supposed trial." He bases his argument on what he calls the "two delivery texts" in Mark 14:53 and 15:1. The first text shows Jesus being arrested in Gethsemane and delivered to Caiaphas on Thursday night. The second text says that the Jews held another meeting on Friday morning and then delivered Jesus to Pilate. If there was a Thursday night trial, he argues, of what purpose or value would there have been in holding another trial on Friday morning? Cook's answer is that the Thursday night trial was an invention of the Gospel writers. The Friday morning "consultation" was not a full-fledged trial before the Sanhedrin. Regarding this, he says, "Nothing less than a full-fledged trial before the 'supreme court' of the land could possibly suffice and also more clearly implicate the entire Jewish nation in his death!"[5] Given this, the Thursday night account of a convening of the Sanhedrin was fictional and invented as a primitive storyline to make the Sanhedrin responsible for the conviction and execution of Jesus. The Gospel writers had to construct a Sanhedrin trial to absolve the Romans of killing Jesus. Cook says that the Gospel writers "replaced Rome with the Jews as the villains."[6] Pilate, the true villain, was replaced with the Jewish high priest who became the determiner of Jesus' death.[7] Cook acknowledges that volumes have been written about the violations and illegalities of the Sanhedrin procedures at Jesus' trial. He says that this is of no consequence because the Sanhedrin account is nothing more than created history. It never happened! Cook's final word is a warning that "Jewish scholars should not accept at face value a literal reading of emotionally charged ancient texts that have been used down the centuries to perpetuate hatred of Jews."[8]

Samuel Sandmel does not speak to the competency of the Sanhedrin at the trial of Jesus. Like Cook, however, he challenges the truth of the canonical Gospels. He says, "How authentic are accounts of a trial which contains so many contradictions and differences, such as two trials by the Sanhedrin in Mark, against one in Matthew and Luke, and none in John?"[9] He contends that the Gospel writers cleverly shifted the responsibility for Jesus' death from Pilate to the Jews. For him, the Gospels offer no objective history regarding the trial, and, in fact, they obscure any attempt to arrive at the truth of that event. Although clothed in the Rubix cube rhetoric of academic and Jewish intellectual legalisms, the intent of Cook, Sandmel, and others is immediately transparent. If the trial of Jesus was a fabrication of the Gospel writers, then any argument regarding the competency and authority of the Sanhedrin becomes a non-question. What difference does it make if the Sanhedrin had the power to exact a death sentence if such a case never came before them? The defense of the Jews consists of the claim that fictional Gospel data has been accepted as genuine history. Therefore, by default, the Jews seek to absolve themselves of any guilt in the killing of Jesus.

The attitudes of most Jewish scholars to Jesus are hostile and defensive. They lament the fact that the Gospels are the only first-century documents that give us a full account of the Jewish reaction to the trial and death of Jesus. Lacking first-century Jewish counterarguments to the Gospel accounts, they seek to absolve the Jewish people with their claims that the Gospel accounts amount to reckless theorizing, emotionally charged stories, prejudice passing as historical events, and finally, invented stories for the perpetuation of hatred of the Jews. As to the lack of counter-writings in defense of Jewish innocence, the Jews have only themselves to blame. The significance of the trial of Jesus for the Jewish people is undisputed. However, in the first six centuries of the Common Era (AD), there are very few references to Jesus in Talmudic literature. W. Riggans says, "The lack of references to Jesus and the birth and growth of the church must be the result of a conscious decision to avoid and indeed prevent, discussion about Jesus in the Jewish community."[10] By personal choice, the ancient rabbis ignored the person and work of Jesus and the rise of Christianity as a rival religion of Judaism. Peter Schafer says that the "rabbis of rabbinic Judaism did not care much about Jesus."[11]

Schafer says that the climax of Jewish scholarly literature about Jesus in the Talmud is reflected in Johann Maier's book of 1978, *Jesus von Nazareth in der talmudischen Uberlieferung* (*Jesus of Nazareth in the Talmudian Delivery*). Schafer provides this summary of Maier's book: "The rabbis did not care about Jesus, they did not know anything reliable about him, and what they might have alluded to is legendary at best and rubbish at worst—not worthy of any serious scholarly attention."[12] The attitudes of the Jewish rabbis/writers/scholars of the first six centuries AD confirm their rejection of Jesus. They are convicted by the Old Testament scriptures that describe and define them as a "stiff-necked" and "stubborn" people (Exodus 33:5; 34:9; Deuteronomy 9:6; 9:13). Before Stephen was stoned to death, presumably with the approval of the high priest and the Sanhedrin (Acts 7:1, 58), he called the Jews "You stiff-necked people, uncircumcised in heart and ears, you always resist the Holy Spirit" (Acts 7:51).

The absence of Jewish writings about Jesus does not provide proof that the Gospel writers invented trial stories that confirmed Jewish guilt in the killing of Jesus. To the contrary, it confirms the "stiff-necked" resistance and national hubris of the Jews at large and their leaders in particular. It shows that in the time of Jesus, they were still as stiff-necked as they were when wandering in the wilderness and murmuring against God and Moses. Stephen's charge against them resonates with the Old Testament charges against the Jews. Bruce says, "Moses and the prophets had described the fathers in these terms; they are equally true, says

Stephen, of their children of the contemporary generation."[13]

When Jewish writings did appear about Jesus, they were scurrilous in content and mocked Jesus' life story as presented in the Gospels. These writings were known as the *Toldot Yeshu* (*The Chronicles of Jesus*). The date of this work is uncertain. It could have appeared in written form as early as the sixth century AD but almost certainly circulated in oral form much earlier than that. Riggans says that the *Toldot Yeshu*

> became the prime, if not the sole, source of the Jewish community's knowledge of Jesus from the early Middle Ages to the early twentieth century in Eastern Europe. The narrative is made up of stories of Jesus' illegitimacy, blasphemy, immorality and hubris, presenting him as a thoroughly reprobate Jewish man, one of whom the Jewish community should be ashamed, and at whose actions and attitudes it should be outraged.[14]

Unable to absolve themselves of the death of Jesus, the Jews have historically sought to deny and delegitimize the life and work of the One of whom the heavenly voice (bath quol) said, "Thou art my beloved Son; with thee I am well pleased" (Mark 1:11). The fact that Jewish scholars continue to deny the historicity of the Gospels is a clear indicator that they will always seek to vindicate the Judaism that was responsible for the killing of Jesus.

Haim Cohn, on the Trial and Death of Jesus

Haim Cohn was a lawyer and a member of the Supreme Court of Israel. He wrote *The Trial and Death of Jesus* in 1968. He died in 2002 at age ninety-one. Cohn is but one of the many lawyer types who sought to apply modern legal procedures to the reconstruction of the trial of Jesus. The purpose of his book was to prove that it was the Romans, not the Sanhedrin, who tried, convicted, and executed Jesus. In the Introduction, Cohn claims that non-lawyers, theologians, and historians have produced unreliable accounts of the trial of Jesus. As sons of the Church, they have been unable to emancipate themselves from the "dogma of the Gospel truth."[15] Cohn's hubris is evident from the beginning as he claims that he will date the Gospels and accurately do what the experts in exegesis and textual criticism have done so poorly and so inaccurately! He categorically states that the authors of the Gospels did not have any testimony or information from eyewitnesses during the stages of the arrest, trial, or crucifixion of Jesus. He dismisses as unreliable Luke's claim that his Gospel contains the witness of the early community "just as they were delivered to us by those who from the beginning were eyewitnesses and ministers of the word" (Luke 1:1-4). He also dismisses the witness of John 19:35 regarding the events of the crucifixion: "He who saw it has borne witness—his testimony is true, and he knows that he tells the truth—that you also may believe." Cohn says that this testimony is imprecise and of no evidentiary value because the identity of the witness is undisclosed.

Cohn does not know, or deliberately overlooks a testimony that proves him wrong. Perhaps he is withholding evidence uncovered in the discovery phase of his trial scenario. He has said that the Gospel writers did not have access to anything written about the death of Jesus prior to AD 70. He also said that Paul, who must have known the facts, doesn't say a word about the Jews having any blame for the killing of Jesus. In fact, Paul says, "For you, brethren, became imitators of the churches of God in Christ Jesus which are in Judea; for you suffered the same things from your own countrymen as they did from the Jews, who killed both the Lord Jesus and the prophets" (1 Thessalonians 2:14-15). First Thessalonians was written in AD 50s; therefore, Cohn is wrong as to pre-AD 70 witnesses as well as Paul's blame of the Jews. What we see here is a lawyer at work whose only objective is to defend his client. He admits that what the Gospel writers report could conceivably have happened. He adds that this concession does not necessarily mean that it did, in fact, happen. He says, "We are concerned not so much with the historicity of the events as with the evidentiary worth of the tradition."[16]

As if giving an opening statement at a modern-day trial, Cohn says, "Our purpose is to show that neither Pharisees nor Sadducees, neither priests nor elders, neither scribes nor any Jews, had any reasonable cause to seek the death of Jesus or his removal."[17] In modern legal form, he begins by contending that there was no motive that would prompt any Jew or Jewish official to kill Jesus. In fact, Cohn says that the Jews brought Jesus before the Sanhedrin in order to "prevent the crucifixion of a Jew by the Romans and, more particularly, of a Jew who enjoyed the love and affection of the people."[18] He says that the account of the high priest tearing his clothes was not because he thought that Jesus had uttered blasphemy. Rather, he tore his clothes because he was grieved that Jesus would not defend himself, and he knew that his silence would ensure that the Romans would convict and kill him. The constant theme of Cohn's book is one that demands us to believe that the Jews loved Jesus as one of their own and did everything within their power to save him from death at the hands of the Romans. He says, "They did all that they possibly could to save Jesus, whom they dearly loved and cherished as one of their own, from his tragic end at the hands of the Roman oppressor."[19] He calls the trial "the perversion of justice," but contends that it was the Jews and not Jesus who were treated unjustly.

It is difficult to understand how a man who is intelligent enough to sit as a member of the Supreme Court of Israel could be so irrational in his reconstruction of the trial of Jesus. While totally stripping the Gospel accounts of any measure of truth, he says: "Never in the chronicles of mankind has a trial been so widely and so skillfully reported, and never was a false report invested with higher and more exalted authority."[20] He would have us believe that those who accepted that the blood of Jesus was on their hands (Matthew 27:24), did their utmost to keep Jesus safe from the murderous hands of Rome! Refusing to accept any historical value regarding the canonical Gospels, he doubles and redoubles his efforts to free the Jews completely from any responsibility in the trial and crucifixion of Jesus. Cohn's argument, while fascinating and meticulously constructed in its attention to detail, is utterly unbelievable. It is based upon historical speculation, unproven assumptions and is often devoid of logic. He writes as a defense lawyer who is passionately dedicated to proving the innocence of his client. His sole purpose is to free his accused client from the dock of justice and to attempt to make irrational pleas sound convincing. His reconstruction of the trial of Jesus is an interesting but unconvincing fantasy tale. It shows many of the same fallacies of similar books attempting to reconstruct the trial of Jesus. They consist largely of a collection of legal discussions (briefs) that deal with the intricacies of jurisprudence based on the rabbinic interpretation of Jewish law that was not operative prior to AD 70. They also rely upon or reference current legal procedures that are not compatible with the law as it might have been applied at the trial of Jesus.

As a concluding observation, it is interesting to note that Cohn does believe that the Sanhedrin had the power of capital jurisdiction during the time of Jesus. He says that he starts

> from the premise that the Sanhedrin had retained all the capital jurisdiction that it had ever possessed under Jewish law, and that there was no jurisdictional obstacle to its proceeding against Jesus for any offense under and in any manner compatible with that law.[21]

Based on this statement, we can assume that the Sanhedrin had the power to execute Jesus if its intent was to prosecute him rather than defend him.

Pre-AD 70 and Post-AD 70 Competence and Authority of the Sanhedrin

For any understanding of the competence and authority of the Sanhedrin, it is important to recognize the political climate of Judea before and after AD 70. Prior to AD 70, there were no codified rules that demanded accountability for legal details and judicial plausibility. It is possible that the trial of Jesus before the Sanhedrin was more of a "kangaroo court" than an official act of jurisprudence. Alice Camille goes so far as to say that "what passed for a trial was probably an abuse of power by every measure: the few speaking for the many, rogue schemers plotting to do secretly what they could not do in the whole assembly."[22] Some of this sort of intrigue may have taken place, but that cannot be claimed with any certainty. However, Camille's statement serves to alert us that the conduct of the pre-AD 70 Sanhedrin surely was not governed by the rules laid down by post-AD 70 Mishnah. The rules governing the Sanhedrin were not written down in the Mishnah earlier than AD 70. David Instone-Brewer suggests that nothing was written prior to AD 190-200.[23] Outside the report of the Gospels, we have very little knowledge of how Jewish trial procedures functioned during the lifetime of Jesus. In fact, we have no reliable knowledge of Jewish origin as to whether the Sanhedrin had a systematized body of traditional law prior to AD 70. This lack of enough data means that any account of the competency and authority of the Sanhedrin other than what we find in the canonical Gospels is speculative at best.

The year AD 70 is important in considering the competency of the Sanhedrin because that year marks the destruction of both the temple and the city of Jerusalem. This resulted in great physical and human loss, but the Jews continued to survive. In the aftermath of this destruction, a tax was levied on the Jews, but the Romans continued to recognize Judaism as a lawful religion and exempted it from emperor worship. With no temple to serve as a center of worship, rabbinic Judaism emerged as a force for leadership. It took as its central task the development of the legal component of the Torah.[24] The Sanhedrin regained control over Jewish law, was reconstituted as the high court, and assumed all legislative and regulatory functions. It is important to remember that the precisely defined rules of legal adjudication that were instituted by the post-AD 70 Sanhedrin were not operative during the trial of Jesus. This means that all the arguments regarding the illegal procedures of the Sanhedrin during the trial of Jesus are meaningless. Lohse provides a list of the rules of the Halakha (laws to regulate daily life and conduct) that are usually claimed to have been broken:

1. Capital trials were only to be held by day according to Sanhedrin,4,1,but the Sanhedrin met at night to judge Jesus.

2. No legal proceedings were to take place on the Sabbath or feast days, but the trial of Jesus before the Sanhedrin took place on the eve of the Passover.

3. Sanhedrin, 4,1 lays down that sentence of death was never to be passed on the day of the trial itself but only on the following day, but here, the Sanhedrin condemned Jesus at once to death.

4. According to Sanhedrin, 7, 5, the blasphemy which to be punished by death is pronouncing the divine name, but here Jesus did not pronounce the name of God.

5. The trial was obviously held in the house of the high priest, not in the regular hall of assembly of the Sanhedrin.[25]

Relative to this list, Lohse says, "It should also be noted, however, that the Pharisaic Rabb. Halacha, later codified in the Mishna, cannot have been normative for the Sanhedrin in the period prior to AD 70."[26]

The difference in the political landscape of pre-AD 70 and post-AD 70 is as different as night and day. In pre-AD 70, both the temple and the holy city were intact and fully functioning, but this was not the case immediately thereafter. It was during this post-AD 70 period, and probably more during the late second century and early third century, that the Mishnah was written down to serve as an instrument to reorient the Jewish government and the religious community which it served. The past was gone, and the Jews were desperate for the development of a trustworthy system of shared existence. The Tractate Sanhedrin was a product of this post-AD 70 reorganization. Far from being functional, it represented a theoretical and idealized construct of what the Jewish leadership wanted to achieve. The language of the post-AD 70 Mishnah in no way reflected the political and judicial climate at the time of the trial of Jesus. Howard Clark Kee says that the language and grammar of the post-AD 70 Mishnah reflects a "world of discourse quite separate from the concrete realities of a given time, place, or society."[27]

What we are confronted with is the tension that exists between the authority of the Sanhedrin of the Gospels, and the authority of the post-AD 70 Tractate Sanhedrin. In either case, it appears that the Jews could, and did, do as they pleased. Since Tractate Sanhedrin of the Mishnah was not written during the lifetime of Jesus, we may confidently conclude that any Sanhedrin referenced in the Gospels was not bound by post-AD 70 regulations. However, supposing that it was bound by those regulations, it has been successfully argued that the Jews did not abide by their own rules. George Barton argues that it was the Saducean element of the Sanhedrin (the house of Annas and Caiaphas), that was responsible for the arrest and trial of Jesus. Based on this, he says, "Even if the rules of procedure laid down more than two hundred years later in the Mishna were then in their incipiency (of which there is no certainty), the Sadducees would be the least likely carefully to observe them."[28]

Driven by their human motives to preserve their power and the privileges afforded them by the Roman government, and of their hatred and rejection of Jesus, the competency and authority of the Sanhedrin was selectively exercised at the discretion of the Jews. They could do as they pleased and had carte blanche to violate their own rules if that became necessary. Clearly, the political and judicial order of the day was one of "the ends justify the means." This is seen and established in Caiaphas' declaration: "You do not understand that it is expedient for you that one man dies for the people, and that the whole nation should not perish" (John 11:49-50).

John Dominic Crossan: A Non-Traditional Position

I cannot fail to mention John Dominic Crossan's book, *Who Killed Jesus? Exposing the Roots of Anti-Semitism in the Gospel Story of the Death of Jesus* (1995). It was the primary title of his book that prompted me to initiate the research and study, which I have also entitled *Who Killed Jesus?* While our titles suggest exact or similar concerns, nothing could be further from the truth. Crossan's subtitle best describes his primary intent. His subtitle is *Exploring the Roots of Anti-Semitism in the Gospel Story of the Death of Jesus*. His motivating interest is not in answering the question of who killed Jesus; he wants to prove that the canonical Gospel accounts are void of any historical value. He says, "This book is about anti-Semitism. It is about the accuracy and honesty of Christian scholarship in its best reconstruction of these ancient yet ever-present events."[29] His claim is that the Gospel accounts do not reflect history remembered; rather, they represent prophecy historicized. He is sure that the Gospel accounts could not have been based on memory because the companions of Jesus didn't know what happened. They all ran away. They could not have known what happened at any trial or interrogation or even if there were any such events. It was only after they were out of harm's way and looking back that they became interested in what had happened. They began to search for Old Testament texts that could be applied to and/or associated with what was rumored to have happened. In other words, they decided what they wanted to have happened and then attempted to proof-text scripture to support their wishful and imaginative claims.

Crossan's appeal to the *Gospel of Peter* as a primary instigator of anti-Semitism is a major source in support of his "prophecy historicized" contention. He claims that it was written in the late AD 40's and that it contains information which he calls the "Cross Gospel."[30] Crossan says that it is this Cross Gospel within the *Gospel of Peter* that became the single source of the passion narratives of the canonical Gospels. His reliance on fragmented, non-canonical writing goes against the mainstream scholarship, which dates from the mid to late second century. In fact, the *Gospel of Peter* appears to consolidate all the passion narrative information contained in the canonical Gospels into one continuous narrative. It seems likely that the writer had access to the canonicals, had knowledge of some stories about Jesus, and then added his own touches to this information. Bart Ehrman says, "In this case, the touches involve some intriguing legendary accretions— especially about the giant resurrected Jesus and the walking cross that speaks to the skies."[31] It is unbelievable that a scholar such as Crossan would rely so heavily on an apocryphal gospel pseudonymously attributed to Peter.

Wilhelm Schneermelcher made the following assessment of the *Gospel of Peter*: "The amount of readable text is so scrappy we do not gain much help for the text of the Gos.Pet. Any speculation about the structure of the rest of the content of the Gos.Pet. as a whole is in the present state of our knowledge meaningless."[32] According to Spivey and Smith, the *Gospel of Peter* is "fundamentally valueless,"[33] and Brown says that the *Gospel of Peter* is later than the canonical Gospels and does not "add a single historical fact to what we can know of the passion from the canonical

Gospels."[34]

It doesn't seem to bother Crossan that the *Gospel of Peter* contains events that can only be described as having been created by a wildly rich imagination. For instance, it has an account of a cross that walks and talks and two angels whose heads extend into the heavens. These accounts are ludicrous, absurd, and defy belief. Paul Foster says, "It must be squarely acknowledged that a cross that emerges from the tomb and speaks is a highly creative embellishment to the canonical tradition."[35]

Crossan's criticism of the Gospels is brutal and unrelenting. He says that the Jewish demands for crucifixion and Pilate's insistence on the innocence of Jesus has nothing to do with history and is nothing less than Christian propaganda. As such, all of it amounts to popular storytelling. His criticism can be crude and tasteless, as it is in his comments regarding Jesus being placed in the tomb provided by Joseph of Arimathea (John 19:38-41). He does not believe that Jesus was placed in Joseph's tomb. Crossan believes that he was either left on the cross for the birds and the dogs to eat, or he was placed in a shallow grave and the dogs dug him up and ate the body.[36]

In defense of the truth of the Gospel accounts, Brown stated that "What is logically surmised to have happened more often than not actually did happen."[37] Crossan responded to Brown with this mocking paraphrase: "Just because you made it up does not mean it did not happen."[38] His flippant, insulting response is less than would be expected of a scholar-to-scholar exchange, but it does reflect his attitude throughout the book. His cynicism is unmistakable. He reduces the Gospels to what he calls the repetition of the "longest lie, and for our own integrity, we Christians must at least name it as such."[39] This is all based on his claim that the Gospel narratives are "prophecy historicized." He speculates that historicization led to popularization, which resulted in actualization.

When these three processes progressively coalesced into one stream of thought, the result was acceptance and belief in them by the ordinary Christians who embraced the stories as a matter of faith. Crossan says that the ultimate outcome of these creative polemics undergirding faith can be described like this: "Jesus rises, Roman authority converts, Jewish authority lies to deceive its own people."[40] In a display of maximum intellectual hubris, Crossan tells us that "learned scholars and scribal exegetes" understand that this three-stage process is a false construct and that it is only the "ordinary Christians" who embrace and perpetuate the lie. It seems fair to challenge and question this assumption. Is there no connection between exegesis and story? Is there no connection between pastoral preaching and scholarship? Apparently, he believes the Church Fathers were irresponsible in their education of the "ordinary Christians."

Crossan makes no mention of the Sanhedrin and its competency as an adjudicatory body in the time of Jesus. This is not surprising, considering that he does not believe there was a trial before Caiaphas or Pilate. He says, "For me, the received tradition is not a core of memory recalling what happened to Jesus under trial but a core of prophecy replacing memory's absence. In the case of Jesus, there may well have been Arrest and Execution but no trial whatsoever in between."[41]

In a rare show of confidence in admitting that the death of Jesus actually happened, Crossan says, "I take it as historical that Jesus was executed by some conjunction of Jewish and Roman authority."[42] If there was no trial by the Sanhedrin, as Crossan claims, did he believe that the Sanhedrin had the authority to convict and execute if there had been a trial in the time of Jesus? I believe that the following comment gives some evidence that Crossan would confirm the authority of the pre-AD 70 Sanhedrin to try, convict, and execute Jesus: "Stoning to death could be done by the people, but crucifixion demanded brutal expertise particular to executioners."⁴³ While my conclusion consists of an extrapolation of Crossan's statement, I believe that it strongly suggests that he would support the claim that the Sanhedrin had the authority to impose capital punishment in the time of Jesus but lacked the expertise to initiate and carry out a crucifixion.

Arguments for the Authority of the Sanhedrin

Brown references a work by Jean Juster and points out that it has influenced many scholars in arguing that the Sanhedrin's power was not limited regarding imposing capital punishment.⁴⁴ Juster was a Jewish author who offered what has been called the most important discussion of the twentieth century pertaining to the trial of Jesus. His major work on this subject is entitled, *The Jews in the Roman Empire*.⁴⁵ While Juster was not a theologian, his comments on the trial of Jesus attracted the attention of Hans Lietzmann, a German Protestant theologian. Juster's work dealt with the study of how the Jews have historically functioned and survived within whatever environment they found themselves in. He examined their methods of dealing with conflict and how they attempted to resolve the many conflicts they faced. When he wrote about the Jews in pagan and Christian literature, he could not avoid dealing with the Jews and their relationship to the trial of Jesus.

One would not expect Juster to be a primary subject involved in a theological debate. His involvement is centered solely on his challenge of the comment of the Jews in John 18:31 when they said to Pilate, "It is not lawful for us to put any man to death." Disputing the claim of the Jews, Juster maintains that the Sanhedrin did have the power to impose and execute the death penalty during the trial of Jesus. The often-held claim that the right to pronounce sentences of life and death was taken away from the Sanhedrin some forty years before the destruction of the temple presents no obstacle for Juster. He says that this cannot be proved and is, in fact, a misinterpretation and inaccurate deduction drawn from the following entry in the Babylonian Talmud:

> Say not that cases of fines ceased, but that capital cases ceased. Why? Because when the Sanhedrin saw that murderers were so prevalent that they could not be properly dealt with judicially, they said: Rather let us be exiled from place to place than pronounce them guilty of capital offenses for it is written (Deuteronomy 17:10) and thou shalt do according to the sentence, which they of that place which the Lord shall choose shall tell thee which implies that it is the place that matters.[46]

Juster makes his case upon the claim that the Sanhedrin was "exiled from place to place" to avoid having to adjudicate on capital cases. By moving the Sanhedrin out of the temple, the Sanhedrin would never have to pass a sentence on any case requiring a death sentence. This faulty reasoning was based on the belief that capital sentences could be passed and imposed only in the temple.[47] Of course, the temple was intact and in full use at the time of Jesus' trial; therefore, the prohibition of Abodah Zorah, 8b could not have applied to the pre-AD 70 Sanhedrin. Juster recognized that this "exile from place to place" of the Sanhedrin never occurred during the time of the Roman-appointed governors.

As an expert in Roman law and knowledgeable of Jewish law derived from his Talmudic studies, Juster examined the legal history of the pre-AD 70 period and found several executions ordered and carried out by Jewish authorities. Among these were the stoning of Stephen in the AD 30s, the stoning of James in the AD 60s, and the threatened stoning of the adulteress in John 8:3-5. Paul's refusal to be tried by the Sanhedrin in Jerusalem and his appeal to Rome suggests that he believed a guilty charge at the hands of the Sanhedrin would result in death by stoning (Acts 25:9-11).

As I have stated before, it is essential to recognize the difference between the political climate of pre-AD 70 and post-AD 70. We can safely assume that Roman control of Jewish governing institutions was far more rigid after the destruction of the temple than before the destruction. We know that Mishnah rules and regulations were not written down prior to AD 70. We also know that the pre-AD 70 Sanhedrin was a "free-wheeling" legal force that was not impeded by any counterforce of checks and balances. Juster, operating under pre-AD 70 guidelines, concluded that the Sanhedrin in Jerusalem, the highest Jewish court before AD 70, had the right to indict Jews who were accused of capital charges and to execute capital punishment.[48]

In a similar fashion as that of Juster, Lightfoot challenges the claim made by the Jews in John 18:31. He says that the statement, "It is not lawful for us to put any man to death," has been misunderstood to mean that the Romans stripped the Sanhedrin of the authority to exercise the power of capital punishment. He says that it may have fallen into disuse, but it was not taken away from them by the Romans.[49] Rather than an unlawful act, their claim was an evasion of their responsibility. If, in the case of Jesus, they were so sensitive about breaking one of their laws, Lightfoot asks, "How came they then to stone the protomartyr Stephen? How came they to stone Ben Satda at Lydda? How came they to burn the priest's daughter alive that was taken in adultery?"[50] The claim of the Jews seems to be one of convenience more than fact. Since there was no Roman prohibition in force, the Sanhedrin could order death by stoning, burning, strangulation, or execution by the sword. Neither of these methods served their purpose in the case of Jesus. They wanted him to hang publicly in shame and dishonor, and this could only be achieved by way of crucifixion. They used all their clever powers of coercion and political persuasion to manipulate Pilate and achieve their desired end. They involved Rome in the method of execution, but in reality, the Jews killed Jesus.

It has also been argued that the Jews unwittingly fulfilled the prophecy of Jesus when they insisted on killing him by crucifixion. Jesus had told the Pharisees, the crowd, and his disciples that he would be killed by "being lifted up from the earth" (John 12:32-33). The insistence of the Sanhedrin that Jesus be crucified was in accordance with God's plan for the salvation of the world. The "lifting up" of Jesus would "draw all men to him" and ensure that "all those believing in him should not perish but have eternal life" (John 3:16). The Jews had not lost the right of capital punishment and could have killed Jesus by stoning or another of the authorized precedents for capital punishment. Being "lifted up" fulfilled both the plan of God and the intent of the Jews. Jesus became the means of salvation for the world, and the Jews fulfilled their desire to humiliate Jesus and render him accursed by God according to their scriptures.

Two Fathers of the Church, Augustine and Chrysostom, gave their understanding of John 18:31. Augustine says that the claim of the Jews that "It is not lawful for us to put any man to death" does not mean that they cannot adjudicate capital cases. He associates this claim with the refusal of the Jews to enter the praetorium to avoid being defiled when Jesus was taken before Pilate (John 18:28). Augustine says,

> We are, however, to understand that they said it was not lawful for them to put any man to death, on account of the sanctity of the festal day, which they had just begun to celebrate, and on which account they were afraid of being defiled even by entering the pretorium.[51]

If Augustine is right, it is clear that the Jews were not forbidden to pass sentences of death. They voluntarily refrained from exercising their right to avoid defiling a holy day and depriving themselves of participating in the Passover celebration.

Chrysostom explains the actions of the Jews in the same way as

Augustine. He says,

> But if they say, "It is not lawful for us to put any man to death," they say it with reference to that season. For that they did slay men, and that they slew them in a different way, Stephen shows, being stoned. But they desired to crucify Him, that they might make a display of the manner of His death."[52]

He further confirms that there were no restrictions on the authority of the Sanhedrin during the time of Jesus. He says,

> The Jews assemble a Sanhedrin themselves and slay whom they please. Thus in fact they put Stephen to death, thus they beat the apostles, not taking them before rulers. Thus also they were about to put Paul to death, had not the chief captain thrown himself upon them. For this took place while the priests, while the temple, while the ritual, the sacrifices were yet standing.[53]

If the temple was yet standing, then Chrysostom is referring to a time prior to AD 70. This is a further confirmation that the Sanhedrin had the authority to exercise capital punishment in the time of Jesus.

T. A. Burkill argues unequivocally that the Sanhedrin was competent and had the authority to inflict capital punishment upon a convicted criminal.[54] Two examples from his extensive argument are important in recognizing the competency of the Sanhedrin in the time of Jesus. The first is a letter from Agrippa to Caligula, and the second is an inscription discovered by Clermont-Ganneau in 1871. Agrippa's letter, written in AD 40, informs Caligula of the Jewish response to anyone violating the ancient customs associated with the inmost part of the temple. He writes,

> And if anyone else, I will not say of the Jews, but even of the priests, and those not of the lowest order, but even those who are in the rank, next to the first, should go in there, either with him or after him, or even if the very high priest himself should enter in thither on two days in the year, or three or four times on the same day, he is subjected to inevitable death for his impiety.[55]

The letter, written before AD 70, states that the Jews would impose the death penalty on the violators identified therein. Burkill says, "This passage plainly shows that the Sanhedrin during the procuratorial period enjoyed the competence to punish certain religious offenses with death."⁵⁶

The inscription discovered by Clermont-Ganneau in 1871 is a temple warning inscription that hung outside the sanctuary of the Second Temple in Jerusalem. The inscription reads: "No foreigner may enter within the balustrade and enclosure surrounding the sanctuary. And whoever is caught so doing will have himself to blame that his death ensues."⁵⁷ This shows that the Sanhedrin was entitled to put any Gentile to death if they violated the mandate of the inscription. Josephus tells us that there is more to this inscription than meets the eye. Titus reminds the Jews that they have the support of Rome in protecting the temple from desecration. Titus says,

> Have not you been allowed to put up the pillars thereto belonging at due distances, and on it to engrave in Greek and in your own letters, this prohibition that no foreigner should go beyond that wall? Have not we given you leave to kill such as go beyond it, though he were a Roman?⁵⁸

It is remarkable and beyond reasonable disputation that the Jews have a special authority to kill any Roman who ignored the inscribed warning and proceeded to violate the temple. This authority was in effect prior to the destruction of the temple in AD 70. Undoubtedly, there was cooperation between the Jewish and Roman authorities in the pre-AD 70 time period. Claims that the Sanhedrin was not competent to deal with all capital cases are unlikely. Burkill says,

> For if in certain circumstances the Jewish authorities could put a Roman citizen to death, a right which was not even enjoyed by the procurator himself, surely they would be formally empowered to pass and execute a capital sentence on any ordinary Jewish

citizen who was found guilty of a religious offense for which the law of Moses required the infliction of the death penalty.⁵⁹"

Paul Winter agrees with Burkill on the matter of the competency of the Sanhedrin in the time of Jesus. While the power and membership of the Sanhedrin may have varied under changing political circumstances, it was never denied the authority to rule over capital cases during the pre-AD 70 period. Winter says that it is not true that the authority of the Sanhedrin existed as a bifurcated authority. This is in response to those who argue that while the Sanhedrin had the right to pass sentences of death, it had no right to carry out such sentences.⁶⁰ He emphasizes the fact that during the time of procuratorial rule, from AD 6 to AD 70, Jewish law courts passed and carried out death sentences. He adds that even after AD 70, it was not unusual for the Jewish law courts to clandestinely administer the death sentence.

The Romans tried to avoid getting involved in the religious affairs of the nations they occupied. It should not be surprising that they preferred that occupied governments should have enough autonomy to manage their own internal affairs. This does not mean that a procurator withdrew completely from the scene of the provincial government. In the case of Pilate, it appears that his cooperation was designed to maintain peace and order without yielding the initiative beyond his control. Winter says, "There is abundant evidence that even in the period after the death of Jesus, the supreme council of the Jewish nation exercised the function of a judicial tribunal in trying Jews on charges which involved the death penalty."⁶¹

The Gospel accounts tell us that the high priest presided over the Sanhedrin that convicted and sentenced Jesus to be killed. Rather than stone him according to their own law, the Sanhedrin chose to involve Pontius Pilate solely as a means of securing crucifixion as the method of death. While there is a connection between the high priest, the Sanhedrin, and Pontius Pilate, it does not absolutely follow that the Sanhedrin was functioning as an instrument of Roman imperial authority. On the contrary, Roman authority via Pontius Pilate refused to convict and sentence Jesus. In this case, it appears that Roman imperial authority functioned as an instrument of the Sanhedrin. The arguments denying that the Sanhedrin lacked the independent competence and authority to try, sentence, and execute Jesus depend entirely on post-AD 70 Mishnah regulations. The canonical Gospels provide us with cogent and credible narratives. The early Fathers of the Church believed that the Gospel accounts were true records of the trial, death, and resurrection of Jesus. In the face of all arguments, I believe that Winter's final analysis confirms with certainty the competency and authority of the Sanhedrin in the time of Jesus. Without evasion or hesitation, Winter says,

The conclusion is inescapable: before the year 70 CE, the Sanhedrin had full jurisdiction over Jews charged with offenses against Jewish religious law, and had the authority openly to pronounce and carry out sentences of death where such penalty was provided in Jewish legislation. Not before 70 CE was the Sanhedrin deprived of its right to administer capital punishment to persons it had tried and sentenced to death.[62]

Chapter Six

Excursus: Martin Luther's Hatred of the Jews

An excursus is defined as a digression that contains a further exposition of some point or topic. While researching information on the authority of the Sanhedrin during the time of Jesus, I became curious as to what Martin Luther might have said relative to this topic. To my surprise, I did not find any information provided by him on this subject. This doesn't mean that he was oblivious to the role of the Sanhedrin in the history of Israel. He was, after all, a distinguished professor of Old Testament at the University of Wittenberg. He assembled a group of scholars to assist him in translating the Scriptures into the German language, and he referred to this translation committee as his "Sanhedrin."

Surprising Discoveries

What I did discover about Luther left me somewhat jaded in my opinion of his life and work. I slowly realized that the authority of the Sanhedrin at the trial of Jesus held no interest for Luther because he had already decided beyond doubt or argument that the Jews killed Jesus. As I read page after page, I began to realize the intensity of Luther's hatred of the Jews. The question that occurred to me was, "Why isn't this aspect of

Luther's life and work common knowledge among Protestant Christians?" It appears that the general public is mostly unaware of Luther's hatred of the Jews. Perhaps we should not find this surprising; however, it is unforgivable that responsible, educated clergy and students of theology and church history should ignore this contemptible aspect of Luther's life and career. To remain silent in the knowledge of such hatred of an entire race of people is a violation of the very Gospel message that Jesus commands us to embrace and reflect in our daily lives.

The story of Luther that was forming in my mind was very different from the one that had been presented in church history classes offered during my seminary studies. I thought that perhaps I had not been listening carefully when lectures and assignments reflecting Luther's hatred of the Jews were discussed. I reviewed my church history textbooks and lecture notes and found nothing but praises for the great Reformer and his courage in breaking away from the corrupt papal power as represented by the Roman Catholic Church of his day. I once again read the theological positions that established the foundations of Protestantism throughout the world. They were not foreign to me and had, indeed, been proclaimed in my preaching and teaching across fifty years of ministry as a parish minister and military chaplain.

Notable Critics of Luther

The first paper I wrote for a church history class in seminary was a paper comparing Martin Luther to John Wesley. As a United Methodist, I was very interested in Wesleyan theology. I knew that Wesley had referenced Luther's Epistle to the Romans as having a great influence on his own spiritual journey. Wesley wrote the following in his personal journal,

> In the evening, I went very unwillingly to a society in Aldersgate-Street, where one was reading Luther's preface to the Epistle to

the Romans. About a quarter before nine, while he was describing the change that God works in the heart through faith in Christ, I felt my heart strangely warmed. I felt I did trust in Christ, Christ alone for salvation: And an assurance was given me, that he had taken away *my* sins, even *mine*, and saved *me* from the law of sin and death. I began to pray with all my might for those who had, in a more special manner, despitefully used me and persecuted me.[1]

Wesley's reaction makes it clear that Luther's doctrine of justification by faith in Christ greatly influenced his spiritual life. It is no small thing that he testified that on that occasion, he received assurance of salvation. One might conclude that Wesley was in total agreement with Luther from that experience forward, but that is not the case. He does acknowledge the importance of Luther's work in establishing the foundations of the Reformation. In comparison to himself, he refers to Luther as a "much greater man."[2] Notwithstanding his generous comparison, a close reading of Wesley suggests that he was not completely satisfied with Luther's theology and his attitude and personality as a servant of Jesus Christ.

Wesley did not find the same satisfaction with Luther's *Commentary on the Epistle to the Galatians* as he did with the preface to *The Epistle to the Romans*. Concerning *Galatians,* he said, "Why, not only that the author makes nothing out, clears up not one considerable difficulty; that he is quite shallow in his remarks on many passages, and muddy and confused on almost all; but that he is deeply tinctured with Mysticism, and hence often dangerously wrong."[3] Furthermore, Wesley finds Luther's rejection of reason and good works to be a serious shortcoming of his theology. He says,

> How does he decry reason, right or wrong, as an irreconcilable enemy to the Gospel of Christ! Whereas what is reason (the faculty so called) but the power of apprehending, judging, and discoursing? Which power is no more to be condemned in the

gross, than seeing, hearing, or feeling. Again, how blasphemously does he speak of good works and of the Law of God; constantly coupling the Law with sin, death, hell, or the devil; and teaching that Christ delivers us from them all alike. Whereas, it can no more be proved by Scripture that Christ delivers us from the Law of God, than that he delivers us from holiness or from heaven.[4]

I believe that Wesley recognized something in Luther's writings that suggested an unhealthy influence of the doctrine of justification by faith alone (*sola fide*) on the totality of his theology. Unlike Wesley, Luther seems to ignore the relationship of faith to other aspects of the Gospel, such as love (*agape*), grace, and the efficacy of Christ's sacrifice. A disciple might not understand, or might even reject Luther's concept of *sola fide* as the sole determining factor of a relationship to Jesus Christ and yet remain a beneficiary of other means of saving grace. While recognizing the Reformation victory resulting from Luther's work, Wesley is aware of a polemical turmoil that exists and is produced and sustained by Luther's rigid personality. As I will suggest later, Luther's personality goes beyond mere rigidity and can be defined as pathological.

Wesley clearly questions the validity of Luther's insistence that faith is the single requirement for experiencing the grace of God in Jesus Christ. He speaks of offering the grace of God on one occasion to about fifteen hundred persons through the preaching of the Gospel. He says that the act of people praying for each other and confessing their faults to each other is a powerful vehicle for conveying and experiencing God's grace. He says, "How dare any man deny this to be (as to the substance of it) a means of grace ordained by God?"[5] Wesley then clearly criticizes Luther's rigid commitment to *sola fide* to the exclusion of all other means of grace. He indicates that Luther, "in the fury of his Solifidianism," has become oblivious to the relationship of faith to love and grace.[6] Solifidianism is the doctrine that faith alone and completely void of the performance of any good works is all that is necessary for personal salvation.

The *Epistle of James* presents a strong argument against this claim that "faith alone" is the singular dynamic at work in salvation through Jesus Christ. It highlights and emphasizes the importance of works in the life of a disciple. James says, " So faith by itself, if it has no works, is dead. But someone will say 'You have faith and I have works.' Show me your faith apart from your works, and I by my works will show you my faith" (*James* 2:17-18). Luther took extreme issue with the *Epistle of James*, referring to it as "an epistle of straw" and void of any connection to the Gospel or to Christ. He says,

> We should throw the *Epistle of James* out of this school (i.e., out of the University of Wittenberg), for it doesn't amount to much. It contains not a syllable about Christ. Not once does it mention Christ, except at the beginning (JAS. 1:1; 2:1). ***I maintain that some Jew wrote it*** (bold italics mine) who probably heard about Christian people but never encountered any. Since he heard that Christians place great weight on faith in Christ, he thought, 'Wait a moment! I'll oppose them and urge works alone.' This he did. He wrote not a word about the suffering and resurrection of Christ, although this is what all the apostles preached about. Besides, there's no order or method in the epistle. Now he discusses clothing and then he writes about wrath and is constantly shifting from one to the other.[7]

Wesley is correct in referring to Luther's rigid affirmation of *sola fide* as the "fury of his Solifidianism." His rejection of the *Epistle of James* gives further insight into his pathological attraction and commitment to his faith without a works position. While I have not yet addressed Luther's hatred of the Jews, in the above quotation, I have emphasized the pejorative tone of Luther's claim of, "I maintain that some Jew wrote it." In this statement, his contempt for the Jews is palpable. But his "fury" continues as he turns his opinion into a fact. The anonymous Jew now becomes a real "he" who was motivated to oppose Christians by championing works over faith in Christ! While calling *James* an epistle of straw, he creates his own fictitious character of straw in an effort to discredit the canonical validity of *James*. If we permit ourselves to look and think beyond an easy and customary acceptance of Luther as nothing less than a Reformation hero, we are able to begin to perceive some evidence of the psychological and emotional conflicts that influenced his life and work. Wesley clearly perceived this conflict and identified it as a shortcoming in Luther's work and ministry. He says, "But O! What pity that he had no faithful friend! None that would, at all hazards, rebuke him plainly and sharply, for his rough, untractable spirit, and bitter zeal for opinions, so greatly obstructive of the work of God![8]

Psychological and Emotional Turmoil

Erik Erikson, a leading figure in the field of psychoanalysis and human development, says that Luther was "beset with a syndrome of conflicts."[9] Luther was conflicted in his personal, spiritual, and political life. In every area, he was tormented by guilt. He suffered from a chronic identity crisis which he was never able to resolve to his own peace and satisfaction. His unhappiness began early in his childhood because of his father's excessive control of his life[10]. It is not unusual for a son to experience a period of conflict regarding his identity with his father; however, in Luther's case, the identity conflict involved relationships with three father figures. He could not escape his feeling that his biological father, the Pope, and God all required his loyalty. The demands of these father figures, as he perceived them, created overwhelming multifaceted conflicts and initiated within him a "special mental state bordering on the pathological."[11] Luther's sensitivity to his own emotional instability may have caused him to wonder if he was suffering from demon possession. While serving in the choir at the monastery at Erfurt, Luther fell to the floor and raved like a madman and shouted, "It isn't me!" He did this upon hearing the reading of Mark 9:17-18 which says, "Teacher, I brought my son to you, for he has a dumb spirit; and wherever it seizes him, it dashes him down; and he foams and grinds his teeth and becomes rigid; and I asked your disciples to cast it out, and they were not able." His protestation of, "It isn't me!" is evidence of his concern regarding his own mental and emotional orientation.

Stimulated by his extreme identity crisis and his guilt-ridden nervous system, Luther probably suffered many more erratic displays of emotional instability. Erikson notes that Luther experienced episodes of "terror, sweat, and the fear of fainting."[12] Nervous symptoms often accompanied his preaching. It was not uncommon for him to have spells of dizziness before, during, and after preaching a sermon. He sometimes had nightmares of standing before a congregation and having no plan or concept for the sermon he was expected to preach. In his later years, there were times when he was gripped with anxiety and unable to leave the confines of his house. Applying Freudian psychology, Hartman Guisar portrayed Luther as "a monk obsessed with the lust of the flesh" who became a "pathological, manic-depressive personality."[13] Danish psychiatrist Paul J. Reiter concluded that Luther suffered from a disturbed childhood, a peculiar environment, and workaholism."[14]

Whether or not we agree with the conclusions of these modern psychoanalysts, we can apply the old adage, "Where there is smoke, there must be fire." Also, Luther's own admissions of doubt, despair, and depression quite naturally invite us to construct a personality profile and probe the various incidents that seem to point to a life that frequently exhibited signs of extreme emotional instability. Having said this, I find it necessary to advise that most of us, like Luther, struggle with our own occasions of despair and situational depression as we search for meaning and security in an insecure world. Furthermore, my experience is that those of us among the living generally resist the attempts of those who try to psychoanalyze us and tell us with complete certainty why we do the things we do. We have the prerogative of defending ourselves against these attempts to define us. However, the accused dead no longer have an active voice of self-defense. In light of this and in fairness to Luther, I recognize that it is difficult, if not impossible, to psychoanalyze the dead with any degree of absolute reliable certainty.

We do not have to read very far into the voluminous works of Luther to form some opinions about his character without depending upon the machinations of psychoanalysis. Some things simply speak for themselves. By any standard Luther was stubborn, impulsive, unreasonable and foul-tongued. We do not need the results of psychoanalysis to convince us that he was a rude man who was ready to insult anyone who disagreed with him. This fact is proved by his own admission. He said to his wife, "Wrath just won't turn me loose. Why, I sometimes rage about a piddling thing not worthy of mention. Whoever crosses my path has to suffer for it—I won't say a kind word to anyone. Isn't that a shameful thing?"[15]

On the occasion of meeting Ulrich Zwingli, another influential leader of the Reformation movement, Luther refused to shake hands with Zwingli because he disagreed with his interpretation of the Lord's Supper. In today's vernacular, it appears that Luther was an early advocate of "It's either my way or the highway." As for his despair and depression, he paints a very clear picture for us that requires no complicated psychoanalysis. In his typical crude, anal terms, he speaks of his melancholy response to his life situation:

> When he had for some days felt a pain in his head, he (Martin Luther) said at the table one evening, "Katy, if I don't feel better

tomorrow, I'll have our Hans (their son) brought back from Targau, for I'd like to have him here at my end." Thereupon, Katy said, "See to it, Sir, that you don't imagine things." "No, Katy," the doctor replied, "this is not imagination. I won't die so suddenly. I'll first lie down and be sick, but I won't lie there very long. I'm fed up with the world, and it is fed up with me. I'm quite content with that. The world thinks that if it is only rid of me, everything will be fine, and it will accomplish this. After all, it's as I've often said: I'm like a ripe stool, and the world's a gigantic anus, and so we're about to let go of each other. I thank thee, dear God, that thou dost allow me to stay in thy little flock that suffers persecutions for the sake of thy Word. It's certainly not on account of harlotry or usury that I'm persecuted; of this, I'm sure."[16]

In this single passage, we see Luther's use of crude, anal language and his antipathy for both the Catholic clergy and the Jews. Harlotry was accepted among the clergy, and the Jews were engaged in usury on a grand scale. Luther's persecution complex is obvious in that he is certain that he is being persecuted for his righteousness. This must be so since he does not participate in, nor does he endorse harlotry and usury.

There are other witnesses that suggest that Luther's temperament was not consistent with the Gospel imperatives of love (agape) and forgiveness. He encouraged the people to "take the pope, the cardinals and whatever riffraff belongs to His Idolatrous and Papal Holiness—and tear out their tongues from the back, and nail them on the gallows." Explaining his position, he asked, "Why should we hesitate to use arms against these teachers of perdition, the cardinals, popes, and the whole Roman Sodom, which corrupts the Church of God without end, and wash our hands in their blood?"[17]. This is hardly the rhetoric one would expect from a teacher/preacher/leader steeped in the knowledge of Christ's guidance given in the Sermon on the Mount (Matthew 5:3-7:27).

Those who would say that Luther didn't mean what he said and that he was only speaking figuratively would do well to remember the fate of Thomas Beckett, the Archbishop of Canterbury, who was murdered in AD 1170. When he took a stand against King Henry II, Henry was purported to have said, "Who will rid me of this meddlesome priest?" While the king may not have intended to have issued a direct order, there were those who interpreted it as such. Beckett was hacked to death while kneeling at the altar in Canterbury Cathedral. The voice of any person in whom authority has been vested will always be accompanied by the presumption that the voice provides a license to fulfill the will of that authority figure without any concern for the rhetoric, be it either literal or figurative. In this respect, Luther must accept the charge that he incited his followers to display conduct and behavior contrary to the teachings of Jesus Christ.

John Wesley was not the only notable person who recognized Luther's uncharitable response to anyone who disagreed with him. Georg Wilhelm Friedrich Hegel, one of the greatest systematic thinkers in Western philosophy, accused Luther of creating a system of religion that was just slightly less objectionable than the Roman Catholic Church which he attacked. He saw Luther as a man who had abolished Catholic political authoritarianism only to substitute for it his own ideological authoritarianism.[18] Friedrich Nietzsche also commented on Luther's ill-mannered relationships with people in general. After giving attention to a large collection of Luther's writings, Nietzsche said, "Luther's arrogant, peevishly envious abusiveness—he felt out of sorts unless he was wrathfully spitting upon someone—has quite disgusted me."[19] His assessment of Luther's character was that he lacked good taste and that he was a presumptuous lout. Nietzsche thought that Luther's protests were grounded in his narcissistic arrogance. He said that Luther could not stomach the good etiquette of the church and that he had to raise his voice and insist on being heard. Rather than experience God in the holy of holies, "he wanted above all to speak directly, to speak himself, to speak 'informally' with his God."[20] It should be noted that neither Hegel nor Nietzsche is commenting on Luther's theology. Their observations are based on his qualities of stubborn unreasonableness and vulgar rhetoric. Therefore, their assessments cannot be dismissed on the grounds of religious prejudice and must be seen as valid descriptions of Luther's interactions with people in general, and, more especially, with anyone who disagreed with him.

That Jesus Christ Was Born a Jew

Having considered some of his unattractive personal characteristics, it becomes easier to see how this champion of the Protestant Reformation also had the unhealthy capacity to spew forth an unbridled attack on the Jews. However, this comes after he has spoken of the Jews with favor and with the expectation that they will assuredly embrace Jesus as the Messiah. He expresses this favorable picture of the Jews in his AD 1523 essay entitled *That Jesus Christ Was Born a Jew*. In this essay, he condemned any mistreatment of the Jews. He encouraged Christians to treat Jews kindly with the expectation that upon hearing the Gospel they would convert to Christianity. He said,

> If I had been a Jew and had seen such dolts and blockheads govern and teach the Christian faith, I would sooner have become a hog than a Christian. They have dealt with the Jews as if they were dogs rather than human beings; they have done little else than deride them and seize their property. When they baptize them, they show them nothing of Christian doctrine or life but only subject them to popishness and mockery. . . . If the apostles, who also were Jews, had dealt with us Gentiles as we Gentiles deal with the Jews, there never would have been a Christian among the Gentiles. . . When we are inclined to boast of our position (as

Christians) we should remember that we are but Gentiles, while the Jews are of the lineage of Christ. We are aliens and in-laws; they are blood relatives, cousins, and brothers of our Lord. Therefore, if one is to boast of flesh and blood, the Jews are nearer to Christ than we are. . . . If we really want to help them, we must be guided in our dealings with them not by papal law but by the law of Christian love. We must receive them cordially, and permit them to trade and work with us, that they may have occasion and opportunity to associate with us, hear our Christian teaching, and witness our Christian life. If some of them should prove stiff-necked, what of it? After all, we ourselves are not all good Christians either.[21]

The tolerance and magnanimity reflected in *That Jesus Christ Was Born a Jew* was the exception rather than the rule that defined Luther's life. He held to his own opinions with an attitude of arrogance, rashness, obstinacy, and a non-negotiable demand that others should agree with him without question. Alexander Chalmers says that Luther "poured forth against such as disappointed him, a torrent of invective mingled with contempt."[22] Without revisiting the attempts to psychoanalyze Luther, I will point out that his defensiveness more than likely reflects insecurity and a diminished sense of self-worth. I caution that his boisterous zeal should not be confused with genuine confidence. His demand that his point of view be validated by all is more reflective of self-doubt than it is of personal certitude. However, one thing is certain and that is that anyone who disagreed with Luther instantly became an adversary and an enemy. When contradicted, the violence of his temper seemed to know no bounds. In the German Peasants' War of AD 1524-25, Luther turned against the peasants even though their uprising found its roots in the principles being advocated by Luther's reformation preaching. Luther referred to the peasants as murderous, thieving hordes and directed that they be smitten, stabbed, and slain. As many as one hundred thousand of the peasants were killed, and Luther boasted that his preaching was responsible for defeating them. Luther, the rebel against Roman Catholic authority, took the side of the authoritarian princes against those who looked to him for leadership and support.

On the Jews and Their Lies

Luther's friendly statements about the Jews in *That Jesus Christ Was Born a Jew* were abandoned when the Jews refused to be evangelized and convert to Christianity. As we have seen, Luther simply would not tolerate anyone who failed or refused to conform to his expectations. He turned on the Jews with a vengeance and wrote his treatise entitled *On the Jews and Their Lies*. This treatise was practically unknown in the English-speaking world. A short version was published in English in 1948.[23] The publishers said,

> This translation is the first and only English-language edition of the Great Reformer's treatment of one of the world's most serious problems in human relations. This treatise by Dr. Martin Luther of the Jewish problem has been virtually hidden from the American people and promises to shake, shock, and alert Christian America in a sensational manner.[24]

Furthermore, the publishers reveal that they met with extreme resistance in their attempts to translate Luther's anti-semitic treatise into the English language. They said,

> When we set out to find the book in its original language and when we proceeded to have it translated, we were shocked and amazed at the interference we encountered from a wide variety of sources. Two different translators were made the victims of intimidation, and only after a rather dramatic experience were we able to complete its translation in spite of its brevity.[25]

They concluded that "in effecting the translation of this work, we became increasingly convinced that a well-organized plot to keep this book hidden exists."[26]

My references will be from the translation by Martin H. Bertram which is found in volume 47 of the American version of *Luther's Works*.[27] It is the newest translation of the treatise and includes the complete text. In his preface to the translation, Bertram expresses some concern about making this translation available to the public. He says,

> The thought of possible misuse of this material, to the detriment of either the Jewish people or of Jewish-Christian relations today, has occasioned great misgivings. Both editor and publisher, therefore, wish to make clear at the very outset that publication of this treatise is being undertaken only to make available the necessary documents for scholarly study of this aspect of Luther's thought, which has played so fateful a role in the development of anti-Semitism in Western culture.[28]

Are we to believe that only "scholarly students" are entitled to read the truth about Luther's hatred of the Jews? Or is this an indication that this embarrassing chapter in the history of the churches called Lutheran can only be understood by "scholars" who are capable of making excuses for Luther's vicious attitude toward fellow human beings? This is an insult to anyone capable of reading and interpreting for him/herself what Luther wrote. The irony in suggesting that this treatise is only meant for "scholarly study" is an insult to Luther himself. Wasn't it Luther who insisted that the Scriptures should be translated into the German language so that the common citizen could read them?

The difficulties encountered by the 1948 publishers, along with Bertram's reservations about translating the treatise, confirms my suspicion that the leaders of the Lutheran churches tried to hide the ugly picture of their founder reflected by treatises such as these. In retrospect, I realize that my experience has been that Luther's hatred of the Jews is still unknown to many, if not most, American Protestants. Out of curiosity, I have asked more than 1,000 American church attendees what they know about Martin Luther. They represented many different faith groups and some of them were Lutherans. The standard response was that they were aware of his act of nailing ninety-five theses to a church door. Some mentioned indulgences and/or Luther's quarrel with the Roman Catholic Church of his day. I asked each person if they were aware of Luther's anti-semitic writings and his negative attitude toward the Jews. Not a single person responded in the affirmative. Those who identified themselves as Lutherans were shocked by my question. Some said that they did not believe it to be true. I am not claiming that my limited survey represents a valid scientific study. However, I do suggest that it reflects the suppression of an ugly and reprehensible chapter in the life and work of Martin Luther. His recorded hatred of the Jews raises some questions. Was he the primary voice and authority for promulgating the long, black tradition of Christian mistreatment of Jews? Did his hatred of the Jews inspire the Nazi propagandists whose evil cause resulted in the Holocaust? These questions will be considered after examining Luther's intolerant attitude toward the Jews.

The English translation by Bertram consists of one hundred sixty-nine pages and cannot be fully included here. It falls into four major sections. In the first section, he denounces the Jews as bragging liars. In the second part, he says that the Jews do not know how to accurately exegete and interpret their own Scriptures. In the third part, he lists many of the blasphemies that the Jews have promulgated against Jesus and Mary. The fourth section is the most scathing of all of Luther's attacks on the Jews. He goes so far as to say, "We are at fault for not slaying them."[29] In this section, he moves from a description of the Jewish situation to a prescription of how to deal with it. He makes recommendations to the German church and German political authorities as to what actions should be taken against the Jews. Unfortunately, history has proved that Luther's prescription would have no expiration date and would be refilled, ingested, and implemented by the National Socialists. Karl Jaspers said, "In this treatise, you have the whole Nazi program."[30]

The occasion for Luther's vicious treatise, *On the Jews and Their Lies*, was a request from Count Schlick of Moravia to provide a refutation to a Jewish pamphlet that presented a negative description of Christianity. Luther tells us that prior to this request, he had decided not to write anymore "neither of the Jews or against the Jews."[31] However, he accepted the request to respond to the Jewish attack on Christianity, and he gave the following reason for his decision to again write about the Jews. He said,

> But since I learned that these miserable and accursed people do not cease to lure to themselves even us, that is, the Christians, I have published this little book, so that I might be found among those who opposed such poisonous activities of the Jews and who warned the Christians to be on their guard against them. I would not have believed that a Christian could be duped by the Jews into taking their exile and wretchedness upon himself. However, the Devil is the God of the world, and wherever God's word is absent he has an easy task, not only with the weak, but also with the strong. May God help us. Amen.[32]

At the time of this writing, Luther had abandoned his earlier optimism that the Jews could be converted to Christianity. For him, this had become an impossible task. As a matter of fact, efforts to evangelize them had made them more obstinate. He says, "Therefore, I do not wish to have anything more to do with any Jew. As St. Paul says, they are consigned to wrath; the more one tries to help them, the baser and more stubborn they become. Leave them to their own devices."[33] And what are their devices? He says,

> They are nothing but thieves and robbers who daily eat no morsel and wear no thread of clothing which they have not stolen and pilfered from us by means of their accursed usury. Thus, they live

from day to day, together with wife and child, by theft and robbery, as arch-thieves and robbers, in the most impenitent security. For a usurer is an arch-thief and a robber who should rightly be hanged on the gallows seven times higher than other thieves.[34]

Luther is particularly angered by the self-righteous boasting of the Jews. He says that they consider non-Jews to be heathens, sub-human, and lower than worms in the eyes of God. On the other hand, Jews consider themselves to be so exalted that they can stand before God and pester him as much as they like. Because of who they are, they claim that "God has to endure that in their synagogues, their prayers, songs, doctrines, and their whole life, they come and stand before him and plague him grievously."[35] In fact, Luther says that the Jewish schools are nothing more than the devil's nest where the devil constantly praises himself. The boasting of the Jews is ludicrous and is carried on without any reason for the boasting. They have been conquered and dispersed time and again. Rejected by God, they no longer have the land of Canaan or the city of Jerusalem, and they are without the temple that they so highly prized. They are suffering the consequences of their rebellious conduct. Luther says, "Rejecting the truth of God, they have to believe instead such abominable, stupid, inane lies, and that instead of the beautiful face of the divine word, they have to look into the devil's black, dark, lying behind, and worship his stench."[36]

He accused the Jews of being dishonest with their own Scriptures. When their interpretations did not agree with his, he dismissed them and complained that they had replaced the authority of the Word of God with the teachings of their rabbis. He was particularly critical of the usury which was practiced by the Jews. According to Luther, gold, silver, and jewels represented the only messiah that the Jews respected. He said,

Their breath stinks with lust for the Gentile's gold and silver; for no nation under the sun is greedier than they were, still are, and always will be, as is evident from their accursed usury. So they comfort themselves that when the Messiah comes, he will take the gold and silver of the whole world and divide it among them."[37]

In addition to usury, Luther says that the Talmud and the rabbis claim that Jews can kill non-Jews without committing a sin, break any oath they make to a non-Jew, and steal and rob with impunity. He says, "The Jews still persist in such doctrine to the present day. They imitate their fathers and pervert God's word. They are steeped in greed, in usury, they steal and murder, where they can, and on and ever teach their children to do likewise."[38]

Much of Luther's hatred of the Jews is to be found in the Jewish blasphemies against Jesus and Mary. The Jews called the Virgin Mary a whore. Luther cites one poisonous rabbi who doesn't call Jesus' mother "Maria but calls her Haria, which means a dungheap."[39] They called Jesus the child of a whore whose birth resulted from an adulterous relationship. Luther says that only devils would speak this way and that all of these claims came from the father of the Jews, who was indeed, the Devil.

He says,

Therefore dear Christian, be advised and do not doubt that next to the devil, you have no more bitter, venomous, and vehement foe than a real Jew who earnestly seeks to be a Jew . . . the history books often accuse them of contaminating wells, of kidnaping and piercing children.[40]

The Jews whined and complained that they were victims and said that they were being held captive in Germany. Luther called their complaints a "fine, thick fat lie." He said, "We do not know to the present day which Devil brought them into our country. We surely did not bring them from Jerusalem!"[41] He points out that no one is holding them and that they may leave any time they wish to leave. As a matter of fact, the Germans would like to get rid of the Jews because "They are a heavy burden, a plague, a pestilence, a sheer misfortune for our country."[42] They will not leave because they are enjoying the best of all living conditions in Germany! They get rich off their usury and are "lazy gluttons and guzzlers." The Jews claim that they have no homeland, but they live better in Germany than they could in any homeland of their own. Luther's assessment is that the Jews, being expert robbers and liars, have learned to use the Germans' own wealth to enslave them.

Having described the situation, Luther now writes a prescription for the solution to the Jewish problem. He says, "What shall we Christians do with this rejected and condemned people, the Jews?"[43] His final solution comes in the form of seven recommendations:

1. Set fire to their synagogues or schools and cover with dirt, whatever will not burn, so that no man will ever again see a stone or cinder of them. All who are able toss in sulphur and pitch; it would be good if someone could also throw in some hellfire.

2. I advise that their houses also be razed and destroyed. For they pursue in them the same aims as in their synagogues. Instead, they might be lodged under a roof or in a barn, like the gypsies.

3. I advise that their prayer books and Talmudic writings, in which such idolatry, lies, cursing, and blasphemy are taught, be taken from them.

4. I advise that their rabbis be forbidden to teach henceforth on pain of loss of life and limb.

5. I advise that safe-conduct on the highways be abolished completely for the Jews. They have no business in the countryside. Let them stay at home.

6. I advise that usury be prohibited to them, and that all cash and treasure of silver and gold be taken from them and put aside for

safekeeping. The reason for such a measure is that they have no other means of earning a living than by usury, and by it they have stolen and robbed from us all they possess.

7. I recommend putting a flail, an ax, a hoe, a spade, a distaff, or a spindle into the hands of young, strong Jews and Jewesses and letting them earn their bread in the sweat of their brow. For it is not fitting that they should let us accursed Goyim toil in the sweat of our faces while they, the holy people, idle away their time behind the stove, feasting and farting, and on top of all, boasting blasphemously of their lordship over the Christians by means of our sweat. No, one should toss out these lazy rogues by the seat of their pants.[44]

If these prescribed remedies fail to remedy the Jewish problem, then the Jews should be driven entirely from the country as has happened in France, Spain, Bohemia, and other countries. This should be done because "as we have heard, God's anger with them is so intense that gentle mercy will only tend to make them worse and worse, while sharp mercy will reform them but little. Therefore, in any case, away with them!"[45]

Luther felt no remorse for his harsh final solution. He challenged others to offer an alternative if they didn't like his advice. As for him, he has had enough of the spitting, raving Christ-cursing Jews. He finds it intolerable that the Jews, being guests in their land, spit upon the Lord Jesus Christ and wish for the death and misfortune of all Christians. Luther concludes by reaffirming that the Jews are poisonous vipers and possessed of all the devils. He says, "Finally, I wish to say this for myself: If God were to give me no other Messiah than such as the Jews wish and hope for, I would much, much rather be a sow than a human being."[46]

More Demonization of the Jews

A few weeks after writing *On the Jews and Their Lies*, Luther wrote another scathing and denigrating treatise about the Jews entitled *Vom*

Schem Haphtoras und Vom Geschlecht Christi. The first part, *Vom Schem Hamphoras* is translated as *Of the Unknowable Name,* and the second part, *Vom Geschlecht Christi* is translated as *The Generations of Christ.* It is not surprising that this work is practically unknown among American Protestants. The only complete translation into English is in Gerhard Falk's book, published in 1992 and currently out of print.[47] This treatise is not pleasant to read. It has been said that this is the ugliest and linguistically dirtiest document that Luther had ever written. It is a work of mocking sarcasm and bitter contempt flavored with disgusting scatological flourishes. It displays Luther's unnatural interest in loading his insults with references to excrement and feces. His obscene preoccupation with scatological references can be found throughout this treatise. It appears that Luther believed that the most effective way to insult the Jews and fight the devil was to mock them using "crap/dung/shit and piss."[48]

In the first section, *Of the Unknowable Name,* Luther claims that the Jews made up an unbelievable story about Christ. They said that Christ found a stone in the Jerusalem temple with the Shem Hamphoras (the unknowable name of God) written upon it. He used the stone to perform miracles and became a wicked magician. The Jews learned how Christ had gotten his power through learning the "unknowable name" inscribed on the stone in the temple. Judas Iscariot also found the stone and was empowered to utter the Schem Hamphoras. The Jews sent Judas, armed with this power, to confront the Christ. Judas spoke the magic name and broke the arm of the so-called Christ while wrestling with him. The angry Israelites grabbed the Christ, beat him, and hung him on a large cabbage stem that was strong enough to hold more than one hundred pounds of seed pods.[49] This ridiculous account and many more like it can be found in the *Toldot Yeshu.* For instance, Jesus is called a "bastard and the son of a whore and a menstruating woman."[50] It also says, "The Jesus whom

Christians adore is not God. Rather, he is and was an accused fraud, and his mother Mary, whom Christians worship, was a great whore and a cheap woman."[51]

The *Toldot Yeshu* can be dated to as early as the tenth century, and some scholars date it as early as the fourth century. It had been used to entice Jews who had become Christians to return to Judaism. These awful stories, widely circulated by the Jews, had always been an abomination to Christians who accused the Jews of reciting these lies to increase Jewish-Christian tensions. In part two of his treatise, Luther was reacting against Jews who sought to influence Christians to depart from their faith. Luther, in the most vulgar and offensive terms, mocked the mystical practices and superstitions associated with the magic of the divine name of God. Wondering where the Jews got their secret information, he says, "they looked up the ass of their God."[52] In the event that they didn't find it there, he says, "they found it outside of scripture in the piss of Judas and in their Jewish sweat."[53] Luther criticized the Jews for failing to realize that the Hebrew word "alma" in Isaiah 7:14 refers not to just a young woman, but a young woman who is a virgin. They are so blind that they do not see that the young woman referred to is the Virgin Mary, who is prophesied to give birth to Immanuel (Jesus). He also refuted the claim of the Jews that Jesus was not a part of the tribe of Judah and that he was not descended from the family of David. He said,

> We Christians know (and no devil or Jew can deny it) that the Messiah must come from the house of David. As he does not have a father, but only a mother, the mother must, of course, be David's daughter. Therefore, whoever believes that Jesus, born of the Virgin Mary, is the true Messiah has already acknowledged, sealed, and proved that his mother, Mary must be of the house of David, as certain or more certain as her bridegroom Joseph.[54]

He concludes that the Jewish interpretation is "not more than Jew-piss and Jew-sweat."⁵⁵ Luther's intent is to present the Germans with firm evidence that the Jews were guilty of consistently blaspheming against Jesus Christ, God's chosen Messiah. He hoped that this proof would convince the German Protestant princes to expel the Jews from their lands.

At the beginning of *On the Unknowable Name*, Luther makes it clear that he has no hope of converting the Jews because that would be "about as possible as converting the devil."⁵⁶ He thinks that the Jewish heart is so hard that it cannot be changed by any means. As to their boasting about their lineage, they are completely wrong because they are the devil's children and damned to hell. Having called God a liar and insisting on having their own stiff-necked way, they were conquered many times and finally driven from their homeland. Consequently, Jerusalem was destroyed, and their temple was burned to the ground. Not one stone was left on another. According to Jeremiah, they had been elected to be God's mouth: "If you utter what is precious, and not what is worthless, you shall be as my mouth" (Jeremiah 15:19). Out of the stubbornness of their hearts they disobeyed God and cut themselves off from his protection: "But my people did not listen to my voice; Israel would have none of me. So I gave them over to their stubborn hearts, to follow their own counsels" (Psalm 81:11-12). As to the misfortunes that have befallen the Jews over the years, Luther says that they got what they deserved. They have been polluted and squirted full of devil's filth, which oozes from all parts of their body and their senses. He says that the Jews enjoy their freedom from God. He says, "Yes, that tastes good to them, into their hearts, they smack their lips like swine. That is how they want it. Call more: 'Crucify him, crucify him.' Scream more: 'His blood come upon us and our children'" (Matthew 27:25).

Luther says that if he were asked where the Jews got their information and their interpretation of Scripture that he could only guess that they got it from "looking up a sow's ass."[57] He draws this conclusion based on an image carved on the outer wall of the Wittenberg church. The carving has the Latin-Hebrew inscription: "Rabini Schem Ha Mphoras," which is translated as "The name of God interpreted by a rabbi." Luther says,

> Here in Wittenberg, in our parish church, there is a sow carved into the stone under which lie young pigs and Jews who are sucking; behind the sow stands a rabbi who is lifting up the right leg of the sow, raises the behind of the sow, bows down and looks with great effort into the Talmud under the sow, as if he wanted to read and see something most difficult and exceptional; no doubt they gained their Shem Hamphoras from that place.[58]

The *Judensau* (Jew's sow) motif was widely displayed across medieval Europe. It was an image that mocked Jews and Judaism and promoted hatred of the Jews. The *Judensau* image adorned a wall of the very church where Luther regularly preached. In commenting on the image, Luther proposed that the Jewish rabbis were looking for God in the backside of a sow. For him, the interpretation of the rabbis did not reflect the Word of God because their interpretations were nothing more than the kind of filth that comes out of the belly of a sow.

He continues to demonize the Jews and their rabbis and insists that their teachings come from the devil. He says,

> For that too is their sin, which cannot be worse, for they do not only have contempt for you, the righteous and eternal God, by insubordination and disdain for your word, but seek to make you into the Devil and servant of all the devils, that you, with your magnificent divine power should be witness and serve the Devil in his lies, insults and murder, and whatever else is the Devil's work.[59]

Jews have nothing left of their future but darkness, lies, and miseries. Moses' law is no longer in effect and is to no avail. They think of themselves as "circumcised saints," but circumcision of the flesh no longer accounts for anything because they have become nothing more than outcasts from Israel who pretend as if they were Jews. Luther says, "That they circumcise themselves, that the Turks do also, and is no more a true sign of Jewish kind or blood, but a real den of cutthroats, full of all kinds of meanness and loutishness, to damage country and citizens and to make life hard for them."[60]

Luther was certain that the devil had possessed the Jews and taken them as prisoners. They no longer had any will of their own but were permanently controlled by the devil. His antagonism and hatred continued to the end of his life as is expressed in his last public sermon. On 15 February 1546, three days before his death, he preached his last sermon and ended it with a warning against the Jews. He said,

> This is how the Jews act: every day they blaspheme and insult our Lord Christ. If this is done with our knowledge, we should not allow it. So long as we tolerate those among us who defame, blaspheme and curse our Lord Jesus Christ, we thereby participate in their sins. Indeed I have sins enough of my own. Therefore you rulers should not endure them (the Jews) but instead drive them out. If, however, they convert, give up their usury, and accept Christ, then we should gladly consider them our brothers.

> Nothing will come of it though, for they go too far. They are our public enemies. They endlessly blaspheme Christ, call the Virgin Mary a whore, Christ her bastard. They refer to us as changelings or fatted calves, and if they could kill us all they would do so gladly. And often they do, too, especially those who claim to be doctors, although they occasionally help. But it is the Devil who finishes up their work. This is what makes their practice of medicine so potent. And in foreign countries there are some (Jewish doctors) who can poison someone so that he will die within an hour, a month, or a year, even in ten or twenty years. This is one of their skills.

So don't get involved with them. For they do nothing among you other than horribly blaspheme our dear Lord Jesus Christ and exploit our bodies, our lives and our possessions. As a child of our country I want to end by warning you that you must not participate in the sins of others and I assert this good and truly to the Lord and his subjects. If the Jews wish to convert to us and put an end to their blasphemy and the other things they have done to us, then we will forgive them gladly. Otherwise, we should not tolerate them nor allow them to live among us.[61]

A preoccupation with the Jews—one might say an obsessive-compulsive response to Jews and Judaism—was a life-long issue with Luther. At no point in his life did he consider that the rabbis were committed to a legitimate exegesis and interpretation of the Old Testament. This, along with their practice of usury and their refusal to convert to Christianity, was a source of his increased defamation and demonization of the Jews. Ultimately, he gave up all hope for the Jews. He saw them as the enemies of God who were in league with the devil. He finally said, "Here, I will let it go and have nothing more to do with the Jews."[62]

Has it made any historical difference that Luther expressed hatred of the Jews five hundred years ago? We might conclude that he was a man writing for his own time and shouldn't be held responsible for anything that resulted from his anti-Semitic contributions during his own life. Such a statement would introduce a "double-edged" sword to any assessment. If he is to be remembered and applauded for any positive contributions to history, it necessarily follows that his negative contributions should be considered as well. At the funeral of Julius Caesar, Shakespeare has Mark Antony say, "The evil that men do lives after them; the good is oft interred with their bones."[63] Luther's hateful and disgusting writings about the Jews lived after him. The force of his words served to provide a foundation for brutal, inhuman, evil acts against an entire race of people.

Strangely enough, Luther did not arrive at his hatred through extensive contact and dealings with Jews. When he began his tenure at the University of Wittenberg, there weren't many Jews left in the territory. The larger territories and cities had already expelled their Jewish population. Mark Edwards says, "Only on rare occasions did Luther encounter Jews: He never lived in close proximity to them, but he inherited a tradition, both theological and popular, of hostility toward them."[64] It appears that Luther's hatred was based on popular second-hand rumors and anecdotes, his frustration with the failure of the Jews to accept his Christological interpretation of the Scriptures, and their refusal to convert to his brand of religion.

When seen in this light, it becomes clearer that Luther's hatred was centered in his own stubborn insistence that he should be recognized as the single authoritative word on how the Jews should live and worship. His stubbornness extended beyond the Jews. He considered anyone whose views differed from his own to be a fanatic.[65] He arrogantly assumed that he had the right to censor what happened in someone else's religious meeting. He denied them the right to interpret their own book of worship and labeled their use of the Old Testament as the "filth and piss of Judas."[66] I believe that Alan Dershowitz's modern-day assessment of Luther opens the door for further insight into the impact of Luther's hatred of the Jews over the past five-hundred years. He says,

> Toward the end of his life and at the height of his influence—Luther articulated a specific program against the Jews which served as bible of anti-Jewish actions over the next four centuries, culminating in the Holocaust. In many ways, Luther can be viewed as the spiritual predecessor of Adolf Hitler. Indeed, virtually all the themes that eventually found their way into Hitler's genocidal writings, rantings, and actions are adumbrated in Martin Luther's infamous essay "Concerning the Jews and Their lies." It is shocking that his ignoble name is still honored

rather than forever cursed by mainstream Protestant churches. The continued honoring of Luther conveys a dangerous message, a message that was not lost on Hitler: namely, that a person's other accomplishments will earn him a position of respect in history, even if he has called for the destruction of world Jewry.[67]

From Luther to Hitler to the Holocaust

Is there a direct line from Luther's writings to Hitler and the National Socialist Party? It would be foolish to say that Luther anticipated the rise to power of a Hitlerian character. However, this does not absolve Luther of the twentieth-century treatment of Jews by the Germans. The nature of what I consider to be his culpability will be addressed later. For now, I think it would be foolishly irresponsible to fail to recognize the direct line that does exist between Luther and Hitler's National Socialist Party. For years, the Lutheran churches have tried to ignore and hide Luther's anti-Semitic ravings from the general public. Even their own church members have been shielded from any knowledge of these ugly writings. The editors complained that there was "pressure to omit Luther's anti-Semitic writing from the American version of *Luther's Works.*"[68] One of the reasons for this pressure was the embarrassment that would result from a comparison of Luther's last sermon and Hitler's last testament. Hitler ended his last will with a warning against the Jews, and Luther warned that the Jews were Germany's public enemies who should be driven out.

In November 1938, an organized pogrom against Jews swept across Germany and Austria. It came to be called *The Kristallnacht Pogrom* or *The Night of Broken Glass.* It was a night that brought beatings, riots, looting, and the wholesale destruction of synagogues and Jewish property. Notwithstanding the horrors of this experience, the German Lutheran bishop Martin Sasse rejoiced that the Nazi regime was taking action to rid the Reich of the Jews. As a foreword to the reprint of Luther's treatise *On the Jews And Their Lies,* Sasse wrote,

On 10 November 1938, on Luther's birthday, the synagogues in Germany are aflame . . . the power of the Jews in economic affairs in the new Germany is finally broken by the German people, and thus is capped the blessed struggle of our Leader (Hitler) for the complete liberation of our people. . . . In this hour the voice must be heard of the man, who, as the German prophet in the 16th century, began first out of ignorance as a friend of the Jews and who, driven by his conscience, driven by experience and reality, became the greatest anti-Semite of his time, the warner of his people against the Jews. In this treatise Luther alone should speak to us in his own words. His voice is even today still stronger than the pitiful God-forsaken and elitist international Jew-friends and scholars who know nothing more about Luther's work and will.[69]

Sasse was a prominent leader in the German Christian movement, which consisted of pastors, bishops, theologians, and laypeople. They fully supported Hitler and wanted to create a Nazified German Protestant Church that was anti-Semitic. The movement attracted at least a third of German Protestant church members and organized itself on the model of the Nazi Party. They placed a swastika on the altar next to the cross and gave the Nazi salute at their rallies. Many of the Reich assemblies closed with the singing of Luther's hymn, *A Mighty Fortress Is Our God.*" One verse ends with, "His Kingdom shall last forever."[70] The German word for kingdom is *Reich*. Certainly, Luther was referring to the Kingdom of God, but one doesn't have to stretch the imagination very far to see an excited anti-Semitic congregation of German Protestants subliminally associating Luther's Reich with Hitler's Third Reich. Nietzsche saw the existence of this connection between the people and their commitment to their national Reich prior to the emergence of the National Socialist movement of the twentieth century. He paraphrases a verse from Luther's hymn: "If they take from us, body, goods, honor, child and wife; let it go—the Reich must yet remain to us." He then exclaims, "Yes! Yes! The Reich!"[71] He saw that this love of the "Reich" was actually a love of power, and he believed that lust for power was the demon that drove man to act as he did. Therefore, he was not praising the "Reich," rather, he was denouncing it. The German people had become willing to risk their lives, their treasures, and their children for the power offered them by the "Reich." In nineteen hundred and thirty-nine, Pierre van Passen wrote,

> Germany is much farther on the road to dechristianization than the Soviet Union, even if the churches in the Reich remain open and the incense still rises from the altars. In the place of God has come the would-be almighty state which, insatiable as the Moloch of old, demands man's entire devotion, mentally and physically. Whatever is of service to the state, be it mass murder or the worst of crimes, that alone is good and worthy of emulation and respect.[72]

It was an easy thing for them to merge God's kingdom with their national kingdom so that they became equals in Hitler's National Socialist hierarchy of power. It would be naïve not to think that Luther's great beloved hymn did not excite and bolster the national zeal.

Bishop Sasse was not the only voice that promoted the Nazi cause through the name of Luther. In fact, Martin Luther had become the paradigmatic German Christian among Germans. It should be no surprise that Hitler exploited his name at every opportunity. He regarded Luther as one of the greatest men in German history. In 1932, he said, "Luther, if he could be with us, would give us National Socialists his blessing."[73] Ultimately, any action taken against the Jews could be justified simply by referring to something that Martin Luther had said. Just about every book printed during the Third Reich contained citations referencing quotes by Luther. His picture appeared on postcards and other publications.

The horrors of *Kristallnacht*, also known as *Reich Pogrom Night*, provided the impetus needed to initiate the final solution and propel the evil intentions beyond the point of no return. Diarmaid MacCulloch says,

"Luther's pamphlet on Jews and Their Lies (1543) is a blueprint for the Nazi's *Kristallnacht* of 1938."[74] Indeed, the Nazi template for executing the final solution can be perfectly superimposed upon Luther's prescription for getting rid of the Jews. His blueprint was closely followed as the Nazis first burned synagogues, forbade them to do business as merchants, refused to let them live among them, and took away their homes. Next, they deported them, took their money and valuables from them, and subjected them to forced labor under inhuman conditions. Finally, they killed at least six million Jews. Undoubtedly, they were aware of Luther's lament, "We are at fault in not slaying them. Rather, we allow them to live freely in our midst despite all their murdering, cursing, blaspheming, lying and defaming."[75] A comparison of Luther's prescribed actions against the Jews with what the Nazis actually did shows that there was no crime committed by the Nazis that Luther had not ordered in *On the Jews and Their Lies*. His proposed program of getting rid of the Jews was carried out four hundred years later by Adolf Hitler.

To what extent did Luther's writings influence the crimes committed by Hitler and the Nazis? I tend to agree with Alan Davies who has written: "Without the Church, Hitler would not have been possible."[76] It is a matter of record that within Germany, Luther's word and work had the authority of Scripture. Falk goes so far as to say that the Holocaust is a direct outcome of Luther's teachings.[77] One can hardly deny that the Nazis invoked Luther's protective authority, and it does appear that both Luther's and Hitler's Jew-hatred share a common historic tradition.

It should be noted that Luther did not develop his hatred of the Jews apart from his Catholic origins. His anti-Semitism did not begin with his departure from Rome. He brought his anti-Semitism to his reformation life and simply built upon what he had been taught by the Catholic Church. Although he was finally excommunicated, it may be said that with regard to the Jews, he was a true son of the Catholic Church. This is reflected in his major writings which, in one way or another, touch upon all the anti-Jewish ideas written, spoken, or depicted in the literature, art, and music of the Catholic Church. These teachings and traditions, along with his personality flaws and immense capacity for hatred, fueled his anger against the Jews. Hitler seized the leverage afforded him by Luther's writings, but much of what Hitler did to the Jews had already been done in previous years by the Catholic Church. From the time that the Christian Church was officially recognized by Constantine in AD 325, the Jews had lived in misery and were seen to have been discarded by God because they were "Christ killers." In AD 1215, at the Fourth Lateran Council in Rome, the Catholic Church "finally ordered that all Jews had to wear special clothes and a yellow star to make certain that Christians would not deal with them."[78] Wearing the yellow star of Jewish identity did not originate with Nazi Germany. The Nazis simply adopted one of the humiliating tactics previously used by the Catholic Church.

Both the Catholic Church and the German Lutheran Protestant Church were responsible for Hitler's rise to power and for the subsequent Holocaust that was inflicted upon the Jews of Europe. Hitler did not come to power by usurping any person or institution that was in authority. The Christian Germans voted him into power and supported him with their public festivals and the delirious enthusiasm reflected in their mass rallies. Pope Pius XII remained silent as the Jews were murdered. German Lutherans had been taught by Martin Luther to regard Jews with hatred and suspicion. Luther's influence did not die with him. Richard Gutteridge says that Luther's anti-Semitism "provided each successive Protestant generation with not only the excuse but also the sanction for animosity and persecution."[79]

The Holocaust presents us with, perhaps, the darkest chapter in human history. It has already been suggested that the Holocaust could not have happened without Luther and the Church. This is a strong suggestion, and there are arguments on both sides of that issue. However, what cannot be denied is the fact that Lutheranism at large has attempted to conceal and/or neutralize the culpability of Martin Luther in the misery inflicted on the Jews over the past five hundred years. While Luther's theology has been translated and distributed throughout the world, his disgusting Jew-hating writings have gone untranslated and unavailable to the public at large. Lutheran scholars have turned themselves "inside out" in their efforts to explain away Luther's personality flaws and his obvious hatred of the Jews. The defenses offered by most of these educated Lutheran scholars are laughable and represent convoluted efforts to deny the obvious. For instance, one argument says that Luther's polemic against Judaism does not represent personal hatred of the Jews but is more like the simple corrective measure of "spanking our children."[80] Any comparison such as this is unconscionable!

Professor Roland Bainton (1894-1984) wrote *Here I Stand: A Life of Martin Luther*. His book sold a million copies and is widely used as a textbook. Surprisingly, he largely ignores Luther's vulgar, hate-filled, anti-Semitic writings. Of the 422 pages in the book, Bainton spends less than two pages on the topic of Luther's attitude toward the Jews. He certainly understands the severity of Luther's hatred as is indicated by his comment that "One could wish that Luther had died before ever this tract was written."[81] He justifies Luther's writings by claiming that Luther did not intend to revile the Jews but was actually trying to establish for them "a more secure position than they enjoyed in his day."[82] Such are the ridiculous arguments used to justify Luther's hatred of the Jews.

The Missouri Synod of the Lutheran Church seeks to dissociate itself from Luther's hatred of the Jews by disingenuously placing him in a charitable light. They do this in their "Resolution 3-09, 'To Clarify Position on Anti-Semitism,' of the Missouri Synod of the Lutheran Church, July 1983." They say, "Resolved, That in that light, we personally and individually adopt Luther's final attitude toward the Jewish people, as evidenced in his last sermon: 'We want to treat them with Christian love and to pray for them, so that they might become converted and would receive the Lord.'" This sounds charitable and in keeping with Christian conduct; and it would be if it were not wrapped in a cloak of deceit. The words cited do not represent Luther's complete statement regarding his warning about the Jews. A real acceptance of Luther's final attitude requires a completion of the statement cited. The complete final attitude reads as: "Yet, we will show them Christian love and pray that they may be converted to receive the Lord, whom they should honor properly before us. ***Whoever will not do this is no doubt a malicious Jew who will not stop blaspheming Christ, draining you dry, and if he can, killing you***" (bold italics mine). A few sentences later, Luther concludes, "If the Jews wish to convert to us and put an end to blasphemy and the other things they have done to us, then we will forgive them gladly. ***Otherwise, we should not tolerate them nor allow them to live among us***" (bold italics mine).[83]

To their credit, the Evangelical Lutheran Church in America adopted a position that acknowledged the complicity of their tradition within the history of hatred as reflected in Luther's anti-Semitic writings. They accepted the truth that the Holocaust was connected to Martin Luther. Based on that truth, they declared:

> In the spirit of that truth-telling, we who bear the name and heritage must with pain acknowledge also Luther's anti-Judaic diatribes and violent recommendations of his later writings against the Jews. As did many of Luther's own companions in the sixteenth century, we reject this violent invective, and yet more do

we express our deep and abiding sorrow over its tragic effects on subsequent generations.[84]

Attempts to absolve Luther of his anti-Semitism are shameful. Arguments that insist that his harsh words should be seen in a theological context void of any anti-Semitism are patently false. Luther held a definite relationship between his theology and his hatred of the Jews. They would not accept his Christological interpretation of their own Scriptures, and this infuriated him. More than that, it threatened him psychologically and emotionally. He was insecure in the decisions he had made. He was not certain that he had done the right thing in leaving the Catholic Church. He was not certain that he was absolutely right in his understanding of the Jewish Scriptures. He had doubts about his theology. He required validation by those who strenuously opposed him (i.e., Zwinglians, Catholics, and Jews), and he didn't get validation from either of them. Resistance compounded and amplified his fear of being wrong, and this fired and fueled his anger and hatred. Luther was a sick man. The sickness I refer to is not unlike that which many of us experience from time to time. However, his sickness, unlike our garden-variety sickness, had the power and influence of religious opinion and public policy on thousands of people in many nations.

Try hard as they may, Luther's defenders cannot argue away the factual evidence of his anti-Semitism. He demonized the Jews in vulgar and indecent terms. Resolutions such as the one adopted by the Lutheran Church Missouri Synod seek to avoid embarrassment and defend Luther by repressing and avoiding absolute facts of history. Lucy Dawidowicz is on target when she says, "To be sure, the similarities of Luther's anti-Jewish exhortations with Hitler's racial policies are not merely coincidental."[85] I believe that adjudication of the complicity of Luther's writings in playing a significant role in Hitler's "final solution" requires a verdict of "Guilty." Julius Streicher, an anti-Semite and senior member of the Nazi Party, was executed at Nuremberg for his part in the mass execution of Jews. While awaiting trial, he appealed to the words of Martin Luther in his defense. He said,

> Dr. Martin Luther would very probably sit in my place in the defendants' dock today (29 April 1946), if this book had been taken into consideration by the Prosecution. In the book <u>The Jews and Their Lies</u>, Dr. Martin Luther writes the Jews are a serpents' brood and one should burn down their synagogues and destroy them.[86]

How does one assess and/or assign a measure of culpability to words spoken and printed five hundred years ago? If the consequences of such occurrences were limited to the time in which they were uttered, they could be relegated to past history. Sadly, this is not the case with Martin Luther's hatred of the Jews. His reputation and prestige as a great reformer have bestowed a quality of authority on his vicious writings. The consequences have not disappeared but have continued to impact the lives of people and the pages of history through the centuries. His vision of a Germany free of Jews became the vision embraced by a Germany that ultimately resulted in the murder of more than six million Jews and brought death, destruction, and misery to the entire population of the world. While his writings most certainly had social and political implications, I do not want to indict him on the basis of legal jurisprudence or social ostracism. My criticism is not the kind that would make him culpable or even vulnerable in any man-made court of law. My indictment finds its roots in the very authority that Luther most admired and respected; that is, the Word of God.

Luther was a respected biblical scholar. He was a Doctor of Theology and a professor of Old Testament at the University of Wittenberg. He translated both the Old and New Testaments from their original languages into German. In all that he wrote and taught, I cannot find that he ever explained to his students, his readers, or his congregations the meaning of the one verse of Scripture that was used by all Christians of his day and was the foremost promoter of Jew-hatred. I am referring to the "blood curse" of Matthew 27:25: "And all the people answered, 'His blood be on us and on our children.'" Luther surely knew that the Jews no longer had Scriptural authority to place a curse on themselves. The curse they invoked at the trial of Jesus was not valid at the very moment it was proclaimed, and certainly not into perpetuity.[87] As an Old Testament professor, he must have known that both Jeremiah and Ezekiel had pronounced that the threat of any generational curse had ended and was "no more to be used by you in Israel" (Ezekiel 18:1-4). Had Luther explained this, it would have removed his endorsement of any attempt to support an eternal curse on the Jewish race. Without a doubt, Luther believed that the Jews killed Jesus, but he also knew that Jewish responsibility for his death did not extend beyond the time of his death. His silence became a resounding approval of the perpetual persecution of Jews of every generation.

Some scholars have absolved Luther by claiming that he was defending Jesus Christ and the Church against its enemies. They say that he wanted to put an end to the public slander and blasphemy of which the Jews were accused. Even so, we must not overlook the fact that his defensive tactics were in violation of the conduct one would expect of a Christian leader. The Church was not created to defend God; rather, the Church was commanded to obey God as revealed in His Son, Jesus Christ. I maintain that Luther's culpability is to be found in his failure to respond to the Jews in the manner prescribed by Jesus Christ. Jesus said, "Do not resist one who is evil. But if anyone strikes you on the right cheek, turn to him the other also" (Matthew 5:39). Luke reports that Jesus said, "Love your enemies, do good to those who hate you, bless those who curse you, pray for those who abuse you. To him who strikes you on the cheek, offer the other also" (Luke 6:27-29).

In both the Sermon on the Mount (Matthew 5:3-7:27) and the Sermon on the Plain (Luke 6:20-48), Jesus unequivocally prohibits retaliation. There is no equivocation in his proclamation, "Blessed are you when men revile you and persecute you and utter all kinds of evil against you falsely on my account. Rejoice and be glad for your reward is great in heaven, for so men persecuted the prophets who were before you" (Matthew 5:11-12) He requires the Christian to take positive action to interrupt and prevent a vicious cycle of revenge. He gave us an example while hanging on the cross. With his dying breath, he said, "It is finished" (John 19:30). Jesus had no intention of countering violence with more violence. This does not mean that he was powerless to respond with violence if he chose to do so. He told his disciples that at any time, he could appeal to his Father, who would "at once send me more than twelve legions of angels" (Matthew 26:53). He could have inflicted violent punishment on those who harmed him, but he chose to live and die by his own message of turning the other cheek and praying for those who ridiculed and abused him.

Two other stories from Luke's Gospel condemn Luther's response of hatred for the Jews. John reported to Jesus that they saw a man casting out demons in Jesus' name. This angered John because the man was not a member of their small group. He told Jesus that they had forbidden the man to continue praying in Jesus' name. Jesus indicated that they had acted wrongly, saying, "Do not forbid him; for he who is not against you is for you" (Luke 9:49-50; also Mark 9:38-41). On another occasion, the disciples went ahead to a Samaritan village to prepare for Jesus' arrival. The village would not cooperate and refused to welcome Jesus. The disciples were angry and recommended that Jesus call down fire from heaven and consume them. Jesus rebuked them and told them that they did not understand their own mean-spirited recommendation. He said, "For the Son of man is not come to destroy men's lives but to save them" Luke 9:51-55, KJV).

Luther is to be numbered among those of whom Jesus said, "You know not what manner of spirit you are." His position was one of pride and intolerance. He convinced the German people that they were the people of God and that the Jews had no right to speak of God. He convinced them that they had rights inherent in their homeland status and that the Jews were usurping those rights. He seemed to ignore the teachings of the Lord of the Church that his disciples were not to stand on their own rights but on the love and mercy represented by the cross of Calvary.

Luther's attacks paved the way for recurring violence and retaliation against the Jews for almost five hundred years after his death. He used the Jews as a model for all evil. The German Lutherans of 1933-1945 learned their hatred from Luther's writings. Much of the speech and writings of the Nazi regime were akin to the vicious anti-Semitic content of Luther's hatred of the Jews. Michael Berenbaum wrote *The World Must Know: The History of the Holocaust as Told in the United States Holocaust Memorial Museum*.[88] Regarding Luther's connection to the Holocaust, Berenbaum says, "Luther's diatribes in the sixteenth century are an eerie foreshadowing of Nazi practices four centuries later."[89]

In keeping with the theme of this book, I could have merely affirmed that Luther believed that the Sanhedrin had the authority to kill Jesus and, in fact, that they did kill Jesus. There is ample proof on both counts, and that certainly would have satisfied my search for Luther's position on those two issues. However, Berenbaum's primary title pulled me toward needing to know more about Luther and the Jews. It was his title that prompted me to include this chapter entitled "Martin Luther and His

Hatred of the Jews." As I said at the beginning, this chapter is an excursus, a digression into the little-known account of Luther's attitude toward the Jews. I felt the same sense of urgency that Berenbaum's title expresses, not that "The World Must Know" but that readers of my acquaintance must know the sad, whitewashed truth about Martin Luther. While he may be regarded as the father of the Lutheran churches and the voice that started the Protestant Reformation, we must also know that his hatred of the Jews undermined Christ's moral teachings on the essential worth of every human being. On this issue, he did not contribute a single word to the establishment of God's Kingdom on earth. In fact, he contributed to the monstrous Nazi ideology that plunged the world into the greatest conflagration in the history of mankind. One truth that we may know is that history may, without contradiction, indict Martin Luther on the charge of being profoundly un-Christian in his hatred of the Jews.

CHAPTER SEVEN

FROM THE TIME OF JESUS TO OUR TIME

Perhaps the most effective attempt to improve Jewish and Christian relations occurred during the Second Vatican Council in 1965. The Catholic Church took the first step in acknowledging that the Church has been responsible for fostering an environment of anti-Semitism from the time of Emperor Constantine to the present.[1] The Holocaust is the more proximate reminder of anti-Semitism. The Second World War exacerbated the tension between the Jews and the Catholic Church. Pope Pius XII (Pope, 1939-58) was often referred to as "Hitler's Pope." He did not condemn the atrocities as the Nazis were committing them during the war. His critics claim that "his silence during the genocide made him complicit in the crime."[2] Pius avoided public criticism of Hitler and the Nazi government. When alerted to the genocide of the Jews, Pius told the Spanish Ambassador that "he had a 'special love' for the Germans, adding that he had 'nothing against' Germany, which he loved and admired, nor against the Hitler regime, although he acknowledged he was saddened by some of its measures."[3] Pius XII maintained his silence even after the Nazis murdered more than twenty of his own priests. His public silence was interpreted as a lack of concern for the Jewish people and his approval of anti-Judaism.

The silence of Pope Pius XII during the Nazi atrocities certainly widened the chasm between Jewish and Catholic relationships. In response to critics of Pius, Hans Küng says, "It must be absolutely clearly stated that Nazi anti-Judaism was the work of godless, anti-Christian criminals. . . But it would not have been possible without the almost two thousand years' pre-history of 'Christian' anti-Judaism, which prevented Christians in Germany from organizing a convinced and energetic resistance on a broad front."[4] While the actual atrocities were committed by "godless criminals," the methods used by the Nazis were not new to the world. Many of them, in some form, had been used in the Christian-dominated Middle Ages. Across the span of history, Christian social, political and economic structures had required Jews to wear distinguishing symbols on their clothing, confiscated their property, denied them employment in certain professional disciplines and vocations and expelled them from towns and countries.

It was this history of Jewish persecution that prompted the Church to seek a new rapport with Judaism. In a document entitled *Nostra Aetate (In Our Time)*, the Second Vatican Council focused on Jewish-Christian relationships. The document begins with this statement:

> In our time, when day by day mankind is being drawn together, and the ties between different people are becoming stronger, the Church examines more closely the relationship to non-Christian religions. In her task of promoting unity and love among men, indeed among nations, she considers above all in this declaration what men have in common and what draws them to fellowship.[5]

The title, *In Our Time*, suggests to me a Catholic willingness to employ a form of revisionist history in its attempt to establish a new relationship with Judaism. By this, I mean that the Church is confusing repentance with rewriting what happened at the time of Jesus' death. Paragraph four of the document says, "True, the Jewish authorities and those who followed their lead pressed for the death of Christ, still what happened in His passion cannot be charged against all the Jews, without distinction, then alive, nor against the Jews of today." This statement is, at best, only half true. The evidence of the canonical Gospels does hold the Jews of Jesus time responsible for his death. If we are to speak of the situation "in our time," honesty demands that we recognize the dynamics of the situation "in their time." The Gospels tell us that "all the people" cried out for his death. *Nostra Aetate* is correct in affirming that subsequent generations of Jews cannot be held accountable for the death of Jesus. Filson sensibly says, "Later generations cannot be blamed for what they do not approve."[6]

What have been the results of the relationship between Catholics and Jews since the Second Vatican Council? One can hardly deny the sincerity of the efforts, but much controversy remains. Catholic guilt produced an apology for its silence during the Holocaust. Nevertheless, it remains that Judaism cannot appreciate the continuing efforts to complete the canonization of Pius XII to sainthood. Before his retirement, Pope Benedict XVI was eager to complete Pius' elevation to sainthood before the archives from Pius' papacy were opened to historians. That Benedict XVI is the German-born Cardinal Ratzinger, a member of the Hitler Youth in Nazi Germany, introduces some suspicion regarding his efforts to "fast track" the sainthood of Pius XII. He regarded Pius as a venerated role model. This personal connection raises some questions for Professor Robert Wistrich of the Hebrew University of Jerusalem. In an interview with Israel's News, Wistrich listed some of his concerns:

1. Benedict XVI insists on extolling the "heroic virtues" of Pius XII.
2. The German-born Ratzinger (Benedict XVI) knows that Pius was a passionate Germanophile who was fluent in German language and was surrounded by German aides during and after the war.

3. Ratzinger knew that Pius personally intervened to commute the sentences of convicted German war criminals.
4. He also knew that Pius refused to make public statements against anti-Semitism, even after learning of the atrocities of the death camps.
5. Benedict XVI regards Pius as a soulmate both theologically and politically.[7]

It appears that the German Pope Benedict XVI, before his retirement from the papacy, was determined to beatify the World War Two Pope Pius XII. Was he motivated by the German connection? How could the Jewish community take the actions of Vatican Two seriously when the Church wanted to beatify a Pope who was silent during the Holocaust when the Nazis were mass murdering Jews? So far, *Nostra Aetate* is described as a step toward improving Jewish-Christian relations. However, while positive in tone, the document elicits more unrealized hope than it does realized success. It says both "yes" and "no," and this contradiction is apparent to the Jewish community. David Novak points out that with few exceptions, the document has produced a negative reaction among Jewish leaders. He says, "It has been branded a whitewash, a rationalization of the conduct of the Church during the Holocaust."[8]

The irony of the Jewish-Christian debate is found in the fact that the very person who connects Jews and Christians is also the same person who separates them. Regardless of how many councils are convened and how many documents are produced, two thousand years of history suggests that no agreement about Jesus of Nazareth is in sight. For the Jews, Jesus was and is just that, a Jew from Nazareth. They will accept him on that basis. This acceptance, however, does not include a recognition and acceptance of the Jesus of the Christian religion. For the Church, he is both Jesus of Nazareth and Jesus the Christ, and without this recognition, there is no Christianity. There is a limit to Jewish acknowledgement of

Jesus, and this is the stumbling block that will always impede and bring to a halt the attempts to solidify Jewish and Christian relationships. Saint Paul clearly saw it when he said, "But we preach Christ crucified, a stumbling block to Jews, and folly to the Gentiles, but to those who are called, both Jews and Greeks, Christ the power of God, and the wisdom of God" (1 Corinthians 1:23-24).

Küng quotes the Jewish writer Schalom Ben-Chorin regarding the limits of Jewish acceptance of the Christian Jesus. Ben-Chorin wrote more than thirty books on Jewish historical and cultural themes. In his book *Bruder Jesus* (*Brother Jesus*), he says,

> I feel his brotherly hand which grasps mine, so that I can follow him. It is not the hand of the Messiah, this hand marked with scars. It is certainly not a divine, but a human hand in the lines of which is engraved the most profound suffering. . . .the faith of Jesus unites us, but faith in Jesus divides us.[9]

The unity that Ben-Chorin describes is the unity that I might have with someone I like, someone whose company I enjoy, someone with whom I might agree on political issues or sports teams. But make no mistake about it: that is not the unity that represents my faith in and through Jesus the Christ. I do feel the scars in his hands. When I am under the cloud of a flagging faith, when grief and sorrow knock on the door of my heart, when my conscience is suffering under the stab of sin, I reach out to him, and he offers a nail-scarred hand and says to me as he said to Thomas, "Put your finger here, and see my hands, and put out your hand and place it in my side; do not be faithless but believing" (John 20:27).

There is a marked difference in the "faith of Jesus" and "faith in Jesus." In acknowledging the "faith of Jesus," Ben-Chorin is not making any Jewish deference to Christian faith. In fact, he is saying that Jesus' faith was the faith of a Jew; therefore, he is merely complimenting what he assumes to be the supremacy of his faith, and Jewish faith by extension. This line of thinking implies that Christians have appropriated a valid Jewish faith "of Jesus" and wrongly turned it into a "faith in Jesus."

Other than living together peacefully in a secular society, what is the state of Jewish and Christian relations today? Leander Keck's assessment is correct and to the point. He says, "Jesus has had no influence on Judaism's understanding of God."[10] Meanwhile, Judaism and Christianity will live together as civilized citizens of the world. However, it is likely that attempts to reconcile theological and religious differences will amount to little more than the cynical interpretation of "holding hands and singing Kumbaya around a warm campfire."

CONCLUSION

The starting point for this book was a critical look at the Passion narratives as recorded in the canonical Gospels. While it is true that some differences may be noted among the four Gospels, it is also true that harmonization "should not overly concern us."[1] Each writer may use a different vocabulary or literary style to tell his story, but the fact remains that they agree and attest to what happened to Jesus at the hands of the Jews. They all agree that he was the subject of a Jewish legal inquiry after he was taken into custody. They agree that he was taken to appear before Pilate. All four mention the Sanhedrin by name and agree that some form of a convened Sanhedrin was involved in the death of Jesus (Matthew 26:59, Mark 15:1, Luke 22:66 and John 11:47). In all four Gospels, the relative silence of Jesus is maintained throughout the Passion narratives. We may concede that there are some differences between the Synoptics and John and even between the Synoptics themselves. However, as Brown points out, while absolute harmonization may not be possible, the canonical Gospels reflect an essential compatibility in content and substance. Morris reminds us that they are all speaking about the same Jesus.[2]

The groups of people involved in the trial and death of Jesus were the

Sadducees, Pharisees, scribes, chief priests, elders, elders of the people, the high priest, the crowds and the Jews. They represented the political, religious, economic, and social power structures of their day. They usually opposed each other for various reasons; however, they were united in their hostility for Jesus. Their rejection of him as the messiah of Israel resulted in their active participation in his crucifixion. As a Jew writing to the Jews, Matthew seldom mentions the Jews as such. He does, however, frequently and consistently refer to the crowds. For him, the crowds are representative of the entire population of the Jews.

Mark makes a sweeping condemnation of the Jews as the killers of Jesus. According to him, every kind of Jew played a part in the murder of Jesus of Nazareth. William A. Johnson says, "Every kind of Jew—Pharisees, scribes, priests, Herodians, Herod Antipas, the Sadducees, the High Priest, the Sanhedrin and the crowd—are all of one mind in rejecting Jesus."[3]

Throughout his Gospel, Mark presses home his indictment against the Jews. He never fails to confirm that they ignored every opportunity to acknowledge the Messiahship of Jesus. He points out that the "heavens opened" at the baptism of Jesus. The action depicted is more than a casual opening. The word used for "opening" is from the Greek verb σχίζω which indicates an aggressive splitting, rending or tearing apart.[4] This "rending of the heavens" is followed by the proclamation of "Thou art my beloved Son, with thee I am well pleased" (Mark 1:10-11). This account is Mark's call for the Jews to recognize their own ancient cry unto God as proclaimed by their own prophet: "O that thou wouldst rend the heavens, and come down" (Isaiah 64:1). Their prayer that God would reveal himself in power is happening before their very eyes at the baptism of Jesus.

A few verses later, Mark refers to another rending and tearing apart.

Jesus told the scribes and Pharisees that trying to put a new patch on an old garment would bring unacceptable results. He said that the new patch would tear away from the old, and a worse tear (σχίσμα) is made (Mark 2:21). He is warning them that the Gospel he brings could not be expressed through their ancient rules and regulations. A new thing is breaking upon Israel and the whole world. Mark's Gospel proclaims that it was not God's intention to put a patch on a religion that was no longer sufficient to meet the needs of all the people. Just as there is no agreement between a new patch and an old garment, there is no agreement between the old religion and the new connection being created between God and humanity. In rejecting the new community being established by Jesus and clinging blindly to their ancient religion, the Jews were denying the promises of their own scriptures. What Jesus was bringing was the fulfillment of the prophecy given to Isaiah: "Remember not the former things, nor consider the things of old. Behold, I am doing a new thing; now it springs forth, do you not perceive it?" (Isaiah 43:19).

As Mark nears the conclusion of his Gospel, he reports another rending, splitting and tearing apart. As Jesus breathed his last, "the curtain of the temple was torn in two (σχίζω) from top to bottom" (Mark 15:38). The rending of the curtain in the temple was confirmation that the old way of worship was no longer the only path into the presence of God. The person and work of Jesus is not intended to be a patch on the old way of worshiping God. It is an entirely new creation that calls Israel to repentance and participation in the love and grace of God. The rending of the curtain was followed by the confession of the pagan centurion who said, "Truly this man was the Son of God" (Mark 15:29). In this new creation through Jesus, God opened the way of the gospel to the Gentiles. John, in the Book of Revelation, would later recognize this action of God in Jesus for what it really was. He reported that he heard a voice from the throne saying, "Behold, I make (ποιῶ) all things new" (Revelation 21:5).

The literal translation is more complete and more powerful: "Look you! I made all things new, I am making all things new, and I will make all things new!"

Mark repeatedly makes it clear that the Jews have been given every opportunity to recognize and accept Jesus as the promised Messiah. Their own scriptures and the words of their prophets proved his Messiahship. Their rejection of Jesus was a rejection of their own God and the new thing he was doing. From beginning to end, the Gospel of Mark confirms that the Jews were the primary instruments in the killing of Jesus.

Luke's Gospel has often been referred to as the universal Gospel. It invites everyone to enter the Kingdom of God. God's love is portrayed as being available without any preference for race, nationality, gender or status in life. Luke's Jesus has come to preach good news to everyone. He unequivocally proclaims that the Gentiles have unrestricted access to the God of Abraham, Isaac and Jacob. This inclusion of the Gentiles angered the Jews, and it was a source of their rejection of Jesus. They became belligerent and very hostile toward Jesus. They participated in taking him into custody, and they completely supported his arrest. They publicly and vociferously demanded that he should be killed. They mocked him, physically abused him and taunted him to save himself to prove to them that he was the Messiah.

Luke goes to great lengths to show that Pilate did not want to kill Jesus. The hatred of the Jews for Jesus was so overtly evident that Pilate had no difficulty in seeing it. He was unable to discover valid evidence to support the accusations of the Jews. When he questioned Jesus, he found that his brief replies contained no support for any possible reason to find him guilty. If Pilate were an honest broker in adjudicating according to the letter of the law, he would have had no choice but to free Jesus. Unfortunately, Pilate was not such a man. He saw the people of Jerusalem siding with the chief priests and the members of the Sanhedrin. He heard their frenzied and murderous demands that Barabbas be set free and Jesus killed. The decision was Pilate's to make, but he allowed the Jews to participate in the ultimate decision regarding the fate of Jesus. Morris says, "All our evidence shows that Pilate was a weak man all too ready to be pushed by the mob into a course of action, not of his own choosing."[5] It may be inaccurate to call Pilate a weak man. It can more accurately be said that Pilate, like Caiaphas, knew something about political expediency.

Luke's Gospel shows the solidarity of the people with the Sanhedrin officials and with Pilate against Jesus. They are rebellious, murderous and somewhat seditious in their implied threat to impeach Pilate if he did not comply with their desire to crucify Jesus. Luke's account of the rejection and killing of Jesus paints a tragic picture of the Jews as a nation of jealous and petulant children. Unable to accept the possibility that their God would show favor to any people other than themselves as the chosen people of God, they orchestrated the death of the One sent to them by their own God. In the Acts of the Apostles, which Luke also authored, he reinforces his claim that the Jews killed Jesus. He records that Peter, preaching to the Jews, said, "You killed the author of life, whom God raised from the dead" (Acts 3:15). Luke shows that the murderous character of the Jews was fully revealed in their solidarity with Caiaphas and the Sanhedrin. They supported and protected a known murderer and demanded the death of one of their own. Their treatment of Jesus of Nazareth amounted to nothing less than the national sin of Israel.

The primary characters in John's Gospel are the crowd, Pilate, the Jews and Jesus. John seldom makes any specific distinction regarding Pharisees, scribes, elders and chief priests. His preference is to regard all those rejecting Jesus and opposed to his teachings as "the Jews." The Jews insist on claiming their privilege as children of Abraham. They totally embrace and protect the traditions that identify them as the chosen people of God. They have frozen into the past their very ideas of what it means to worship and serve God. The function of priests in the life of Israel had become devoid of any revelatory character. The practice of the presence of God had become little more than a mechanized administration of traditional acts. The religion of the priests had become a system of religious rites that valued the system more than the God it presumed to reveal and worship. Jesus called this system to give an account of itself and placed it under the judgment of God. John tells the Jews that they are spiritually blind and incapable of seeing the hand of God at work in the person of Jesus. Even the raising of Lazarus from death to life does not convince them of the power of God being displayed in the ministry of Jesus.

John portrays Pilate in a similar fashion as does Luke. He regards him as being convinced of the innocence of Jesus. It appears that he wants to be fair. One could expect that an impartial Roman judge would have released any prisoner presented under the same circumstances as Jesus. We can only speculate as to the reasons Pilate acted as he did. Perhaps he lacked the interest or concern to persevere in his insistence that Jesus was innocent. More than likely, his lack of resolve was the result of political pressure applied by the Jews. If it were a contest of the wills, there is no question that the Jews were more resolved to kill Jesus than Pilate was to spare him. Their malevolent intentions and obvious hatred of Jesus were much more powerful than any feelings Pilate might have had for him. While acknowledging that Jesus is innocent, Pilate's concern is minimal, and he is simply going through a formality. He knows what the angry conspiratorial Jews want, and he knows what the outcome will be. Pilate acquiesced to the Jews and handed Jesus over to them, and they led him away to be crucified.

The Gospel of John says that Jesus' final words were, "It is finished," and having said that, "he bowed his head and gave up his spirit" (John 19:30-31). The Jews must have felt the surge of power and satisfaction that comes with winning a victory. However, any sense of victory they might have experienced would be very short-lived. God's work to provide the world with a Savior was finished, but the misery that would be visited upon the Jews was just beginning. Within four decades, their temple would be torn down from top to bottom, and the city of Jerusalem would know the wrath and destructive power of the Roman army. Israel would never again have access to a temple to receive their burnt offerings and support their ancient religious practices. Future generations of Jews would be labeled and ostracized as the people who killed the Son of God. The writer of the Gospel of John leaves no room for doubt about who killed Jesus. In rejecting the kingship of Jesus, the Jews unwittingly rejected their own God. John clearly relieves the Romans of the responsibility for killing Jesus and would have his readers know that the Jews killed Jesus.

In all four canonical Gospels, we find that Pilate gave the Jews the opportunity to execute Jesus (Matthew 27:24, Mark 15:15, Luke 23:24-25 and John 19:6). The offer was genuine, and Pilate was sincere in telling them to take Jesus and kill him themselves. The Jews complained that it was not lawful for them to put any man to death (John 18:31). It would be a mistake to accept this statement at face value. As phrased, it represents an intentional deception on the part of the Jews. According to their law, they had the authority to kill Jesus. What they did not have was the approval of their law to kill him the way they wanted to kill him. The right to capital punishment was doubly authorized in the case of Jesus. The Jews had the autonomous authority of their own law and the additional endorsement and validation of the Roman governor. Pilate, recognizing that the Jews found Jesus guilty and "worthy of death" (Matthew 26:66, Mark 14:64), encouraged them to exercise their

Sanhedrin authority and to kill Jesus in accordance with their own laws. S. G. F. Brandon points out that "Pilate's order to the Jews logically implies that they had the authority to try Jesus."[6]

The fact of the matter is that it wasn't the authority to kill Jesus that the Jews rejected. It was the method of execution under their law that they rejected. Their law prescribed stoning as the method of execution, but they wanted him to be crucified. As pertaining to Jesus, their anger, hatred and cruelty knew no bounds. They wanted Jesus of Nazareth subjected to the agonizing horror of death as it occurred in being affixed to a cross. Martin Hengel spells out some of the human cruelty resident in inflicting death by crucifixion. He says,

> It was carried out publicly. . . It was usually associated with other forms of torture, including at least flogging. . . By the public display of a naked victim at a prominent place—at a crossroads, in the theatre, on high ground, at the place of his crime—crucifixion also represented his uttermost humiliation, which had a numinous dimension to it. With Deuteronomy 21:23 in the background, the Jew in particular was very aware of this.[7]

Jesus was crucified in a place that was geographically so cosmopolitan that the titular attached to his cross was inscribed in Hebrew, Latin and Greek: "Jesus of Nazareth, the King of the Jews" (John 19:19). This is what the Jews wanted; the public humiliation of Jesus and the curse of their law upon his head. He did not die a quiet and painless death. He did not die "old and full of years" like the famous patriarchs of Jewish history and the ancient fathers of his own homeland. He died between two common criminals, like a slave on a cross of shame.

Many of the early Fathers of the Church have left us their understanding of the death of Jesus at the hands of the Jews. Justin Martyr, Origin, John Chrysostom, and Augustine all believed that the Sanhedrin had the power of capital punishment and that they used that power to kill Jesus. Their beliefs were not developed within the comfortable confines of speculating academia. They did not employ the wiles of corrupt political chicanery as a means of self-preservation and safety. They arrived at and defended their faith and the history of their Savior through the power of prayer and the path of martyrdom when required. They hung their destiny on the cross where Jesus was nailed down, and they were seized and transformed by what he did on that cross. They bet their lives that God, through Jesus, who was called the Christ, was doing something of eternal value for the human race. Their testimonies regarding the murderers of Jesus and the competence and authority of the Sanhedrin are to be believed.

Attempts to reconstruct the authority of the Sanhedrin in capital cases are futile unless we recognize its character before and after AD 70. Unfortunately, many scholars superimpose the rules and regulations of post-AD 70 Sanhedrin procedures upon the character of the Sanhedrin as it functioned in the time of Jesus. Other than the trial of Jesus as portrayed in the Gospels, there are no extant documents to serve as precedents for Sanhedrin's action during that time frame. The history of the rules and regulations of the Sanhedrin was written almost entirely after the destruction of the temple in AD 70. This means that any interpretation of pre-AD 70 trials using post-AD 70 guidelines and protocols would be based on theoretical deductions rather than from observation or personal experience.

As for Roman authority, it is often argued that the Roman governors assigned to the various provinces in the time of Jesus would have been provided a list of rules that reflected the will of the emperor. Any such argument is pointless since, as in the case of the pre-AD 70 Sanhedrin, there are no extant copies of any such rules. What is more likely is that the governors/procurators did whatever they had to do to assert Roman authority and maintain order. Pilate's hatred of the Jews did not mean that he did not recognize the pragmatic necessity of a certain degree of cooperation with Caiaphas and the members of the Sanhedrin. Pilate was crude and brutal, and Caiaphas was clever and calculating. Both knew how to manipulate situations to accommodate their own best interests and support their tactics for self-preservation. The security of their careers demanded that each defer to the other in matters that threatened that security. When necessary, the relationship between the procurator and high priest was one of "one hand washes the other." Crossan says, "We must presume that the Romans and Caiaphas worked well together. . . It is not unfairly cynical to presume that there was close cooperation between Caiaphas and Pilate."[8] It is not unreasonable to assume that the Jewish court and the Roman governor had no doubt that they could work together to get rid of Jesus. The combination of Pilate's power and Caiaphas' clever plotting did not bode well for any hope that justice would prevail in the case of Jesus.

It is transparently obvious that this alliance of governmental power and political chicanery defined the character of the pre-AD 70 Sanhedrin. Nevertheless, it was not this collusion between Pilate and Caiaphas that afforded the Sanhedrin the competency and authority to try, convict and exercise capital punishment in the time of Jesus. The Sanhedrin did not need the help of Pilate to kill Jesus. It cannot be overemphasized that what they did need was the help of Pilate to kill Jesus by crucifixion.

We are left with the question of why so many studies about the trial of Jesus assume that the Sanhedrin did not have the authority to carry out sentences of capital punishment? The simple and yet totally accurate answer is that too many scholars begin with and proceed on the assumption that the legal guidelines of the post-AD 70 Mishnah represent and govern the procedures of the Sanhedrin during the time of Jesus. The problem with this approach is that there are no documents or reports that remotely suggest that any kind of legal code denying the Sanhedrin the right of capital punishment was in force during the pre-AD 70 period. It was only in the aftermath of the destruction of the temple that Jewish questions began to appear regarding the killing of Jesus. It is not unlikely that the Jews were reminded that at the trial of Jesus, all the people had accepted guilt for his death: "And all the people answered, 'His blood be on us and on our children!'" (Matthew 27:25). Christianity has no excuse for the harmful way this verse of scripture has been used against the Jews. That is not to say that Christianity is wrong in recognizing that in AD 30 or AD 33 the Jews killed Jesus. It is, however, wrong to blame Jews of all time for the death of Jesus. When they thought they were self-cursing themselves, little did they know that the blood they called for would be the blood that transcended all curses. It was not the blood of vengeance that cried out from the ground as a curse on Cain for killing his brother Abel (Genesis 4:8-14). The blood of Jesus does not cry out for revenge or punishment. It is not poured out as a curse on anyone. There is a very great irony in the fact that the blood the Jews thought would curse them forever became the blood that offered them redemption and salvation.

With the destruction of the temple and the Sanhedrin, Judaism needed a legal structure to guide and inform the transition from pre-AD 70 to post-AD 70 government. The reshaping of Jewish identity began with the emergence of rabbinic Judaism. It took as its central task "the development of the legal component of Torah."[9] The first record of these rabbinic legal procedures date from the late second century AD. It was during this time that Judaism was trying to follow an established rabbinic halakhah. Using this late second-century code, they made the mistake of implying that it had been in force and followed by everyone prior to AD 70. Instone-Brewer says, "In the second century, it was possible to rewrite history," and he points out that the "traditions about the trials of Jesus and his disciples were brought into the Talmudic discussions early in the third century."[10] Clearly, applying post-AD 70 rules to the trial of Jesus is of no historical value. Lester Grabbe says, "There is no need to assume that the rabbinic picture is anything more than a later invention of rabbinic ideology."[11] Not only are they of no historical value, we may also assume that they reflect "deliberate misrepresentations by later Jews."[12]

The attempts of lawyers to recreate the trial of Jesus amount to the expression of "trying to put toothpaste back into the tube." They are laborious, disingenuous exercises that circumvent truth and facts to arrive at a pre-determined conclusion. Haim Cohn's book, *The Trial and Death of Jesus*, is an example of the failure of applying a mix of post-AD 70 Mishnah rules and modern legal procedures to conclude that the Jews did not kill Jesus. The legal experts invariably claim that non-lawyers, theologians and historians are not capable of producing reliable accounts of the trial of Jesus. They subject the pre-AD 70 trial to a multitude of forensic gymnastics. Using courthouse tactics, they go a long way around to prove their points and yet never get "there," wherever "there" is for them! Their processes are filled with speculations, objections and whimsical "would haves, could haves and should haves." All their efforts are meaningless because their arguments are based primarily on post-AD 70 rules, regulations and protocols that were either unknown or ignored during the trial of Jesus. Hans Conzelmann says that at the trial of Jesus, "there was scarcely any feeling of accountability for legal detail and judicial plausibility."[13] Lacking any records other than the Gospel accounts of the trial of Jesus, it is senseless to validate as truth those later polemical documents that were created to fictitiously absolve the Jews of the killing of Jesus. The writers of the canonical Gospels each had their own way of presenting what would later be referred to as,

That which was from the beginning, which we have heard, which we have seen with our eyes, which we have looked upon and touched with our hands, concerning the word of life—the life was made manifest and we saw it, and testify to it, and proclaim to you the eternal life which was with the Father and was made manifest to us (1 John 1:1-2).

Among the many voices spoken since the trial and killing of Jesus, the only plausible guidance that can be given is "Let the Gospels speak!"

Who killed Jesus? This book concludes with the claim that the Jews killed Jesus. While Jewish hands may not have driven the crucifixion nails, there is no doubt that they orchestrated the beginning and the end of the murderous affair. Israel's guilt throughout the Gospels is unmistakable. Jesus is identified as "that righteous man," but the Jews preferred Barabbas, a known murderer, over the righteous Jesus. If any guilt is due, some would argue that it applied to the leaders of the Jewish people and not to the whole population. Those who seek to exonerate the rank-and-file citizens fail to see or acknowledge that the ordinary people of Israel played a prominent role in delivering Jesus into the hands of the designated executioner. The whole of Israel, not just its governing authorities, is complicit in the murder. The ownership of the Kingdom was held by all of Israel, and it was ultimately taken away from all of them. Jesus had said, "Therefore, I tell you the kingdom of God will be taken away from you and given to a nation producing the fruits of it" (Matthew 21:43).

The Passion narratives of the canonical Gospels uniformly show that it is the chief priests, elders, scribes, the Sanhedrin (council), the rulers of the people, the crowds and the Jews who put Jesus to death. There is no separation between the Sanhedrin and the people. They are partners and of one voice in their demand to kill Jesus. Who killed Jesus? It wasn't the Romans. They only served to provide crucifixion as the method of death that the Jews required. Ultimately, a Jewish Sanhedrin empowered with the authority to exercise capital punishment, in collaboration with a nation of Jews motivated by the demands of angry crowds, killed Jesus. He was killed at the hands of a nation of people who were so blinded by tradition and nationalism that they did not recognize the presence of their own God in their midst.

END NOTES

INTRODUCTION

¹ William Barclay, *The Gospel of Matthew*, vol. 1 (Philadelphia: The Westminster Press, 1975), 1.

² All scriptural quotes and references are taken from the *Revised Standard Version (RSV)* unless otherwise noted. Reference to the *Septuagint* is noted as *LXX*. *Greek New Testament* 3rd ed., edited by Kurt Aland, et.al., United Bible Societies, 1975 is used in this study.

CHAPTER ONE

¹ Bruce M. Metzger, *The New Testament: Its Background, Growth and Content* (Nashville: Abingdon Press, 1965), 18-19.

² W. C. Allen, *A Critical and Exegetical Commentary on the Gospel According to Matthew*, 3RD ed. (Edinburgh: T.&T. Clarke, 1912), lix.

³ Origen, "From the First Book of the Commentary on Matthew," in *The Anti-Nicene Fathers*, ed. Allan Menzies, vol. 9 (1897; 2d repr. Peabody, Massachusetts: Hendrickson Publishers, 1995), 412.

⁴ Eusebius, "The Writings of Papias," in *Nicene and Post Nicene Fathers*, ed. Philip Schaff and Henry Wace, vol 9, chapter 39, vs. 16 (1890; 2d series, Peabody, Massachusetts: Hendrickson Publishers, 1995), 173.

⁵ Eusebius, "The Statements of Irenaeus in Regard to the Divine Scriptures," in *Nicene and Post-Nicene Fathers*, ed. Philip Schaff and Henry Wace, vol. 9, book 5, chapter 8, vs. 2 (1890; 2d series, Peabody, Massachusetts: Hendrickson Publishers, 1995), 222.

Endnotes…

[6] Flavius Josephus, *The Works of Flavius Josephus in Four Volumes*, trans. William Whiston, vol. 1, book 1, chapter 5, section 2, "The Wars of the Jews," (1974; repr. Grand Rapids, Michigan: Baker Book House, 1974), 23. All future references will be shown with abbreviated title and cited as: Josephus, *Works: Subtitle,* Arabic numerals reflecting volume, book, chapter, section, page; e.g., Josephus, *Works: Antiquities,* 1.2.3.4.100.

[7] Robert A. Spivey and D. Moody Smith, Jr., *Anatomy of the New Testament* (New York: The Macmillan Co., 1970), 14.

[8] Josephus, *Works: Antiquities* 4.18.1.3.3.

[9] Josephus, *Works: Antiquities* 3.17.2.4.475.

[10] Josephus, *Works: The Life of Flavious Josephus*, vol. 2, p. 38.

[11] Werner Forester, "ὄφις," in *Theological Dictionary of the New Testament*, ed. Gerhard Kittel and Gerhard Friedrich, trans. and ed. Geoffrey Bromiley, vol. 5 (Grand Rapids: Wm. B. Eerdmans, 1967), 579. All future citations will be shown as *TDNT* for *Theological Dictionary of the New Testament*.

[12] Walter Bauer, *A Greek-English Lexicon of the New Testament and Other Early Christian Literature*, rev. and ed. William F. Arndt and F. Wilbur Gingrich, 4th revised and augmented ed. (Chicago: University of Chicago Press, 1957), 605. All future citations will be shown as Bauer, *Greek-English Lexicon*.

[13] Werner Forester, "ἔχιδνα" in *TDNT*, ed. Gerhard Kittel, trans. Geoffrey W. Bromiley, vol. 2 (Grand Rapids: Wm. B. Eerdmans, 1964), 815-816.

[14] Josephus, *Works: Antiquities* 3.13.10.5.252.

[15] *Ibid.*, 3.13.10.6.253.

[16] L. H. Schiffman, *From Text to Tradition: A History of Second Temple and Rabbinic Judaism* (Hoboken, NJ: KTAV, 1991), 110-111.

[17] Rudolf Meyer, "Σαδδουκαῖος," in *TDNT*, ed. Gerhard Kittel and Gerhard Friedrich, trans. Geoffrey W. Bromiley, vol. 7 (Grand Rapids: Wm. B. Eerdmans, 1971), 36-44.

[18] Barclay, *Matthew*, 1: 275.

[19] Josephus, *Works: Antiquities* 4.18.1.4.3-4.

[20] *Ibid.*

[21] Meyer, "Σαδδουκαῖος," in *TDNT*, 7:46

Endnotes...

[22] Robert H. Gundry, *A Survey of the New Testament* (Grand Rapids: Zondervan Publishing House, 1970), 49.

[23] Sherman E. Johnson, "The Gospel According to Saint Matthew: Introduction and Exegesis," in *The Interpreter's Bible*, vol. 7 (Nashville: Abingdon Press, 1951), 265.

[24] Joachim Jeremias, "γραμματεὺς," in *TDNT*, ed. Gerhard Kittel, trans. Geoffrey W. Bromiley, vol. 1 (Grand Rapids: Wm. B. Eerdmans, 1964), 740.

[25] Helmer Ringgren, *Israelite Religion*, trans. David E. Green (Philadelphia: Fortress Press, 1966), 302.

[26] Gerhard von Rad, *Old Testament Theology*, vol. 1, trans. D. M. G. Stalker (New York: Harper & Row, 1965, 90.

[27] *Ibid*, 91.

[28] Ringgren, *Israelite Religion*, 303.

[29] Anthony Saldorini, "Comparing the Traditions: New Testament and Rabbinic Literature," *Bulletin for Biblical Research* 7 (1997): 203.

[30] Robert M. Seltzer, *Jewish People, Jewish Thought: The Jewish Experience in History* (New York: Macmillan Publishing Co., 1980), 130.

[31] Gerhard von Rad, *Old Testament Theology*, 1:102.

[32] Walther Eichrodt, *Theology of the Old Testament*, vol. 1, trans. J. A. Baker (Philadelphia: Westminster Press, 1961), 401.

[33] Rudolf Bultmann, *Theology of the New Testament: Complete in One Volume*, 2 vols., trans. Kendrick Grobel (New York: Charles Scribner's Sons, 1951-1955), 1:25-26.

[34] Barclay, Matthew, vol.1, 132.

[35] Bultmann, Theology of the New Testament, 1:13.

[36] Jeremias, "γραμματεὺς," in *TDNT*, 1:741.

[37] Metzger, *The New Testament*, 47.

[38] Walther Eichrodt, *Theology of the Old Testament*, vol. 2, trans. J. A. Baker (Philadelphia: Westminster Press, 1967), 261-262.

[39] Josephus, *Works: Antiquities* 4.20.11.2.148.

Endnotes…

[40] Joachim Jeremias, *Jerusalem in the Time of Jesus*, trans. F. H. and C. F. Cave (Philadelphia: Fortress Press, 1969), 236.

[41] Jeremias, *Jerusalem,* 243.

[42] Metzger, *The New Testament*, 47.

[43] Jeremias, *Jerusalem*, 236.

[44] Gerhard von Rad, *Old Testament Theology*, vol. 1:244.

[45] Josephus, *Works: Antiquities* 4.20.10.1.143-145.

[46] Gudry, *A Survey of the New Testament*, 5.

[47] Gottlieb Schrenk, "ἀρχιερεύς," in *TDNT*, ed. Gerhard Kittel, trans. Geoffrey W. Bromiley, vol. 3 (Grand Rapids: Wm. B. Eerdmans, 1965), 268.

[48] *Ibid*, 2699.

[49] Jeremias, *Jerusalem*, 203.

[50] Schrenk, "ἀρχιερεύς," in *TDNT*, 3:270.

[51] Jeremias, *Jerusalem*, 160.

[52] Josephus, *Works: Antiquities* 4.20.10.1.146.

[53] M. H. Shepherd, Jr., "Priests in the NT," *Interpreter's Dictionary of the Bible*, 4 vols. (Nashville: Abingdon Press, 1962), 3:890.

[54] Ringgren, *Israelite Religion*, 234.

[55] Eichrodt, *Theology of the Old Testament*, 1:403.

[56] Josephus, *Works: Antiquities* 4.18.2.1.6.

[57] Josephus, *Works: Antiquities* 4.18.4.3.16.

[58] Spivey and Smith, *Anatomy*, 10-11.

[59] Raymond E. Brown, *The Death of the Messiah: From Gethsemane to the Grave*, vol. 1 (New York: Doubleday, 1994), 372.

[60] Philo of Alexandria, "On the Embassy to Gaius," in *The Works of Philo: New Updated Edition Complete and Unabridged in One Volume*, trans. C. D. Yonge (Peabody, Massachusetts, 1995), 784.

Endnotes…

[61] J. H. Hertz, ed., *The Pentateuch and Haftorahs: Hebrew Text, English Translation and Commentary*, vol. 2 (London: Oxford University Press, 1937), 615).

[62] Jeremias, *Jerusalem*, 222.

[63] Raymond E. Brown, *The Death of the Messiah: From Gethsemane to the Grave*, vol. 2 (New York: Doubleday, 1994). 1429.

[64] Eichrodt, *Theology of the Old Testament*, 1:89.

[65] Josephus, *Works: The Life of Flavius Josephus*, vol. 2, section 9, p. 8.

[66] F. W. Beare, *The Gospel According to Matthew* (New York: Harper & Row, 1981), 357.

[67] H. Strathmann, "ὁ λαὸς," in *TDNT*, ed. Gerhard Kittel, trans. Geoffrey W. Bromiley, vol. 4 (Grand Rapids: Wm. B. Eerdmans, 1967), 32.

[68] Gunther Bornkamm, "πρεσβύτερος," in *TDNT*, ed. Gerhard Kittel and Gerhard Friedrich, trans. Geoffrey W. Bromiley, vol. 6 (Grand Rapids: Wm. B. Eerdmans, 1968), 655.

[69] Gerhard von Rad, *Old Testament Theology*, 1:95.

[70] *Ibid.*, 99.

[71] Martin Noth, *Numbers: A Commentary* (Philadelphia: Westminster Press, 1968), 87.

[72] Bornkamm, "πρεσβύτερος," in *TDNT*, 6:659.

[73] *Ibid.*, 6:659, n. 45.

[74] Bultmann, *Theology of the New Testament*, 2:101.

[75] Strathmann, "ὁ λαὸς," in *TDNT, 4:53.*

[76] J. D. Kingsbury, *The Parables of Jesus in Matthew 13* (Richmond: John Knox, 1969), 24-28.

[77] Warren Carter, "The Crowds in Matthew's Gospel," *The Catholic Biblical Quarterly* 55, no. 1 (January 1993): 54, n. 3.

[78] Ulrich Luz, *Matthew 1-7*, trans. William C. Linss (Minneapolis: Augsburg, 1989), 456.

[79] Paul Minear, "The Disciples and the Crowds in the Gospel of Matthew," *Anglican Theological Review*, Supplementary Series 3 (1974): 30.

Endnotes...

[80] Beare, *The Gospel According to Matthew*, 122.

[81] Andries van Aarde, "Jesus' Mission to All of Israel Emplotted in Matthew's Story," *Neotestamentica* 41, no. 2 (2007): 418.

[82] Rudolf Meyer, "ὄχλος," in *TDNT*, ed. Gerhard Kittel and Gerhard Friedrich, trans. Geoffrey W. Bromiley, vol. 5 (Grand Rapids: Wm. B. Eerdmans, 1967), 583.

[83] *Ibid.*, 582.

[84] *Ibid.*

[85] Gerhard Kittel, "ἀκολουθέω," in *TDNT*, ed., Gerhard Kittel, trans. Geoffrey W. Bromiley, vol. 1 (Grand Rapids: Wm. B. Eerdmans, 1964), 210-216.

[86] *Ibid.*, 214.

[87] Carter, "The Crowds in the Gospel of Matthew," 61.

[88] R. C. Cousland, *The Crowds in the Gospel of Matthew* (Brill: Leiden, 2002), 35.

[89] *Ibid.*, 302.

[90] H. E. Dana and Julius R. Mantey, *A Manual Grammar of the Greek New Testament* (Toronto: The Macmillan Co., 1955), 144; Bauer, "πας," in *A Greek-English Lexicon*, 637.

[91] J. A. Fitzmeyer, "Anti-Semitism and the Cry of 'All the People' (Mt. 27:25)," *Theological Studies* 26 (1965): 669.

[92] Luz, *Matthew 1-7*, 121.

[93] A. J. Saldarini, *Matthew's Christian-Jewish Community (Studies in the History of Judaism)* (Chicago: Chicago University Press, 1994), 33.

[94] Jeremias, *Jerusalem*, 84.

[95] Josephus, *Works: Wars of the Jews* 1.2.12.1-2.160-161.

[96] Bauer, "καλος," in *A Greek-English Lexicon*, 401.

[97] John Keats, *Endymion*.

[98] Floyd Filson, *The Gospel According to Matthew*, 2nd ed. (1960; repr., London: Adam & Charles Black, 1977), 272.

[99] Gerhard Delling, "καιρός," in *TDNT*, ed. Gerhard Kittel, trans. Geoffrey, vol. 1 (Grand Rapids: Wm. B. Eeerdmans, 1965), 460.

Endnotes...

[100] Heinrich Schlier, "Ἀμὴν," in *TDNT*, ed. Gerhard Kittel, trans. Geoffrey W. Bromiley, vol. 1 (Grand Rapids: Wm. B. Eerdmans, 1964), 338.

[101] Filson, *The Gospel According to St. Matthew*, 273.

[102] *Ibid.*, 278.

[103] Leonard Goppelt, "ποτήριον," in *TDNT*, ed. Gerhard Kittel and Gerhard Friedrich, trans. Geoffrey W. Bromiley, vol. 6 (Grand Rapids: Wm. B. Eerdmans, 1968), 163.

[104] Karl Barth, The Doctrine of Reconciliation," in *Church Dogmatics*, trans. G. W. Bromiley, vol. 4, part 1 (1956; repr., Edinburgh: T. & T. Clark, 1980), 269.

[105] James Mays, "'Now I Know': An Exposition of Genesis 22:1-19 and Matthew 26:36-46." *Theology Today* 58, no. 4 (January 2002): 521.

[106] Allen, *Matthew*, 284.

[107] W. F. Albright and C. S. Mann, *Matthew: A New Translation with Introduction and Commentary* (New York: Doubleday, 1971), 333.

[108] Eduard Lohse, "συνέδριον," in *TDNT*, ed. Gerhard Kittel and Gerhard Friedrich, trans. Geoffrey W. Bromiley, vol. 7 (Grand Rapids: Wm. B. Eerdmans, 1971), 870, n. 9.

[109] Karl Barth, "The Doctrine of Creation," in *Church Dogmatics*, trans. G. W. Bromiley, vol. 3 part 2 (1960; repr., Edinburgh: T. & T. Clarke, 1980), 503.

[110] Allen, *Matthew*, 286.

[111] Barclay, *Matthew*, 2:347.

[112] J. Behm, "μετανοέω," in *TDNT*, ed. Gerhard Kittel, trans. Geoffrey W. Bromiley, vol. 4 (Grand Rapids: Wm. B. Eerdmans 1967), 1000.

[113] O. Michel, "μεταμέλομαι," in *TDNT*, ed. Gerhard Kittel, trans. Geoffrey W. Bromiley, vol.4 (Grand Rapids: Wm. B. Eerdmans 1967), 628.

[114] Werner Beider, "ῥιψτω," in *TDNT*, ed. Gerhard Kittel and Gerhard Friedrich, trans. Geoffrey W. Bromiley, vol. 6 (Grand Rapids: WM. B. Eerdmans, 1968), 991.

[115] Beider, "ῥιψτω," in *TDNT,* 6:99.

[116] Brevard Childs, *The New Testament as Canon: An Introduction* (Philadelphia: Fortress Press, 1984), 70.

[117] Albright and Mann, *Matthew*, 344.

Endnotes…

[118] Filson, *The Gospel According to Saint Matthew*, 290.

[119] Barclay, *Matthew*, 2:362.

[120] R. T. France, *Matthew: An Introduction and Commentary* (Downers Grove, Illinois: IVP Academic, 2015), 507, https//scribd.com/read/377941273.

[121] Fitzmeyer, "Anti-Semitism," 668.

[122] Brown, *Death of the Messiah*, 2:831, n. 22.

[123] Walter Zimmerli, *Ezekiel 1: A Commentary on the Book of the Prophet Ezekiel, Chapters 1-24*, trans. Ronald E. Clements and ed. Frank Moore Cross (Philadelphia: Fortress Press, 1979), 378.

[124] Fitzmeyer, "Anti-Semitism," 671.

[125] Beare, *The Gospel According to Matthew*, 531.

[126] Filson, *The Gospel According to Saint Matthew*, 295.

[127] Johnson, "The Gospel According to Saint Matthew," 608.

[128] Bauer, *A Greek-English Lexicon*, 125.

[129] Rudolf Bultmann, "αφίημι," in *TDNT*, ed. Gerhard Kittel, trans. Geoffrey W. Bromiley, vol. 1 (Grand Rapids: Wm. B. Eerdmans, 1965), 443.

[130] *Ibid.*, 510.

[131] *Ibid.*, 512.

[132] Carl Schneider, "καθήμεναι," in *TDNT*, ed. Gerhard Kittel, trans. Geoffrey W. Bromiley, vol. 3 (Grand Rapids: Wm. B. Eerdmans, 1965), 443.

CHAPTER TWO

[1] Werner Georg Kümmel, *Introduction to the New Testament: An English Translation*, 14th ed., trans., A. J. Mattill, Jr., (Nashville: Abingdon Press, 1965), 70.

[2] Spivey and Smith, *Anatomy*, 71.

[3] C. S. Mann, *Mark: A New Translation with Introduction and Commentary* (New York: Doubleday, 1986), 243.

[4] Vincent Taylor, *The Gospel According to St. Mark: The Greek Text with Introduction, Notes and Indexes*, 2nd ed. (New York: St. Martin's Press, 1966), 403.

Endnotes…

[5] Eduard Lohse, "Ἰερουσαλήμ," in *TDNT*, 7:330.

[6] Hugh Anderson, *The Gospel of Mark* (London: Oliphants, 1976), 6.

[7] D. E. Nineham, *The Gospel of Saint Mark* (London: Penguin Books, 1963), 91.

[8] Taylor, *The Gospel According to St. Mark*, 472.

[9] Barclay, *The Gospel of Mark* (Philadelphia: The Westminster Press, 1975), 283.

[10] Anderson, *The Gospel of Mark*, 336.

[11] Ezra P. Gould, *A Critical and Exegetical Commentary on the Gospel According to St. Mark* (Edinburgh: T. & T. Clarke, 1896), 285.

[12] Barclay, *Mark*, 357.

[13] Nineham, *The Gospel of Saint Mark*, 412.

[14] Meyer, "ὄχλος," in *TDNT*, 5:583.

[15] Barclay, *Mark*, 357.

[16] Elias Canetti, *Crowds and Power*, trans., Carol Stewart (New York: Continuum, 1973), 51.

[17] *Ibid.*

[18] *Ibid.*, 52.

[19] Nineham, *The Gospel of Saint Mark*, 412.

CHAPTER THREE

[1] G. B. Caird, *Saint Luke* (Baltimore: Penguin Books, 1972), 16.

[2] Kummel, *Introduction to the New Testament*, 100.

[3] *Ibid.*, 89.

[4] John Lightfoot, *A Commentary on the New Testament from the Talmud and Hebraica, Matthew--1 Corinthians*, vol. 3, *Luke—John* (1859; repr., Peabody: Massachusetts: Hendrickson Publishers, 1997), 76.

[5] Joseph A. Fitzmyer, *The Gospel According to Luke: A New Translation with Introduction and Commentary: X-XXIV*, vol. 2 (New York: Doubleday, 1985), 1233.

[6] Alfred Plummer, *A Critical and Exegetical Commentary on the Gospel According to S. Luke*, 5th ed. (Edinburgh: T. & T. Clarke, 1922), 440.

Endnotes...

[7] *Ibid.*, 443.

[8] J. Kodell, "Luke's Use of LAOS, 'People,' Especially in the Jerusalem Narrative (LK 19,28-24,53)," *Catholic Biblical Quarterly* 31, (1969): 333.

[9] Caird, *Saint Luke*, 241.

[10] Klaus Baltzer, *Deutero-Isaiah: A Commentary on Isaiah 40-55*, trans. Margaret Kohl, ed. Peter Machinist (Minneapolis: Fortress Press, 2001), 429.

[11] *Ibid.*, 407.

[12] Claus Westermann, *Isaiah 40-66: A Commentary* (Philadelphia: The Westminster Press, 1977), 262.

[13] Baltzer, *Deuter-Isaiah*, 407

[14] Westermann, *Isaiah 40-66*, 269.

[15] Fitzmyer, *The Gospel According to Luke*, 2:1451.

[16] Lightfoot, *Luke-John*, 3:376.

[17] Fitzmyer, *The Gospel According to Luke*, 2:1456.

[18] David Lestis Matson, "Pacifist Jesus? The (Mis)Translation of εᾶτε ἕως τούτου in Luke 22:51," *Journal of Biblical Literature* 134, no. 1 (2015): 157.

[19] *Ibid.*, 165.

[20] Georg Bertram, "διαστρέφω," in *TDNT*, ed. Gerhard Kittel and Gerhard Friedrich, trans., Geoffrey W. Bromiley, vol. 7 (Grand Rapids: Wm. B. Eerdmans, 1971), 718.

[21] Kodell, "Luke's Use of LAOS," 328.

[22] John J. Kilgallen, "Jesus' First Trial: Messiah and Son of God," (Luke 22, 66-71)," *Biblica* 80, no. 3 (1999): 403.

[23] Caird, *Saint Luke*, 247.

[24] S. MacLean Gilmour, "The Gospel According to Saint Luke: Introduction and Exegesis," in *The Interpreter's Bible*, vol. 8 (Nashville: Abingdon Press, 1952), 403.

[25] Fitzmyer, *The Gospel According to Luke*, 2:1496.

[26] *Ibid.*, 2:1504.

Endnotes...

[27] A. R. C. Leaney, *The Gospel According to Luke*, 2nd ed. (London: Adam and Charles Black, 1966), 279.

[28] Caird, *Saint Luke*, 243.

CHAPTER FOUR

[1] D. Moody Smith, *John Among the Gospels: The Relationship in Twentieth-Century Research* (Minneapolis: Fortress Press, 1993).

[2] F. F. Bruce, *The Gospel of John* (Grand Rapids: Eerdmans, 1983), 12.

[3] Walter A. Elwell and Robert W. Yarbrough, *Encounters in the New Testament: A Historical and Theological Survey*, 2nd ed. (Grand Rapids, Michigan: Baker Academic, 2005), 110.

[4] Rudolf Bultmann, *The Gospel of John: A Commentary*, trans., G. R. Beasley Murray (Philadelphia: The Westminster Press, (1971), 230.

[5] *Ibid.*, 229, n. 4.

[6] *Ibid.*, 444.

[7] J. H. Bernard, *A Critical and Exegetical Commentary on the Gospel According to St. John*, vol. 1 (Edinburgh: T. & T. Clarke, 7th impression, 1969), 269.

[8] J. H. Bernard, *A Critical and Exegetical Commentary on the Gospel According to John*, vol. 2 (1928 repr.; Edinburgh: T. & T. Clarke, 1972), 299.

[9] Bultmann, *The Gospel of John*, 446.

[10] *Ibid.* 443

[11] Raymond F. Brown, *The Gospel According to John I-XII: A New Translation with Introduction and Commentary*, vol. 1 (New York: Doubleday, 1966) 374.

[12] Bruce, *The Gospel of John*, 219.

[13] Brown, *The Gospel According to John*, 1:399.

[14] C. K. Barrett, *The Gospel According to St. John: An Introduction with Commentary and Notes on the Greek Text* (London: S.P.C.K., 1965), 314.

[15] William Barclay, *The Gospel of John*, vol. 2 (Philadelphia: The Westminster Press, 1975), 104.

[16] Bultmann, *The Gospel of John*, 411.

[17] Bernard, *John*, 2:590.

Endnotes...

[18] Barclay, *John*, 2:226.

[19] Lynn Carter Boughton, "The Priestly Perspective of the Johannine Trial Narratives," *Revue Biblique* 110, no. 4 (October 2003): 518.

[20] Brown, *The Gospel According to John*, 2:829.

[21] Lightfoot, *Luke-John*, 3:415.

[22] Brown, *The Gospel According to John*, 2:844.

[23] Bultmann, *The Gospel of John*, 642.

[24] *Ibid.*, 641.

[25] Brown, *The Gospel According to John*, 2:832.

[26] Bernard, *John*, 2:607.

[27] Bultmann, *The Gospel of John*, 662.

[28] Smith, *John Among the Gospels*, 130.

[29] Barrett, *The Gospel According to St. John*, 458.

[30] Bultmann, *The Gospel of John*, 671.

[31] Brown, *The Gospel According to John*, 2:929.

[32] Bultmann, *The Gospel of John*, 674-675.

[33] Karl Barth, "Index Volume with Aids for the Preacher," in *Church Dogmatics*, ed. G. W. Bromiley and T. F. Torrance, index vol. (Edinburgh: T. & T. Clarke, 1977, 378.

[34] Walter Gutbrod, "Ιουδαῖος," in *TDNT*, ED. Gerhard Kittel, trans., G. W. Bromiley, vol. 3 (Grand Rapids: Wm. B. Eerdmans, 1965), 379.

CHAPTER FIVE

[1] A. M. Okorie, "Who Crucified Jesus?," *Communio Viatoriam* 38, no. 2 (1996): 106.

[2] Werner Georg Kümmel, *The Theology of the New Testament According to Its Major Witnesses: Jesus—Paul—John*, trans., John E. Steely (Nashville: Abingdon Press, 1973), 71.

[3] S. G. F. Brandon, *The Trial of Jesus of Nazareth* (New York: Stein and Day, 1968), 6.

Endnotes...

[4] Michael J, Cook, "Where Jewish Scholars on Jesus Go Awry: Last Supper, Sanhedrin, Blasphemy, Barabbas," *Shofar* 28, no. 3 (2010): 70.

[5] *Ibid.*, 79.

[6] *Ibid.*, 75.

[7] *Ibid.*

[8] James M. Somerville, "Modern Jews Engage the New Testament: Enhancing Jewish Well-Being in A Christian Environment," *Theology Today* 66, no. 2 (July 2009): 252.

[9] Samuel Sandmel, *We Jews and Jesus: Exploring Theological Differences for Mutual Understanding* (Woodstock, Vermont: Jewish Lights Publishing, 2006), 197.

[10] W. Riggans, "The Jewish Reclamation of Jesus and Its Implications for Jewish-Christian Relations," *Themelios* 18, no. 1 (October 1992): 10.

[11] Peter Schafer, *Jesus In the Talmud* (Princeton: Princeton University Press, 2007), 17.

[12] *Ibid.*, 21.

[13] F. F. Bruce, *The Book of the Acts*, (Grand Rapids: Wm. Eerdmans, 1976), 162.

[14] Riggans, "The Jewish Reclamation of Jesus," 10.

[15] Haim Cohn, *The Trial and Death of Jesus* (1971; repr., Old Saybrook, CT: Konecky & Konecky, 2000), xii.

[16] *Ibid.*, xxi.

[17] *Ibid.*, 38.

[18] *Ibid.*, 114.

[19] *Ibid.*, 331.

[20] *Ibid.*, 327.

[21] *Ibid.*, 31-32.

[22] Alice Camille, "Seventy Angry Men," *U. S. Catholic* 78, no. 4 (April 2013): 46.

[23] David Instone-Brewer, "Jesus of Nazareth's Trial in the Uncensored Talmud," *Tyndale Bulletin* 62, no. 2 (2011): 278.

[24] Seltzer, *The Jewish People, Jewish Thought*, 245.

Endnotes…

[25] Eduard Lohse, "συνέδριον," in *TDNT*, 7:868.

[26] *Ibid.*, 868.

[27] Howard Clark Key, "Central Authority in Second Temple Judaism and Subsequently from Synedrion to Sanhedrin," *The Annual of Rabbinic Judaism* 2 (1999): 58.

[28] George A. Barton, "On the Trial of Jesus Before the Sanhedrin," *Journal of Biblical Literature* 41, no. 3-4 (1992): 209.

[29] John Dominic Crossan, *Who Killed Jesus? Exposing the Roots of Anti-Semitism in the Gospel Story of the Death of Jesus* (San Francisco: HarperSanFrancisco, 1995), ix.

[30] *Ibid.*, 223.

[31] Bart Ehrman, *Lost Christianities: The Battle for Scripture and the Faiths We Never Knew* (New York: Oxford University Press (2003), 20.

[32] Wilhelm Schneermelcher, *New Testament Apocrypha, I: Gospels and Related Writings* (Louisville: John Knox, 1991), 217.

[33] Spivey and Smith, *Anatomy*, 173.

[34] Brown, *Death of the Messiah*, 1:5.

[35] Paul Foster, "Do Crosses Walk and Talk? A Reconsideration of Gospel of Peter 10:39-42," *The Journal of Theological Studies* 64, no. 1 (April 2013: 100.

[36] Crossan, *Who Killed Jesus?*, 187-188.

[37] Brown, *Death of the Messiah*, 2:1274.

[38] Crossan, *Who Killed Jesus?*, 37.

[39] *Ibid.*, xii

[40] *Ibid.*, 106.

[41] *Ibid.*, 117.

[42] *Ibid.*, 147.

[43] *Ibid.*, 96.

[44] Brown, *The Gospel According to John*, 2: 849.

[45] Jean Juster, *Les Juifs Dans l'Empire Romain,(Jews in the Roman Empire)*, 2 vols. (Paris: Paul Geuthner, 1914). This book does not have an English translation.

Endnotes...

[46] *Babylonian Talmud, Tractate Aboda Zara*, 8b.

[47] Barrett, *The Gospel According to St. John*, 445.

[48] Juster, *Les Juifs*, 2:132-145.

[49] Lightfoot, *Luke-John*, 3:424.

[50] *Ibid.*, 428.

[51] Augustine, ""Homilies on the Gospel of John," in *Nicene and Post-Nicene Fathers*, ed. Philip Schaff, 2nd printing, vol. 7 (Peabody, Massachusetts: Hendrickson Publishing, 1995), 421.

[52] Chrysostom, "Homilies on the Gospel of Saint John and the Epistle to the Hebrews," in *Nicene and Post-Nicene Fathers*, ed. Philip Schaff, 2nd printing, vol 14 (Peabody, Massachusetts: Hendrickson Publishers, 1995), 310.

[53] *Ibid.*, 365.

[54] T. A. Burkill, "The Competence of the Sanhedrin," *Vigiliae Christianae* 10, no. 2 (April 1956): 80-96.

[55] Philo, "On the Embassy to Gaius," 785.

[56] Burkill, "Competence," 95.

[57] *Ibid.*

[58] Josephus, *Works: The Wars of the Jews* 1.6.2.4.434.

[59] Burkill, "Competence," 96.

[60] Paul Winter, "The Trial of Jesus," *Commentary* (September 1964): 39.

[61] Paul Winter. "Marginal Notes on the Trial of Jesus," *Zeitschrift für die Neutestamentliche und die Kunderalteran Kirche* 50, no. 1-2 (1959): 17.

[62] *Ibid.*, 33.

CHAPTER SIX

[1] John Wesley, *The Works of John Wesley*, vol. 1, *Journals from October 14, 1735 to November 29,* 1745, 3rd ed. (1872; repr., Grand Rapids, Michigan: Baker Book House, 1978), 103.

[2] John Wesley, *The Works of John Wesley*, vol. 13, *Letters*, 3rd ed. (1872; repr., Grand Rapids, Michigan: Baker Book House, 1978, 300.

[3] Wesley, *Works*, vol. 1, 315.

Endnotes…

⁴ *Ibid.*

⁵ *Ibid.,* 185-186.

⁶ *Ibid.,* 186.

⁷ Martin Luther, *Luther's Works,* ed. and trans. Theodore G. Tappert, vol. 54, *Table Talk* (Philadelphia: Fortress Press, 1967), 424-425.

⁸ John Wesley, *The Works of John Wesley,* vol. 2, *Journals from December 2, 1745 to May 5, 1760,* 3rd ed. (1872; repr., Grand Rapids, Michigan: Baker Book House, 1978), 142.

⁹ Erik H. Erikson, *Young Man Luther: A Study in Psychoanalysis and History* (New York: W. W. Norton & Company, 1958), 15.

¹⁰ *Ibid.*, 28.

¹¹ *Ibid.*, 97.

¹² *Ibid.*, 37.

¹³ Eric Gritsch, "The Unrefined Reformer," *Christian History* 39 (1993): no pagination.

¹⁴ *Ibid.*

¹⁵ *Ibid.*

¹⁶ Luther, *Luther's Works*, vol. 54, 448. Note: This quote is from the American Version which has "cleaned up"Luther's language. The literal translation from *Tischedren*, Weimar Ausgaben, V, no. 5537 is "I am like ripe shit and the world is a gigantic asshole."

¹⁷ Gritsch, "The Unrefined Reformer," no pagination.

¹⁸ Michael Harrington, *The Politics at God's Funeral: The Spiritual Crisis of Western Civilization* (New York: Holt, Rinehart and Winston, 1983), 59.

¹⁹ Daniel Conway, ed., *Nietzsche: Critical Assessments* (London and New York: Routledge, 1998), 12.

²⁰ Walter Kaufmann, ed. and trans., *The Basic Writings of Nietzsche* (New York: The Modern Library, 1968), 581.

²¹ Martin Luther, *Luther's Works,* ed. Helmut T. Lehmann and James Atkinson, trans. Walter L. Brandt, vol. 45, *That Jesus Christ Was Born A Jew* (Philadelphia: Fortress Press, 1962), 200-204.

Endnotes...

[22] Alexander Chalmers, *The Life of Martin Luther*, ed. and trans. William Hazlitt (London: H. G. Bohn, York Street, Covent Garden, 1856), 94.

[23] Christian National Crusade, *On the Jews and Their Lies, First English Translation Published in the U.S.A.* (Las Angeles, California: Christian National Crusade, May 1948).

[24] *Ibid.*, cover page.

[25] *Ibid.*, 3.

[26] *Ibid.*

[27] Martin Luther, *Luther's Works*, ed by Franklin Sherman, trans. Martin H. Bertram, vol. 47, *The Christian in Society IV* (Philadelphia: Fortress Press, 1971).

[28] *Ibid.*, 123.

[29] Luther, *Luther's Works*, vol. 47, 267.

[30] Sherman Franklin, *Faith Transformed: Christian Encounters with Jews and Judaism*, ed. John C. Merkle (Collegeville, Minnesota: Liturgical Press, 2003), 63-64.

[31] Luther, *Luther's Works*, vol. 47, 137.

[32] *Ibid.*

[33] *Ibid.*, 192.

[34] *Ibid.*, 242

[35] *Ibid.*, 140.

[36] *Ibid.*, 256.

[37] *Ibid*, 211.

[38] *Ibid.*, 227.

[39] *Ibid.*, 261

[40] *Ibid.*, 217.

[41] *Ibid.*, 265.

[42] *Ibid.*

[43] *Ibid.*, 268.

[44] *Ibid.*, 268-272, 285-286.

Endnotes…

[45] *Ibid.*, 272.

[46] *Ibid.*, 292.

[47] Gerhard Falk, *The Jew in Christian Theology: Martin Luther's Anti-Jewish Vom Schem Hamphoras, Previously Unpublished in English, and Other Milestones in Church Doctrine Concerning Judaism* (Jefferson, North Carolina: McFarland, 1992), 163-224.

[48] Brooks Schramm, "Luther's Schem Hamphoras," *Dialog: A Journal of Theology* 56, no. 2 (June 2017): 154.

[49] Peter Schafer, Michael Meerson and Yaccov Deutsch, ed., *Toldot Yeshu: The Life Story of Jesus Rewritten* (Tubingen, Germany: Mohr Siebeck, 2011), 186.

[50] Schafer, *Toldot*, 65.

[51] *Ibid.*, 306.

[52] Falk, 214.

[53] *Ibid.*

[54] *Ibid.*, 192.

[55] *Ibid.*, 215.

[56] *Ibid.*, 166.

[57] *Ibid.*, 239. "*Der Sau im (grab heraus) Hinterns.*"

[58] *Ibid.*, 182-183.

[59] *Ibid.*, 186.

[60] *Ibid.*, 195.

[61] Robert Michael, "Luther, Luther Scholars and the Jews," *Encounter* 46, no. 4 (Autumn 1985): 351-352.

[62] Falk, 224.

[63] William Shakespeare, *Julius Caesar*, Act 3, Scene 2, line 75.

[64] Mark Edwards, *Luther's Last Battles: Politics and Polemics 1531-46* (Ithaca and London: Cornell University Press, 1983), 121.

[65] Falk, 224, n. 7.

[66] *Ibid.*, 222.

Endnotes…

[67] Alan Dershowitz, *Chutzpah* (Boston: Little, Brown and Company, 1991), 106-107.

[68] Michael, "Luther, Luther Scholars and the Jews," 346.

[69] Mark Edwards, "Martin Luther and the Jews: Is There a Holocaust Connection?" *Shofar* 1, no. 4 (Summer 1983), 14.

[70] *Das Reich muss uns doch bleiben* is literally translated as "the Kingdom must stay with us."

[71] Walter Kaufmann, *Nietzsche: Philosopher, Psychologist, Antichrist* (Princeton: Princeton University Press, 1974), 198.

[72] Pierre van Passen, *Days of Our Years*, (Garden City, New York: Garden City Publishing Co., Inc., 1940), 176.

[73] Robert Michael, *Holy Hatred: Christianity, Antisemitism and the Holocaust* (New York: Palgrave Macmillan, 2006), 169.

[74] Diarmaid MacCulloch, *Reformation: Europe's House Divided:* (London: Penguin Books, 2003), 666-667.

[75] Luther, *Luther's Works*, vol. 47, 267.

[76] Alan Davies, *Anti-Semitism and the Christian Mind* (New York: Herder and Herder, 1969), 59.

[77] Falk, 55.

[78] *Ibid.*, 65.

[79] Richard Gutteridge, *The German Evangelical Church and the Jews 1879-1950* (New York: Harper and Row, 1976), 3.

[80] Ronald F. Marshall, "Luther's Alleged Anti-Semitism," *Logia* 21, no. 4 (2012): 5.

[81] Roland Bainton, *Here I Stand: A Life of Martin Luther* (Nashville: Abingdon Press, 1950), 379.

[82] *Ibid.*, 380.

[83] Martin Luther, *Luther's Works*, ed. Christopher Boyd Brown, vol. 58, *Sermons V* (Saint Louis: Concordia Publishing House, 2010), 458-459.

[84] The Church Council of the Evangelical Lutheran Church in America, April 18, 1994.

Endnotes…

[85] Lucy Dawidowicz, *The War Against the Jews 1933-1945* (New York: Holt, Rinehart and Winston, 1975), 23.

[86] Michael, "Luther, Luther Scholars and the Jews," 349.

[87] See pages 59-62 in Chapter One above.

[88] Michael Berenbaum, *The World Must Know: The History of the Holocaust as Told in the United States Holocaust Memorial Museum* (Boston: Little, Brown and Company, 1992).

[89] *Ibid.*, 14.

Chapter Seven

[1] Seltzer, *The Jewish People, Jewish Thought*, 607-612.

[2] Frank J. Coppa, "Pope Pius: From the Diplomacy of Impartiality to the Silence of the Holocaust," *Journal of Church and State* 55, no. 2 (June 2013): 286.

[3] *Ibid.*, 300.

[4] Hans Küng, *On Being a Christian* (Glasgow: William Collins and Sons, 1978), 169.

[5] *Nostra Aetate, Declaration on the Relationship of the Church to Non-Christian Religions, Second Vatican Council,* October 28, 1965.

[6] Filson, *The Gospel According to Saint Matthew*, 291.

[7] Robert Wistrich, "Why Has Pope Benedict Chosen Now to Beatify Nazi-Era Pontiff?" http://www.haaretz.com/1.4834284, December 28, 2009).

[8] David Novak, "Jews and Catholics: Beyond Apologies," *First Things* 89 (January 1999): 20.

[9] Küng, *On Being a Christian*, 173.

[10] Leander Keck, *Who Is Jesus? History in Perfect Tense* (Minneapolis: Fortress Press, 2001), 207.

Conclusion

[1] Brown, *The Gospel According to John*, 2:832.

[2] Leon Morris, *Studies in the Fourth Gospel* (Grand Rapids: Wm. B. Eerdmans, 1969), 63.

Endnotes...

[3] William A. Johnson, "The Jews in Saint Mark's Gospel," *Religion and Intellectual Life* 6, no. 3-4 (Spring-Summer 1989): 183.

[4] Christian Maurer, "σχίζω," in *TDNT*, ed. Gerhard Kittel and Gerhard Friedrich, trans. Geoffrey W. Bromiley, vol. 7 (Grand Rapids: Wm. B. Eerdmans, 1971), 995.

[5] Morris, *Studies in the Fourth Gospel*, 195.

[6] Brandon, *The Trial of Jesus of Nazareth*, 90.

[7] Martin Hengel, *Crucifixion in the Ancient World and the Folly of the Message of the Cross* (Philadelphia: Fortress Press, 1977), 86-87.

[8] Crossan, *Who Killed Jesus?* 148.

[9] Seltzer, *The Jewish People, Jewish Thought*, 245.

[10] Instone-Brewer, "Jesus of Nazareth's Trial in the Uncensored Talmud," 290-294.

[11] Lester L. Grabbe, "Sanhedrin, Sanhedriyyot, or Mere Invention," *Journal for the Study of Judaism* 39, no. 1 (2008): 19.

[12] Instone-Brewer, "Jesus of Nazareth's Trial in the Uncensored Talmud," 273.

[13] Hans Conzelmann, *Jesus* (Philadelphia: Fortress Press, 1973), 86.

BIBLIOGRAPHY

Aland, Kurt, Matthew Black, Carlo Martini, Bruce M. Metzger, and Allen Wikgren, eds., *The Greek New Testament*. New York: American Bible Society, 1975.

Albright, W. F. and C. S. Mann. *Matthew: A New Translation with Introduction and Commentary*. New York: Doubleday, 1971.

Allen, W. C. *A Critical and Exegetical Commentary on the Gospel According to Matthew*. 3rd ed. Edinburgh: T.&T. Clark, 1912.

Anderson, Hugh. *The Gospel of Mark*. London: Oliphants, 1976.

Augustine. "Homilies on the Gospel of John." In *Nicene and Post-Nicene Fathers*. Edited by Philip Schaff. 7th Printing, Vol. 7: Peabody, Massachusetts: Hendrickson Publishing, 1995.

Bainton, Roland. *Here I Stand: A Life of Martin Luther*. Nashville: Abingdon Press, 1950.

Baltzer, Klaus. *Deutero-Isaiah: A Commentary on Isaiah 40-55*. Translated by Margaret Kohl and Edited by Peter Machinist. Minneapolis: Fortress Press, 2001.

Barclay, William. *The Gospel of John*. Vol. 2. Philadelphia: The Westminster Press, 1975.

_____. *The Gospel of Mark*. Philadelphia: The Westminster Press, 1975.

_____. *The Gospel of Matthew*. Vol. 1. Philadelphia: The Westminster Press, 1975.

Barrett, C. K. *The Gospel According to St. John: An Introduction with Commentary and Notes on the Greek Text*. London: S.P.C.K.

Barth, Karl. "The Doctrine of Creation." In *Church Dogmatics*. Translated by G. W. Bromiley. Vol. 3, part 2. 1960. Reprint, Edinburgh: T.&T. Clark, 1980.

_____. "Index Volume with Aids for the Preacher." In *Church Dogmatics*. Edited by G. W. Bromiley and T. F. Torrance. Index Vol. Edinburgh: T.&T. Clarke, 1980.

_____. "The Doctrine of Reconciliation." In *Church Dogmatics*. Translated by G. W. Bromiley. Vol.4, part 1. 1956. Reprint, Edinburgh: T.&T. Clarke, 1977.

Barton, George A. "On the Trial of Jesus Before the Sanhedrin." *Journal of Biblical Literature* 41, no. 3-4 (1992): 205-211.

Bauer, Walter. *A Greek-English Lexicon of the New Testament and Other Early Christian Literature*. 4th revised and augmented edition. Translated and Edited by William F. Arndt and F. Wilbur Gingrich. Chicago: University of Chicago Press, 1957.

Beare, F. W. *The Gospel According to Matthew*. New York: Harper & Row, 1981.

Behm, J. "μετανοέω." *Theological Dictionary of the New Testament*. Translated by Geoffrey W. Bromiley and Edited by Gerhard Kittel. Vol.4. Grand Rapids: Wm. B. Eerdmans, 1967: 975-1022.

Beider, Werner. "ριψτω." *Theological Dictionary of the New Testament*. Translated by Geoffrey W. Bromiley and Edited by Gerhard Kittel and Gerhard Friedrich. Vol. 6. Grand Rapids: Wm. B. Eerdmans, 1968: 991-993.

Berenbaum, Michael. *The World Must Know: The History of the Holocaust as Told in the United States Holocaust Memorial Museum*. Boston: Little, Brown and Company, 1992.

Bernard, J. H. *A Critical and Exegetical Commentary on the Gospel According to St. John*. Vol. 1. Edinburgh: T.&T. Clark, 1969.

Bernard, J. H. *A Critical and Exegetical Commentary on the Gospel According to St. John*. Vol. 2. 1928. Reprint, Edinburgh: T.&T. Clark, 1972

Bertram, Georg. "διαστρέφω." *Theological Dictionary of the New Testament*. Translated by Geoffrey W. Bromiley and Edited by Gerhard Kittel and Gerhard Friedrich. Vol 7. Grand Rapids: Wm. B. Eerdmans, 1971: 714-729.

Boughton, Lynn Carter. "The Priestly Perspective of the Johannine Trial Narratives." *Revue Biblique* 110, no 4 (October 2003): 517-551.

Brandon, S. G. F. *The Trial of Jesus of Nazareth*. New York: Stein and Day, 1968.

Brown, Raymond E. *The Death of the Messiah: From Gethsemane to the Grave*. vol. 1. New York: Doubleday, 1994: vii-877.

_____. *The Death of the Messiah: From Gethsemane to the Grave*. Vol. 2. New York: Doubleday, 1994: vii-877.

_____. *The Gospel According to John I-XII: A New Translation with Introduction and Commentary*. Vol. 1. New York: Doubleday, 1966: v-538.

Bruce, F. F. *The Book of Acts*. Grand Rapids: Wm. B. Eerdmans, 1976.

_____. *The Gospel of John*. Grand Rapids: Wm. B. Eerdmans, 1983.

Bultmann, Rudolf. *The Gospel of John: A Commentary*. Translated by G. R. Beasley Murray. Philadelphia: The Westminster Press, 1971.

_____. "ἀφίημι." *Theological Dictionary of the New Testament*. Translated by Geoffrey W. Bromiley and Edited by Gerhard Kittel. Vol. 1. Grand Rapids: Wm B. Eerdmans, 1965: 509-512.

_____. *Theology of the New Testament: Complete in One Volume*. Translated by Kendrick Grobel. 2 Vols. New York: Charles Scribner's Sons, 1951-1955.

Burkill, T. A. "The Competence of the Sanhedrin." *Vigiliae Christianae* 10, no. 2 (April 1956): 80-96.

Caird, G. B. *Saint Luke*. Baltimore: Penguin Books, 1972.

Camille, Alice. "Seventy Angry Men." *U. S. Catholic* 78, no. 4 (April 2013): 44-46.

Canetti, Elias. *Crowds and Power.* Translated by Carol Stewart. New York: Continuum, 1973.

Carter, Warren. "The Crowds in Matthew's Gospel." *The Catholic Biblical Quarterly* 55, no. 1 January 1993): 54-67.

Chalmers, Alexander. *The Life of Martin Luther.* Edited and Translated by William Hazlitt. London: H. G. Bohn, York Street, Covent Garden, 1856.

Childs, Brevard. *The New Testament as Canon: An Introduction.* Philadelphia Fortress Press, 1984.

Christian National Crusade. *On the Jews and Their Lies, First English Translation in the U.S.A.* Las Angeles, California: Christian National Crusade, Publishers , May 1948.

Cohn, Haim. *The Trial and Death of Jesus.* 1971. Reprint, Old Saybrook CT: Konecky & Konecky, 2000.

Conway, Daniel, ed. *Nietzsche: Critical Assessments.* London and New York: Routledge, 1998.

Conzelmann, Hans. *Jesus*. Philadelphia: Fortress Press, 1973.

Cook, Michael J. "Where Jewish Scholars on Jesus Go Awry: Last Supper, Sanhedrin, Blasphemy, Barabbas." *Shofar* 28, no. 3 (2010): 70-77.

Coppa, Frank J. "Pope Pius: From the Diplomacy of Impartiality to the Silence of the Holocaust." *Journal of Church and State* 55, no. 2 (June 2013): 256-306.

Crossan, John Dominic. *Who Killed Jesus?: Exposing the Roots of Anti-Semitism in the Gospel Story of the Death of Jesus.* San Francisco: HarperSanFrancisco, 1995.

Cousland, R. C. *The Crowds in the Gospel of Matthew.* Brill: Leiden, 2002.

Chrysostom. "Homilies on the Gospel of Saint John and the Epistle to the Hebrews." In *Nicene and Post-Nicene Fathers.* Edited by Philip Schaff.

2nd Printing, Vol. 14. Peabody, Massachusetts: Hendrickson Publishers, 1995.

Dana, H. E. and Julius R. Mantey. *A Manual Grammar of the Greek New Testament.* Toronto: The Macmillan Co., 1955.

Davies, Alan. *Anti-Semitism and the Christian Mind.* New York: Herder and Herder, 1969.

Dawidowicz, Lucy. *The War Against the Jews 1933-1945.* New York: Holt, Rinehart and Winston, 1975.

Delling, Gerhard. "καιρός." *Theological Dictionary of the New Testament.* Translated by Geoffrey W. Bromiley and Edited by Gerhard Kittel. Vol. 3. Grand Rapids: Wm. B. Eerdmans, 1965: 455-464.

Dershowitz, Alan. *Chutzpah.* Boston: Little, Brown and Company, 1991.

Edwards, Mark. *Luther's Last Battles: Politics and Polemics.* Ithaca and London: Cornell University Press, 1983.

_____. "Martin Luther and the Jews: Is There a Holocaust Connection?" *Shofar* 1, no. 4 (Summer 1983): 14-16.

Ehrman, Bart. *Lost Christianities: The Battle for Scripture and the Faiths We Never Knew.* New York: Oxford University Press, 2003.

Eichrodt, Walther. *Theology of the Old Testament.* Translated by J. A. Baker. Vol. 1. Philadelphia: Westminster Press, 1961.

_____. *Theology of the Old Testament.* Translated by J. A. Baker. Vol. 2. Philadelphia: Westminster Press, 1967.

Elwell, Walter A. and Robert W. Yarbrough. *Encounters in the New Testament: A Historical and Theological Survey.* 2nd Edition. Grand Rapids: Baker Academic, 2005.

Erikson, Erik H, *Young Man Luther: A Study in Psychoanalysis and History.* New York: W. W. Norton & Company, 1958.

Eusebious. "The Statements of Irenaeus in Regard to the Divine Scriptures." In *Nicene and Post-Nicene Fathers.* Edited by Philip Schaff and Henry Wace. Vol. 9, 322. Peabody, Massachusetts: Hendrickson Publishers, 1995.

_____. "The Writings of Papias." In *Nicene and Post-Nicene Fathers*. Edited by Philip Schaff and Henry Wace. Vol. 9, 170-173. Peabody, Massachusetts: Hendrickson Publishers, 1995.

Falk, Gerhard. *The Jew in Christian Theology: Martin Luther's Anti-Jewish Vom Schem Hamphoras, Previously Unpublished in English, and Other Milestones in Church Doctrine Concerning Judaism*. Jefferson, North Carolina: McFarland, 1992.

Filson, Floyd. *The Gospel According to Matthew*. London: Adam & Charles Black, 1977.

Fitzmyer, J. A. "Anti-Semitism and the Cry of 'All the People' (Mt. 27:25)." *Theological Studies* 26 (1965): 667-671.

_____. *The Gospel According to Luke: A New Translation with Introduction and Commentary: X-XXIV*. Vol. 2. New York: Doubleday, 1985.

Forester, Werner. "ἔχιδνα." *Theological Dictionary of the New Testament*. Translated by Geoffrey W. Bromiley and Edited by Gerhard Kittel. Vol. 2. Grand Rapids: Wm. B. Eerdmans, 1964: 815-816.

_____. "ὄφις." *Theological Dictionary of the New Testament*. Translated by Geoffrey Bromiley and Edited by Gerhard Kittel and Gerhard Friedrich. Vol. 5. Grand Rapids: Wm. B. Eerdmans, 1967: 576-582.

Foster, Paul. "Do Crosses Walk and Talk? A Reconsideration of Gospel of Peter 10:39-42." *The Journal of Theological Studies* 64, no. 1 (April 2013): 89-104.

France, R. T. *Matthew: An Introduction and Commentary*. Downers Grove, Illinois: IVP Academic, 507. https//scribd.com.

Franklin, Sherman. *Faith Transformed: Christian Encounters with Jews and Judaism*. Edited by John C. Merkle. Collegeville, Minnesota: Liturgical Press, 2003.

Gilmour, S. MacLean. "The Gospel According to Saint Luke: Introduction and Exegesis." In *The Interpreter's Bible*. Vol. 8. Nashville: Abingdon Press, 1952.

Goppelt, Leonard. "ποτήριον." *Theological Dictionary of the New Testament*. Translated by Geoffrey W. Bromiley and Edited by Gerhard Kittel and Gerhard Friedrich. Vol. 6. Grand Rapids: Wm. B. Eerdmans,1968: 148-160.

Gould, Ezra P. *A Critical and Exegetical Commentary on the Gospel According to Saint Mark*. Edinburgh: T.&T. Clarke, 1896.

Grabbe, Lester L. "Sanhedrin, Sanhedriyyot, or Mere Invention." *Journal for the Study of Judaism* 39, no. 1 (2008): 1-19.

Gritsch, Eric. "The Unrefined Reformer," *Christian History* 39 (1993): no pagination.

Gundry, Robert H. *A Survey of the New Testament*. Grand Rapids: Zondervan, 1970.

Gutbrod, Walter. "Ἰουδαῖος." *Theological Dictionary of the New Testament*. Translated by G. W. Bromiley and Edited by Gerhard Kittel. Vol. 3. Grand Rapids: Wm. B. Eerdmans, 1965: 369-391.

Gutteridge, Richard. *The German Evangelical Church and the Jews 1879-1950*. New York: Harper and Row, 1976.

Harrington, Michael. *The Politics at God's Funeral: The Spiritual Crisis of Western Civilization*. New York: Holt, Rinehart and Winston, 1983.

Hengel, Martin. *Crucifixion in the Ancient World and the Folly of the Message of the Cross*. Philadelphia: Fortress Press, 1977.

Hertz, J. H., Editor. *The Pentateuch and Haftorahs: Hebrew Text, English Translation and Commentary*. Vol. 2. London: Oxford University Press, 1937.

Instone-Brewer, David. "Jesus of Nazareth's Trial in the Uncensored Talmud." *Tyndale Bulletin* 62, no. 2 (2011): 269-294.

Jeremias, Joachim. "γραμματεύς." *Theological Dictionary of the New Testament*. Translated by Geoffrey W. Bromiley and Edited by Gerhard Kittel. Vol. 1. Grand Rapids: Wm. B. Eerdmans, 1964: 740-742.

_____. *Jerusalem in the Time of Jesus*. Translated by F. H. and C. F. Cave. Philadelphia: Fortress Press, 1969.

Jewish Virtual Library. *Babylonian Talmud: Tractate Abada Zarah 8b.* https://jewish virtuallibrary.org/tractate-avodah-zara.

Johnson, Sherman E. "The Gospel According to Saint Matthew: Introduction and Exegesis." In *The Interpreter's Bible*. Vol. 7. Nashville: Abingdon Press, 1951.

Johnson, William A. "The Jews in Saint Mark's Gospel." *Religion and Intellectual Life* 6, no. 3-4 (Spring-Summer 1989): 181-192.

Josephus, Flavius. *The Works of Flavious Josephus in Four Volumes.* Translated by William Whiston. Vol. 1. *The Wars of the Jews* and *Josephus and Masada*. Grand Rapids: Baker Book House, 1974.

———. *The Works of Flavius Josephus in Four Volumes.* Translated by William Whiston. Vol. 2. *The Life of Flavious Josephus* and *Antiquities of the Jews Books 1-8*. Grand Rapids: Baker Book House, 1974.

———. *The Works of Flavius Josephus in Four Volumes.* Translated by William Whiston. Vol. 3. *The Life of Flavious Josephus* and *Antiquities of the Jews Books 9-17*. Rapids: Baker Book House, 1974.

———. *The Works of Flavius Josephus in Four Volumes.* Translated by William Whiston. Vol. 4. *Antiquities of the Jews Books 18-20*. Grand Rapids: Baker Book House, 1974.

Juster, Jean. *Les Juifs Dans l'Empire Romain*. 2 vols. Paris: Paul Geuthner, 1914. (This book does not have an English Translation).

Kaufmann, Walter. *Nietzsche: Philosopher, Psychologist, Antichrist.* Princeton: Princeton University Press, 1974.

———. Editor and Translator. *The Basic Writings of Nietzsche.* New York: The Modern Library, 1968.

Keck, Leander. *Who Is Jesus?: History in Perfect Tense.* Minneapolis: Fortress Press, 2001.

Key, Howard Clark. "Central Authority in Second Temple Judaism and Subsequently from Synedrion to Sanhedrin." *The Annual of Rabbinic Judaism* 2 (1999): 51-63.

Kilgallen, John J. "Jesus' First Trial: Messiah and Son of God (Luke 22:66-71)." *Biblica* 80, no. 3 (1999): 401-414.

Kingsbury, J. D. *The Parables of Jesus in Matthew 13*. Richmond: John Knox, 1969.

Kittel, Gerhard. "ἀκολουθέω," *Theological Dictionary of the New Testament*. Translated by Geoffrey W. Bromiley and Edited by Gerhard Kittel. Vol. 1. Grand Rapids: Wm. B. Eerdmans, 1964: 210-216.

Kodell, J. "Luke's Use of LAOS, 'People,' Especially in the Jerusalem Narrative (LK 19:28-24:53)." *Catholic Biblical Quarterly* 31, (1969): 327-343.

Kümmel, Werner Georg. *Introduction to the New Testament: An English Translation*. Translated by A. J. Mattill, Jr. Nashville: Abingdon Press, 1965.

_____. *The Theology of the New Testament According to Its Major Witnesses: Jesus—Paul—John*. Translated by John E. Steely. Nashville: Abingdon Press, 1973.

Küng, Hans. *On Being a Christian*. Glasgow: William Collins and Sons, 1978.

Leaney, A. R. C. *The Gospel According to Luke*. 2nd Edition. London: Adam and Charles Black, 1966.

Lightfoot, John. *A Commentary on the New Testament from the Talmud and Hebraica, Matthew—1 Corinthians, Luke-John*. Vol. 3. 1859, Reprint. Peabody: Massachusetts: Hendrickson Publishers, 1997.

Lohse, Eduard. "συνέδριον." *Theological Dictionary of the New Testament*. Translated by Geoffrey W. Bromiley and Edited by Gerhard Kittel and Gerhard Friedrich. Vol. 7. Grand Rapids: Wm. B. Eerdmans, 1971: 860-871.

Luther, Martin. *Luther's Works*. Edited and Translated by G. T. Tappert, Vol. 54, *Table Talk*. Philadelphia: Fortress Press, 1967.

_____. *Luther's Works*. Edited by Helmut T. Lehmann, James Atkinson and Translated by Walter L. Brandt. Vol. 45, *The Christian in Society II*. Philadelphia: Fortress Press, 1962.

_____. *Luther's Works*. Edited by Franklin Sherman and Translated by Martin H. Bertram. Vol. 47, *The Christian in Society IV*, Philadelphia: Fortress Press, 1971.

_____. *Luther's Works*. Edited by Christopher Boyd Brown. Vol. 58,*Sermons V*, Saint Louis: Concordia Publishing House, 2010.

Luz, Ulrich. *Matthew 1-7*. Translated by William C. Linss. Minneapolis: Augsburg, 1989.

MacCulloch, Diarmaid. *Reformation: Europe's House Divided*. London: Penguin Books, 2003.

Mann, C. S. Mark: *A New Translation with Introduction and Commentary*. New York: Doubleday, 1986.

Marshall, Ronald F. "Luther's Alleged Anti-Semitism." *Logia* 21, no. 4 (2012): 5-8.

May, Herbert and Bruce Metzger, eds. *The New Oxford Annotated Bible with the Apocrypha: Revised Standard Version*. New York: Oxford University Press, 1977.

Mays, James. "'Now I Know': An Exposition of Genesis 22:1-19 and Matthew 26:36-46." *Theology Today* 58, no. 4 (January 2002): 172-189.

Matson, David Lestis. "Pacifist Jesus? The (Mis)Translation of εᾶτε ἕως τούτου in Luke 22:51." *Journal of Biblical Literature* 134, no. 1 (2015): 157-176.

Maurer, Christian. "σχίζω." *Theological Dictionary of the New Testament*. Translated by Geoffrey W. Bromiley and Edited by Gerhard Kittel and Gerhard Friedrich. Vol. 7. Grand Rapids: Wm. B. Eerdmans, 1971: 35-54.

Metzger, Bruce M. *The New Testament: Its Background, Growth and Content*. Nashville: Abingdon Press, 1965.

Meyer, Rudolf. "ὄχλος." *Theological Dictionary of the New Testament*. Translated by Geoffrey W. Bromiley and Edited by Gerhard Kittel and Gerhard Friedrich. Vol. 5. Grand Rapids: Wm. B. Eerdmans, 1967: 582-590.

_____. Rudolf. "Σαδδουκαῖος." *Theological Dictionary of the New Testament*. Translated by Geoffrey W. Bromiley and Edited by Gerhard Kittel and Gerhard Friedrich. Vol. 5. Grand Rapids: Wm. B. Eerdmans, 1967: 582-590.

Michael, Robert. *Holy Hatred: Christianity, Antisemitism and the Holocaust*. New York: Palgrave Macmillan, 2006.

_____. "Luther, Luther Scholars and the Jews." *Encounter* 46, no. 4 (Autumn 1985): 339-356.

Michel. O. "μεταμέλομα." *Theological Dictionary of the New Testament*. Translated by Geoffrey W. Bromiley and Edited by Gerhard Kittel. Vol. 4. Grand Rapids: Wm. B. Eerdmans, 1967: 626-629.

Minear, Paul. "The Disciples and the Crowds in the Gospel of Matthew." *Anglican Theological Review*. Supplementary Series 3 (1974): 28-44.

Morris, Leon. *Studies in the Fourth Gospel*. Grand Rapids: Wm. B. Eerdmans, 1969.

Nineham, D. E. *The Gospel of Saint Mark*. London: Penguin Books, 1963.

Noth, Martin. *Numbers: A Commentary*. Philadelphia: The Westminster Press, 1968.

Novak, David. "Jews and Catholics: Beyond Apologies." *First Things* 89 (January 1999): 120-125.

Okorie, A. M. "Who Crucified Jesus?" *Communio Viatoriam* 38, no. 2 (1996): 101-109.

Origen. "From the First Book of the Commentary on Matthew." In *Anti-Nicene Fathers*. Edited by Allan Menzies. Vol. 9, 412. Peabody, Massachusetts: Hendrickson Publishers, 1995.

Philo of Alexandria. "On the Embassy to Gaius." In *The Works of Philo: New Updated Edition Complete and Unabridged in One Volume*. Translated by C. D. Yonge. Peabody, MA: Hendrickson, 1995.

Plummer, Alfred. *A Critical and Exegetical Commentary on the Gospel According to S. Luke*. 5th Edition. Edinburgh: T.&T. Clarke, 1922.

Riggans, W. "The Jewish Reclamation of Jesus and Its Implications for Jewish-Christian Relations." *Themelios* 18, no. 1 (October 1992): 9-16.

Ringgren, Helmer. *Israelite Religion*. Translated by David E. Green. Philadelphia: Fortress Press, 1966.

Saldarini, Anthony. "Comparing the Traditions: New Testament and Rabbinic Literature." *Bulletin for Biblical Research* 7 (1997): 195-204.

_____. *Matthew's Christian-Jewish Community (Studies in the History of Judaism)*. Chicago: Chicago University Press, 1994.

Sandmel, Samuel. *We Jews and Jesus: Exploring Theological Differences for Mutual Understanding*. Woodstock, Vermont: Jewish Lights Publishing, 2006.

Second Vatican Council. *Nostra Aetate, Declaration on the Relationship of the Church to Non-Christian Religions, Second Vatican Council*, October 28, 1965.

Schafer, Peter. *Jesus in the Talmud*. Princeton: Princeton University Press, 2007.

Shafer, Peter and Michael Meerson, Yaccov Deutsch, Ed. *Toldot Yeshu:The Life Story of Jesus Rewritten*. Tubingen, Germany: Mohr Siebeck, 2011.

Schiffman, L. H. *From Text to Tradition: A History of Second Temple and Rabbinic Judaism*. Hoboken: New Jersey: KTAV, 1991.

Schlier, Heinrich. "Ἀμήν." *Theological Dictionary of the New Testament*. Translated by Geoffrey W. Bromiley and Edited by Gerhard Kittel. Vol. 1. Grand Rapids: Wm. B. Eerdmans, 1964: 335-338.

Schneermelcher, Wilhelm. *New Testament Apocrypha I: Gospels and Related Writings*. Louisville: John Knox, 1991.

Schneider, Carl. "καθήμεναι." *Theological Dictionary of the New Testament.* Translated by Geoffrey W. Bromiley and Edited by Gerhard Kittel. Vol. 3. Grand Rapids: Wm. B. Eerdmans, 1965: 440-443.

Schramm, Brooks. "Luther's Schem Hamphoras." *Dialog: A Journal of Theology* 56, no. 2 (June 2017): 151-155.

Schrenk, Gottlieb, "ἀρχιερεύς." *Theological Dictionary of the New Testament.* Translated by Geoffrey W. Bromiley and Edited by Gerhard Kittel. Vol. 3. Grand Rapids: Wm. B. Eerdmans, 1965: 221-283.

Seltzer, Robert M. *Jewish People, Jewish Thought: The Jewish Experience in History.* New York: Macmillan Publishing Co., 1980.

Shepherd, M. H. "Priests in the New Testament." In *Interpreter's Dictionary of the Bible.* Vol. 2. Nashville: Abingdon Press, 1962.

Smith, D. Moody. *John Among the Gospels: The Relationship in Twentieth-Century Research.* Minneapolis: Fortress Press, 1993.

Somerville, James M. "Modern Jews Engage the New Testament: Enhancing Jewish Well-Being in a Christian Environment." *Theology Today* 66, no. 2 (July 2009): 248-252.

Spivey, Robert A. and D. Moody Smith, Jr. *Anatomy of the New Testament.* New York: The Macmillan Co., 1970.

Strathman, H. "ὁ λαός." *Theological Dictionary of the New Testament.* Translated by Geoffrey Bromiley and Edited by Gerhard Kittel. Vol. 4. Grand Rapids: Wm. B. Eerdmans, 1967: 29-39.

Taylor, Vincent. *The Gospel According to St. Mark: The Greek Text with Introduction, Notes and Indexes.* 2nd Edition. New York: St. Martin's Press, 1966.

The Church Council of the Evangelical Lutheran Church in America, April 18, 1994.

Van Aarde, Andries. "Jesus' Mission to All of Israel Emplotted in Matthew's Story." *Neotestamentica* 41, no. 2 (2007): 14-33.

Van Passen, Pierre. *Days of Our Years.* Garden City, New York: Garden City Publishing Co., Inc., 1940.

Von Rad, Gerhard. *Old Testament Theology*. Translated by D. M. G. Stalker. Vol. 1. New York: Harper & Row, 1965.

Wesley, John. *The Works of John Wesley*. Vol. 1, *Journals from October 14, 1735 to November 29, 1745*, 3rd ed. 1872 Reprint, Grand Rapids, Michigan: Baker Book House, 1978.

_____. *The Works of John Wesley*. Vol. 2, *Journals from December 2, 1745 to May 5, 1760*, 3rd ed. 1872 Reprint, Grand Rapids, Michigan: Baker Book House, 1978.

_____. *The Works of John Wesley*. Vol. 13, *Letters*, 3rd ed. 1872 Reprint, Grand Rapids, Michigan: Baker Book House, 1978.

Westerman, Claus. *Isaiah 40-66: A Commentary*. Philadelphia: The Westminster Press, 1977.

Winter, Paul. "Marginal Notes on the Trial of Jesus." *Zeitschrift für die Neutestament liche und die Kunderalteran Kirche* 50, no. 1-2 (1959): 14-33.

_____. The Trial of Jesus." *Commentary*. (September 1964): 35-41.

Wistrich, Robert. "Why Has Pope Benedict Chosen Now to Beatify Nazi-Era Pontiff?" http://www.haaretz.com/1.4834284, December 28, 2009.

Zimmerli, Walter. *Ezekiel 1: A Commentary on the Book of the Prophet Ezekiel, Chapters 1-24*. Translated by Ronald E. Clements and Edited by Frank Moore Cross. Philadelphia: Fortress Press, 1979.

Zondervan. *The Septuagint Version of the Old Testament and Apocrypha with an English Translation*. Zondervan Publishing House, 1975.

INDEX

A. M. Okorie, *114*, *210*, 230

A. R. C. Leaney, *89*, *209*, 228

Aaron, *24*, 27

Abraham, *21*, *96*, 97, *100*, *188*, *189*

Agrippa's letter, *135*

Alan Davies, *169*, *217*

Alan Dershowitz, *165*, *217*, 224

Alexander Chalmers, *150*, *215*, 223

Alice Camille, *124*, *211*

Allen, *11*, *51*, *53*, *199*, *205*, *220*

Amen, *45*, *154*

Andries van Aarde, *36*, *204*, 232

Annas, *102*, 103, 104, *126*

Anthony Saldarini, *40*

anti-Semitic, 151, 153, *164*, *166*, *167*, *171*, 172, *177*

anti-Semitism, 5, 127, *128*, 152, *169*, *170*, 172, *173*, *179*, *182*, 204, 206, 212, 217, 223, 224, 225, 229, 230

Augustine, *134*, *135*, *192*, *213*, *220*

Babylonian captivity, *25*, *32*

Bainton, *171*, *217*, *220*

Barabbas, *34*, *57*, 74, *75*, *76*, *77*, *88*, *106*, *117*, *189*, *197*, *211*, *223*

Barclay, *6*, *54*, *57*, *73*, *75*, *76*, *101*, *103*, *199*, *200*, *201*, *205*, *206*, *207*, *209*, *210*, *220*

Bart Ehrman, *128*, *212*

Beare, *32*, *35*, *60*, *203*, *204*, *206*, *221*

beautiful thing, *42*

blindness, *97*, 98

blood curse, 58, *175*

Bornkamm, *33*, *203*

Brevard Childs, *56, 205*

brood of vipers, *13*

Bruce Metzger, *23*, 199, 201, 202, 220, *229*

Bruder Jesus (Brother Jesus), *183*

Bultmann, *22, 34, 65, 95, 97, 101, 104, 107, 109, 110,* 201, *203, 206, 209, 210, 222*

C. S. Mann, *56, 71, 205, 206, 220*

Caesar, *87, 88, 107,* 108, *164, 216*

Caiaphas, *1, 28, 29,* 30, *31, 32, 41, 51, 54, 100,* 101, *102, 103, 104, 107, 117, 126, 127, 130, 189, 194*

Canetti, *76, 77, 207, 223*

Catholic Church, *3, 5, 140, 148, 153, 169,* 170, *173, 179*

centurion, *66, 89, 187*

Christological interpretation of the Scriptures, *165*

chronic identity crisis, *144*

Chrysostom, *134, 135, 192, 213, 223*

Claus Westermann, *83, 208*

Constantine, *170, 179*

Cook, *116, 117, 118, 211, 223*

Count Schlick of Moravia, *154*

Cousland, *39, 204, 223*

cross, *41, 59, 61, 62, 63, 65, 66, 72, 85,* 108, *109, 110, 111, 128, 129, 167, 176, 177, 192, 193,* 226

Crossan, *5, 127, 128, 129,* 130, 131, *194, 212, 219, 223*

crowd, *18, 19, 35, 36, 37, 38, 39, 40, 41, 50, 56, 57,* 70, *74, 75, 76, 77,* 79, *85, 93, 134, 186, 189,* 207

crowds, *12, 13, 14, 34, 35, 36, 37, 38, 39, 40, 41, 50, 51, 72, 74, 81, 87, 93, 111,* 112, *186, 197,* 203, 204, 223, 230

crucifixion, *18, 61, 66, 73, 77, 88, 89, 107, 108, 121, 122, 123, 129, 130,* 131, *133, 134, 137, 186, 192, 194, 197, 219, 226*

culpability, *70,* 79, *93, 107, 166, 171, 174, 175*

D. E. Nineham, *72,* 75, 77, *207,* 230

D. Moody Smith, *91,* 200, 209, 232

darkness, *62, 63, 86, 89, 162*

David Instone-Brewer, *124,* 195, *211,* 219, 226

Devil, 46, 53, 97, 142, *154,* 155, *156,* 158, 159, 160, 161, 162, 163, 164

Eduard Lohse, *72, 205, 207, 212*

Eichrodt, *28, 32, 201, 202, 203, 224*

elders, *1, 11, 12, 31, 32, 33,* 34, *38, 43, 51, 56, 57, 62,* 70, *71, 77,* 79, 93, *111, 113, 122, 186, 189, 197*

elders of the people, *12, 19, 26, 28, 31, 33, 34, 35, 41, 50, 54, 86, 186*

Elijah, *64, 80*

Elisha, *80*

emotional instability, *144, 145*

Epistle of James, *143*

Ezekiel, *59, 175, 206, 233*

Ezra, *19, 74, 113, 207, 226*

F. F. Bruce, *91, 209, 211*

fictional Gospel data, *118*

Filson, *47, 56, 62, 181, 204, 205, 206, 218, 225*

final solution, *157, 158, 168, 169, 173*

form criticism, *6*

Foster, *129, 212, 225*

generational curse, *59, 60, 175*

Georg Wilhelm Friedrich Hegel, *148, 149*

George Barton, *126,* 212, 221

Gerhard Kittel, *37, 200, 201, 202, 203, 204, 205, 206, 208, 210, 219, 221, 222, 224, 225, 226, 228, 229, 230, 231, 232*

Gerhard von Rad, *24, 33, 201, 202, 203, 233*

German Peasants' War of AD 1524-25, *150*

Gethsemane, *46, 48, 49, 50, 92, 117, 202, 203, 222*

greatest anti-Semite of his time, *167*

Gutbrod, *112, 210, 226*

Haim Cohn, *116, 120,* 121, 122, 123, *196, 211,* 223

Hans Conzelmann, *196, 219*

Hans Küng, *180, 183, 218, 228*

He has a demon, 99, *100*

heavenly voice (bath quol), *120*

heresies, *92*

Herod, *1,* 88, 89, 186

high priests, *10, 18,* 26, *102*

His blood be upon us and our children, *58*

Hitler, *165, 166, 167,* 168, *169, 170, 173, 179, 181*

Holocaust, *153, 165, 166, 169, 170,* 171, 172, *177, 179, 181, 182, 217, 218, 221, 223, 224, 230*

Holy of Holies, *28*, *66*, 149

Howard Clark Kee, *126*

Hugh Anderson, *72*, *207*, 220

It is finished, *65*, *110*, *111*, *176*, *191*

J. H. Bernard, *95*, 102, 105, *209*, 210, 221, 222

Jack Kingsbury, *35*, 203, 228

James Mays, *50*, *205*, 229

Jeremiah, *55*, *59*, *60*, *161*, *175*

Jeremias, *19*, *22*, *26*, *32*, *41*, *201*, *202*, *203*, *204*, *226*

Jerusalem, *1*, *10*, *15*, *18*, *19*, *20*, *21*, *23*, *26*, *27*, *29*, *30*, *32*, *34*, *41*, *47*, *56*, *67*, *71*, *72*, *78*, *79*, *82*, *113*, *114*, *124*, *132*, 133, *136*, *155*, *156*, *159*, *161*, *181*, *188*, *191*, *202*, *203*, *204*, *208*, *226*, *228*

Jewish audience, *9*, *10*, *11*, *22*

Jewish legalism, *22*

Jewish schools, *155*

Jews, *1*, *2*, *3*, *4*, *9*, *10*, *11*, *12*, *15*, *18*, *19*, *23*, *24*, *30*, *31*, *32*, *35*, *39*, *40*, *41*, *42*, *55*, *56*, *57*, *58*, *59*, *60*, *61*, *70*, *71*, *72*, *73*, *74*, *75*, *76*, *77*, *79*, *80*, *82*, *83*, *85*, *86*, *87*, *88*, *89*, *90*, *92*, *93*, *94*, *95*, *96*, *97*, *98*, *99*, *100*, *102*, *103*, *105*, *106*, *107*, *108*, *109*, *110*, *111*, *112*, *114*, *115*, *116*, *117*, *118*, *119*, *120*, *121*, *122*, *123*, *124*, *126*, *127*, *131*, *133*, *134*, *135*, *136*, *137*, *138*, *139*, *140*, *143*, *147*, *149*, *151*, *152*, *153*, *154*, *155*, *156*, *157*, *158*, *159*, *160*, *161*, *162*, *163*, *164*, *165*, *166*, *167*, *168*, *169*, *170*, *171*, *173*, *174*, *175*, *176*, *177*, *179*, *180*, *181*, *182*, *185*, *186*, *187*, *188*, *189*, *190*, *191*, *192*, *194*, *195*, *196*, *197*, *200*, *204*, *211*, *213*, *215*, *216*, *217*, *218*, *219*, *224*, *225*, *226*, *227*, *230*, *231*, *232*

Johann Maier, *119*

John Lightfoot, *80*, 84, 104, 133, *207*, 208, 210, 213, 228

John Wesley, *140*, 141, 142, 143, 144, *148*, 213, 214, 233

John., *6*, *91*, *110*, *220*, *221*, *222*, *228*, *233*

Joseph Fitzmyer, *40*, 58, 60, 204, 206

Joseph of Arimathea, *67*, *129*

Josephus, *5*, *12*, *13*, *14*, *16*, *23*, *29*, *32*, *41*, *136*, *200*, *201*, *202*, *203*, *204*, *213*, *227*

Judas Iscariot, *1*, *43*, *159*

Judensau (Jew's sow) motif, *162*

Julius Streicher, *173*

justification by faith alone (*sola fide*), *142*

Justin Martyr, *192*

Karl Barth, *49, 52, 111, 205, 210*, 221

Karl Jaspers, *154*

King Henry II, *148*

King of the Jews, 11, *56, 62, 108, 110, 192*

Klaus Baltzer, *83, 208*, 220

Kristallnacht, 166, 168

Kümmel, *78, 79, 115, 206, 210, 228*

lawyer, *120, 121, 123*

lawyers, *21, 115, 120, 196*

Leander Keck, *184, 218*, 227

Lord's Supper, *46, 146*

Lucy Dawidowicz, *173, 218,* 224

Luke, *4, 6, 59, 65, 78, 79, 80, 81, 82, 85, 86, 87, 88, 89, 90, 93, 113, 118, 121, 175, 176, 185, 188, 189, 190, 191, 207, 208, 209, 210, 213, 222, 225, 228, 229, 231*

Luther, *139, 140, 141, 142, 143, 144, 145, 146, 147, 148, 150, 151, 152, 153, 154, 155, 156, 157, 158, 159, 160, 161, 162, 163, 164, 165, 166, 167, 168, 169, 170, 171, 173, 174, 175, 176, 177, 214, 215, 216, 217, 218, 224, 228, 229, 230, 232*

Luther's and Hitler's Jew-hatred, *169*

Luther's last sermon and Hitler's last testament, *166*

Lutheran churches, *152, 166, 178*

Lutheran scholars, *171*

Lynn Boughton, *104*, 210, 222

Mark, *4, 6, 56, 69, 70, 71, 72, 73, 74, 76, 77, 79, 80, 93, 113, 117, 118, 120, 145, 164, 165, 176, 185, 186, 187, 188, 191, 206, 207, 216, 217, 219, 220, 224, 226, 227, 229, 230, 232*

Martin H. Bertram, *152, 215, 229*

Martin Hengel, *192, 219,* 226

Martin Luther, *139, 140, 146, 151, 153, 165, 168, 170, 171, 174, 177, 214, 215, 216, 217, 220, 223, 224, 225*

Martin Noth, *34, 203,* 230

Martin Sasse, *166,* 167, 168

Mary, *67, 94, 153, 156, 160*

Mary Magdalene, *67*

Matthew, *4, 6, 9, 10, 11, 12, 13, 15, 16, 17, 18, 21, 22, 25, 26, 27, 28, 31, 32, 33, 34, 35, 36, 37, 39, 40, 42, 43, 55, 56, 57,*

58, 60, 61, 62, 64, 65, 66, 67, 68, 69, 70, 74, 79, 93, 113, 118, 123, 147, 161, 175, 176, 185, 186, 191, 195, 197, 199, 200, 201, 203, 204, 205, 206, 207, 218, 220, 221, 223, 225, 227, 228, 229, 230, 231, 232

Mercy Seat, *28*

Michael Berenbaum, *177*, 178, *218*, 221

Michel, *55, 205, 230*

Mishnaic code of legal procedure, *114*

Missouri Synod of the Lutheran Church, *171*

Mosaic law, *16, 17*, 26

My time is at hand, *44*

National Socialist Party, *166*

National Socialists, *154, 168*

Nehemiah, *19, 20*

Nietzsche, *148*, 149, *167, 214, 217, 223, 227*

Nostra Aetate, 5, *180, 181, 182, 218, 231*

Of the Unknowable Name, 159

On the Jews and Their Lies, 151, 154, 158, 166, 169, 215, 223

Origin, 11, *192*

Parable of the Pounds, 81

Parable of the Vineyard and the Tenants, *73*

Passover, *41, 43, 44, 72, 77*, 125, *134*

Paul, *78, 121, 132, 135, 145, 154, 183, 210, 212, 227, 228*

Paul Winter, *137*, 138, *213*, 233

Peter, 4, 37, 47, 48, 49, 52, 53, 54, 89, 95, 128, 189, 208, 212, 225

Pharisees, *12, 13, 14, 15, 16, 17, 18, 19, 21, 22, 26, 35, 39, 68, 69, 71, 79, 93, 98, 100, 111, 113, 122, 134, 186, 187, 189*

Philo, *30, 202, 213, 231*

Pilate, *1, 11, 29, 30, 31, 32, 50, 51, 54, 56, 57, 58, 60, 61, 67, 68, 70, 73, 74, 75, 76, 77, 79, 86, 87, 88, 89, 93, 103, 104, 105, 106, 107, 108, 117, 118, 129, 130, 131, 133, 134, 137, 185, 188, 189, 190, 191, 194*

plot to kill Jesus, 100, *103, 105, 110*

political blackmail, *87*

Pope Benedict XVI, *181, 182*

Pope Pius XII, *170, 179, 180, 182*

post-AD 70 Mishnah, *124, 126, 138, 194, 196*

post-AD 70 Sanhedrin, *125, 193*

power of the crowd, *76*

pre-AD 70 Sanhedrin, *124*, *130*, *132*, *133*, 193, 194

priests, *1*, *11*, *12*, *15*, *19*, *21*, *24*, *25*, *26*, *27*, *28*, *32*, *35*, *41*, *43*, *50*, *54*, *55*, *56*, *57*, *62*, *68*, *71*, *72*, *75*, *76*, *77*, *86*, *87*, *88*, *100*, *106*, *108*, *111*, *122*, *135*, *179*, *186*, *189*, *197*, 202, 232

prophecy historicized, *127*, *128*, *129*

psychological and emotional conflicts, *144*

R. T. France, *58*, *206*, 225

redaction criticism, *6*

Reich, *166*, *167*, 168, *217*

resurrection, *5*, *12*, *16*, *17*, *45*, *47*, *66*, *68*, *96*, *99*, *101*, *138*, *143*

Richard Gutteridge, *170*, *217*, 226

Robert Wistrich, *181*, *218*, 233

Roman authority, *130*, *138*, *193*, 194

Rudolf Meyer, *36*, *37*, *200*, *204*, 207, 230

S. van Tilborg, *35*

Sabbath, *21*, 71, 72, *86*, *96*, *98*, *125*

Sadducees, *12*, *15*, *16*, *17*, *18*, *21*, *34*, *35*, *68*, *69*, *79*, *93*, *100*, *111*, 112, *113*, *122*, *126*, *186*

Samuel Sandmel, *117*, 118, *211*, 231

Sanhedrin, *22*, *26*, *27*, *28*, *32*, *34*, *41*, *51*, *52*, 54, *70*, *71*, *72*, *75*, *79*, *82*, *86*, *87*, *89*, *93*, *100*, 101, *103*, *104*, *105*, *113*, *114*, *115*, *116*, *117*, *119*, *120*, *122*, *123*, *124*, *125*, *126*, *127*, *130*, *131*, *132*, *133*, *134*, *135*, *136*, *137*, *138*, *139*, *177*, *185*, *186*, *189*, *192*, *193*, *194*, *195*, *197*, *211*, *212*, *213*, *219*, *221*, *222*, *223*, *226*, *227*

scatological references, *159*

Schafer, *119*, *211*, *216*, *231*

Schalom Ben-Chorin, *183*

Schlier, *45*, *205*, *231*

scribal religion, *20*, *21*, *22*

scribes, *12*, *18*, *19*, *21*, *22*, *23*, *24*, *26*, *27*, *28*, *32*, *35*, *38*, *51*, *62*, *70*, *71*, *72*, *77*, *86*, *122*, *186*, *187*, *189*, *197*

Second Vatican Council (1965), *5*

seducer of Israel, *37*

Septuagint, *19*, *33*, *44*, *64*, *65*, *95*, *199*, *233*

Sermon on the Mount, *147*, *176*

Sermon on the Plain, *176*

Shakespeare, *164, 216*

shepherd, *39, 46,* 47, *99*

Sherman Johnson, *18,* 201, 227

Simon of Cyrene, *61, 108*

snakes, *13, 14, 17*

Solifidianism, *142,* 143

Son of God, *51, 62, 66, 77, 86, 87, 104, 107, 187, 191, 208, 228*

Son of Man, *50, 51, 71, 72, 87, 88, 104,* 177

source criticism, *6*

Stephen, *119, 132, 133, 135*

suffering Servant, 56, 83

supernatural events, *66*

sword, *47, 50, 82, 84, 85, 133, 164*

swords, *84, 85, 86*

synagogue, *71, 80, 81, 98, 99,* 103, 155, 157, 166, 169, 174

T. A. Burkill, *135,* 136, 137, *213,* 222

temple, *16, 26, 27, 29, 30, 32, 50, 51, 66, 86, 89, 100, 101, 102, 104, 124, 125, 131, 132, 133, 135, 136, 155, 159, 161, 187, 191, 193, 195*

That Jesus Christ Was Born a Jew, *149, 150, 151,* 214

The Generations of Christ, 159

The Trial and Death of Jesus, 116, 120, 196, 211, *223*

The World Must Know, 177, 178, 218, 221

Thomas Beckett, the Archbishop of Canterbury, *148*

three father figures, *144*

Tiberius, *30, 57*

Toldot Yeshu, *120, 159, 160, 216, 231*

tomb, 66, *67, 68, 129*

tormented by guilt, *144*

trial, *5, 9, 10, 18, 22, 28,* 50, *51, 52, 56, 61, 75, 88, 103, 104, 106, 108, 114, 115, 116, 117, 118, 119, 120, 121, 122, 124, 125, 126, 127, 130, 131, 132, 138, 139, 174, 175, 185, 193, 194, 196, 197*

Ulrich Luz, *35, 203*

Ulrich Zwingli, *146*

University of Wittenberg, *139, 143, 165, 174*

usury, *147, 154, 155, 156, 157, 158, 163, 164*

Virgin Mary, *156, 160, 163*

W. Riggans, *118,* 120, *211,* 231

Walter Zimmerli, *59, 206, 233*

Wilhelm Schneermelcher, *128, 212*, 231

You are of your father the devil, 97

Zadok, *15, 24, 26*

Zadokite, *15*, 25, 26

Zealot, *43*

Zechariah, *47, 55*

ABOUT THE AUTHOR

Norman D. Holcomb, Jr. was born in Berwind, McDowell County, West Virginia on July 14, 1944. Before becoming a United Methodist minister and U. S. Navy Chaplain, he served as a U. S. Marine scout sniper and infantryman during the Vietnam War. He has earned doctorates from Vanderbilt University and the Institute of Liberal Arts. In addition to the two doctorates, he has earned master's degrees from Duke University, Eastern Connecticut State University, Saint Luke School of Theology, Salve Regina University, California State University and Troy State University. He has completed other graduate studies at Emory University. He has an undergraduate degree in education from Bluefield State College.

Dr. Holcomb retired from the Navy with the rank of Captain after thirty-three years of service. He is also retired from the United Methodist Church. He is married to the former Mary Beth Austin of Bluefield, West Virginia. They have four children and have been married for fifty-seven years. Norman and Beth reside in Virginia Beach, Virginia.

www.ingramcontent.com/pod-product-compliance
Lightning Source LLC
Chambersburg PA
CBHW041137110526
44590CB00027B/4045